# On the Philosophy of Logic

# On the Philosophy of Logic

## Jennifer Fisher
*University of North Florida*

**THOMSON**

---✦---™

**WADSWORTH**

---

Australia • Brazil • Canada • Mexico • Singapore • Spain
United Kingdom • United States

THOMSON

WADSWORTH

## On the Philosophy of Logic
### Jennifer Fisher

Philosophy Editor: Worth Hawes
Consulting Editor: Robert Talisse
Assistant Editor: Patrick Stockstill
Editorial Assistant: Kamilah Lee
Technology Project Manager:
Julie Aguilar
Marketing Manager: Christina Shea
Marketing Assistant: Mary Anne
Payumo
Project Manager, Editorial Production:
Marti Paul

Creative Director: Rob Hugel
Executive Art Director: Maria Epes
Print Buyer: Linda Hsu
Permissions Editor: Bob Kauser
Production Service: Integra Software
Services Pvt. Ltd., India
Compositor: Integra Software
Services Pvt. Ltd., India
Text and Cover Printer:
Thomson West

Thomson Higher Education
10 Davis Drive
Belmont, CA 94002-3098
USA

For more information about our
products, contact us at:
**Thomson Learning Academic
Resource Center
1-800-423-0563**

For permission to use material
from this text or product,
submit a request online at
**http://www.thomsonrights.com.**
Any additional questions
about permissions can be
submitted by e-mail to
**thomsonrights@thomson.com.**

Library of Congress Control Number:
2007928284

ISBN-13: 978-0-495-00888-0
ISBN-10: 0-495-00888-5

For my mother, Claudia Land, the source of my logical intuitions

# Acknowledgments

First off, I would like to thank Robert Talisse for inviting me to participate in this series. Yvonne Raley, Jared Warren, and Scott Aiken each gave the manuscript a close and thoughtful reading, and I am extremely grateful for their input. Thanks also to Russell Marcus, and Claudia Land, who each read and offered helpful suggestions on portions of the manuscript. Arnold Koslow also read and offered suggestions on select chapters, for which I thank him, but my indebtedness to him goes well beyond this effort on his part. His continued support and his willingness to discuss some of the issues that arose in the writing of this book have been absolutely invaluable to me. Finally, I would like to thank my husband, David Knowles, whose stylistic and thematic input improved the book enormously.

# Contents

## SOME TRADITIONAL PHILOSOPHICAL QUESTIONS RAISED BY LOGIC

# Introduction:
# What is Logic?

Imagine a set of cards, each with a number on one side and a letter on the other. Suppose that four of these cards are laid out on a table in front of you, like this:

Now consider the following rule:

  If there is a vowel on one side, there is an even number on the other.

  Which cards are relevant to this rule's truth or falsity? Or in plainer terms, flipping as few cards as possible, which cards would you have to turn over to see if the rule was true of these four cards?

  The answer is the E and the 7. To see why, just carefully think through the potential results of flipping each card over. You have to turn over the card with the E, because if there is an odd number on it, then the rule is disconfirmed, and you have to turn over the card with the 7 on it because if there is a vowel on the other side the rule will also be disconfirmed. Most people think you have to turn over the 4 as well, but to see why this isn't necessary, imagine that you turned over the card with the 4 and there was a consonant on the other side. The rule would be neither confirmed nor disconfirmed. After all, the rule is, "If there is a vowel on one side there is an even number on the other." It says nothing about what must happen if there is an even number on one side. In other words, it does not say, "If there is even number on one side, then there is a vowel on the other." Some people (though considerably fewer) also think you need to turn over the K, but since the rule doesn't tell you anything about what should happen if there is a consonant on one side, there could be an even number or an odd number on the other side of the K card, and it wouldn't either confirm or disconfirm the rule.

On average, 80–90% of people who take this kind of test don't come up with the right answer. Known as the *Wason selection task*[1] after one of the psychologists who first performed it in 1966, the test was designed to assess ordinary people's logical abilities by measuring their understanding of 'if ___ then ___' sentences. One thing that many concluded from these results is that people frequently don't reason as logically as they should.

But what does " . . . reason as logically as they should" mean? In philosophy, the distinction between what we do and what we should do is referred to as a distinction between the descriptive and the normative. The *descriptive* describes what is the case. For example, from the field of ethics, it is a sad fact of life that there are cases of genocide, where one ethnic or religious group seeks to annihilate another simply because of their ethnic or religious differences. The *normative*, on the other hand, is supposed to prescribe what ought to be the case. So, though genocides do happen, they ought not to, and we feel that in a morally perfect world, they would not. Clearly, those who conclude from the Wason selection task that people don't reason as logically as they should are assuming that logic is normative in the sense that it tells us how we ought to reason.

The normative aspects of any field of thought raise issues of a distinctly philosophical nature. In the study of ethics, many important normative questions are investigated. What actions are right? What makes an action right? Why we should be moral at all? Even seemingly basic questions turn out to be surprisingly difficult to answer in a satisfactory way, and a number of theories and views have been put forth over the centuries that seek to provide an ethical roadmap.

---

[1] All italicized words are listed again in a glossary in the back of the book.

In this book, I will follow the psychologists who designed the Wason selection task, and assume that logic is as normative for belief as ethics is for action. But this assumption is controversial, and in the final chapter I will consider some challenges to it. Until then, however, similar questions arise for the study of logic as did in the study of ethics. What reasoning is right? What makes it right? Why should we be logical at all? And just as in ethics, the answers to these questions are both difficult and far from agreed upon.

The book is divided into three main sections. The first section is designed to introduce logic as a systematic and formal study of reasoning, and to familiarize the reader with some basic logical notions. Chapter 1 introduces some important logical concepts and gives a little of the history of logic. Chapter 2 is a brief introduction to classical logic for those who are completely unacquainted with it. (Readers who have taken or are currently taking a symbolic logic class may want to skip Chapter 2.)

After a brief interlude on the nature of truth, the second section of the book explores some of the more traditional terrain in the philosophy of logic. Chapter 4 explains three important distinctions that will be useful in the discussions that follow. Chapter 5 completes the account of classical logic that was started in Chapter 2, and Chapter 6 discusses a common way to extend this account, along with some of the philosophical issues that the proposed extension raises. In Chapters 7-10, several alternatives to classical logic will be explored, and I will explain and critically evaluate at least some of the reasons that philosophers and logicians have given in favor of their particular suggestions. I then take another brief interlude and discuss some of the philosophical challenges in approaching these many different logics.

In the third section of the book, I explore some traditional philosophical questions that arise in thinking about the many alternative logics canvassed in the second section. Chapter 12 focuses on the metaphysics of logic. *Metaphysics* is the study of the nature of the world beyond what the scientists say. (The term 'meta' literally means after, and the name 'metaphysics' comes from the fact that Aristotle's book on this fundamental aspect of philosophy came after his book on physics.) Here, I examine several accounts of the metaphysical underpinnings of the normativity of logic. Chapter 13 explores the epistemological issues. *Epistemology* is the theory of knowledge (deriving from the ancient Greek 'episteme', which means to know). In this chapter, I discuss some of the difficulties with justifying and revising logic. Finally, in Chapter 14, I take up the assumption that has guided the entire book up until that point, namely whether or not logic really is normative for us and our beliefs. I return to the Wason selection task, and canvas some of the many challenges to both it and its conclusions. In addition I explore an argument that purports to show that logic is not at all relevant to us and how we should reason.

# 1

## Formal Logic—An Introduction

### I—REASONING, INFERENCE, ARGUMENTS, AND LOGIC

*Reasoning* is what people do when they go from one belief or set of beliefs to another belief or set of beliefs. Reasoning is an integral part of our everyday lives, informing myriad small decisions and actions. Let's consider two different examples. First, Jake goes to a movie by a particular director because he has liked two previous movies by that same director. Second, upon coming home and not finding her husband, Hannah forms the belief that her husband has gone to the store because he told her earlier in the day that he would either be at home or at the store when she got home.

Most philosophers believe that both of these examples of reasoning are also examples of people using logic, whether Jake and Hannah know it or not. In each case, the person in question has made an *inference*. In an inference, one belief is thought to follow in some way from another belief or set of beliefs. In the first example, Jake's belief that the two previous movies by the director were good leads to the supposition that the new movie by that same director will also be good. In the second case, Hannah's belief that her husband is either at home or has gone to the store together with the belief that her husband is not at home, leads to the conclusion that her husband must have gone to the store.

Each of these inferences is a particular kind of *argument*. The word 'argument' sometimes connotes yelling and slamming doors, but the sense in which it is used here involves none of that. An argument, for the purposes of this book, is a set of sentences in which one or more sentences are supposed to give some kind of support to another sentence. In an argument, the sentence that is being supported is called the *conclusion*, and the sentences that are supposed to be giving support are called the *premises*.

Jake's and Hannah's inferences can be restated as arguments where we make the premises and the conclusions clearer by using words that help to indicate what sentences are supposed to be premises and what sentences are supposed to be conclusions. For example, using 'so' to indicate which sentence in each argument is supposed to be the conclusion, Jake's and Hannah's inferences become the following arguments:

1. Both of the movies I've seen by the director have been good. So, I expect the next movie by the same director to be good as well.

2. Either my husband is at home or he has gone to the store. He's not at home. So, he must have gone to the store.

These two arguments belong to different branches of reasoning. The first is *inductive* and the second is *deductive*. There are many differences between inductive and deductive reasoning. The main one stems from the level of support that the conclusion receives from the premises. In inductive arguments, the premise or premises are simply supposed to make the conclusion more likely. Even if the two movies by the director that Jake has seen were good, it's possible that he won't like the new one. This is so not only because many people are involved in the making of a movie, and different cinematographers, writers, and actors can make a difference in the overall product, but also because the director, herself, just might not do as good a job this time around. Past accomplishments are a fairly good guide to future accomplishments, but they are no guarantee.

In deductive arguments, on the other hand, the premise or premises are supposed to necessitate or guarantee the truth of the conclusion. If it's true both that Hannah's husband is either at home or he's gone to the store, and that he's not at home when Hannah returns, then he absolutely must have gone to the store. That is, given the truth of the premises, the conclusion has to be true. Of course, the premises themselves might not be true. Perhaps Hannah is mistaken as to her husband's possible whereabouts. Though he told her that he would be in either place, unbeknownst to her, he may have run into a neighbor and went over to help him with some chore. Or perhaps she didn't look thoroughly enough, and neglected to check the basement. In both of these cases, Hannah has a belief that is, in fact, false. But regardless of the actual truth of the premises, the deductive argument still provides a guarantee that IF the premises are true, then the conclusion must also be true.

In this book, the discussion will center on deductive logic. In doing this, I do not mean to imply that inductive logic is less worthy of investigation. The reason for my focus has almost entirely to do with the history of mathematical logic in the 20th Century. Since the most robust developments have been in deductive logic, the philosophical issues that have arisen have also tended to be couched in terms of deductive reasoning.

## II—A LITTLE HISTORY: ARISTOTELIAN LOGIC

Why do philosophers study logic? The answer to this has to do with the role that arguments and reasoning have always played in philosophical thinking. Going all the way back to ancient Greece, philosophers have been especially concerned with arguments and reasoning because these are the philosopher's tools of the trade. Just as it would be important for a carpenter to have tools to facilitate working with many different materials, so too philosophers wanted arguments and reasons to be applicable to many different subjects. This led philosophers to study the underlying structure of arguments, and logic as the systematic study of reasoning was born.

The philosophical urge to distinguish good from bad arguments can be traced back at least to Socrates. Socrates and his student, Plato, thought of philosophy as a search for immutable truths, and they thought that good reasoning could reveal truths about reality and the nature of humankind. For this reason, they were very concerned to distance themselves from a group of thinkers known as the *sophists*. The Greek word 'sophistes' means expert, and it originally applied to anyone with expertise in a subject. By the time of Socrates, however, the expression had come to refer to thinkers with a particular expertise in the art of persuasion. *Sophists* in this more specific sense were known for

## Can a bad argument be more persuasive than a good one?

It is a sad fact, but people are often more persuaded by bad arguments than by good ones. Examples of this are, unfortunately, not hard to find. Politicians will frequently use scare tactics to get voters to vote for them, rather than engaging in a real discussion of the pros and cons of their opponent's views. A famous example of this occurred during the 1964 presidential elections, when Lyndon Johnson's campaign aired its now infamous Daisy ad against Barry Goldwater. The ads featured an image of a little girl holding a flower, and as the commercial progressed the entire image morphed into a mushroom cloud. The ad never mentioned Goldwater by name, though viewers knew the intended target since Goldwater had advocated the use of nuclear weapons as a means of getting out of the war in Indochina. But instead of addressing the reasons either for or against the use of nuclear weapons as a means of getting out of a difficult war, the ad went straight for the heart by juxtaposing the image of the little girl and the mushroom cloud. Any voters persuaded by the ad (which was only shown once by the Johnson campaign, though it was replayed again and again on the major networks because of its controversial tactics) were swayed by emotional factors rather than the force of good reason. One goal of the study of logic and reasoning is to make us aware of our tendency to be moved by reasons that aren't really relevant to or good enough for establishing the conclusion in question. The hope is that by being aware of this all too human tendency, we may be able to overcome it more easily, and so only accept reasons that really are sufficient for establishing their conclusions.

using any argument that would convince a crowd, and they weren't shy about using bad arguments if doing so would be more effective than using good ones. In addition, *sophists* would defend any claim that they were paid to defend, whether or not the claim had any real worth. In other words, instead of only using good reasons in pursuit of the truth, like Plato and Socrates, the *sophists* would use any reasons that were persuasive to convince people of any view regardless of its merit. (Today, you still hear the term *sophistry* used to refer to the practice of making bad arguments sound like good ones.)

Aristotle, who was a student of Plato's, did a great deal of thinking about distinguishing good argument from bad. His research culminated in a theory of the *syllogism*, which is an argument with two premises and one conclusion. The logic that he developed went on to dominate Western and Middle Eastern intellectual development for millennia. Over the centuries, many refinements and improvements were added, and the results came to be known as Aristotelian logic.

The kinds of arguments that Aristotelian logic concerns itself with are what we now call *categorical syllogisms*. These are syllogisms whose premises and conclusion are all *categorical sentences*.[1] A categorical sentence relates things belonging to one group to things belonging to a different group. For example, "All whales are mammals." Here, the group of things that are whales is said to also belong to the group of things that are mammals. The technical term for these groups is *class*. A class is a set of things all of which have share some particular quality. Take the tree outside my window. It belongs to many different classes. Among these are the classes of green things, living things, tall things, mortal things, things on the campus at the university where I work, and so on. A class is specified by a *predicate* in a language (in our case, English). Basically, any term that can be predicated of the tree (including 'is a tree') defines a class that the tree belongs to.

In a categorical sentence, the predicates and noun phrases that denote classes are the *terms* of the sentence. In addition to being arguments with two premises and one conclusion, all of which are categorical sentences, categorical syllogisms can have at most three different terms. Here is an example of a categorical syllogism, where 'whales,' 'mammals' and 'animal that nurse their young' are the argument's terms:

3. All whales are mammals.
   All mammals are animals that nurse their young.
   So, all whales are animals that nurse their young.

---

[1] I should note that philosophers distinguish sentences from propositions, and much ink has been spilled over the question of which is more appropriate for discussions in logic and the philosophy of logic. Roughly speaking, propositions are supposed to be the timeless meanings of the verbal or written sentence. Thus, the two different sentences "Snow is white" and "La neige est blanc" express the same proposition, namely that snow is white. In this book, I will couch all of my discussions in terms of sentences. I do not intend this choice to color my discussion of the issues, nor does it need to. For our purposes, the difference between propositions and sentences can be overlooked because for most of the discussions in this book, one can pretty readily translate talk of propositions into talk of sentences, and vice versa. The one exception to this in Chapter 6 is noted in a footnote.

Notice that both the premises and the conclusion of this argument have the same sentence form: All _____ are _____. In Aristotelian logic, categorical sentences come in four basic types, A, E, I or O. The sentence form of the premises and conclusion of syllogism (1) are all A sentences. Here is the basic sentence form of each type of categorical sentence, where S stands for the subject term and P stands for the predicate term, followed by an example:

A: All S are P          (e.g., All whales are mammals.)
E: No S are P          (e.g., No lizards are warm-blooded.)
I: Some S are P        (e.g., Some dogs are friendly.)
O: Some S are not P  (e.g., Some mammals are not land-dwellers.)

Legend has it that these vowel names derive from the Latin for I affirm, *AffIrmo*, and I deny, *nEgO*. The A sentences affirm of all the things in one class that they belong to some other class and the I sentences affirm of some of the things in one class that they belong to another class. Similarly, the E sentences deny that all the things in one class belong to some other class and O sentences deny that some of the things in one class belong to another class.

Like all categorical syllogisms, (3) is a deductive argument. Recall that a deductive argument is one in which the truth of the conclusion is supposed to be guaranteed by the truth of the premises. When a deductive argument succeeds in providing this guarantee, the argument is said to be *valid*. (3) is a valid argument. If it is true that all whales are mammals, and also that all mammals are animals that nurse their young, then all whales must be animals that nurse their young. Given the truth of the premises, whales can't be animals that don't nurse their young.

One thing to notice about (3) is that its validity doesn't depend on the meaning of the terms involved. That is, its validity has nothing to do with whales, mammals, and animals that nurse their young. Rather, what guarantees the truth of the conclusion, given the truth of the premises, is the argument's logical form. Since the notion of validity and logical form are so central in logic, it's worth spending a little time here to begin to familiarize ourselves with these ideas.

An argument's *logical form* is its basic logical structure, what remains when all non-logical terms are removed, leaving the logical terms in their place. The structure of an argument is like the blueprint for a building. A building's blueprints lay bare the basic elements that give the building the shape it has, but do not specify details like which flooring or fixtures will be used. In this way, different buildings can look very different even if they are based on the same blueprints. Likewise, an argument's logical form specifies what is logically essential to the argument, but does not specify what the terms in question are, thereby allowing many arguments with different terms to nevertheless have the same structures. The logical form of (3), replacing 'whales' with S,[2] 'mammals' with M, and 'animals that nurse their young' with P (these stand for the subject term, middle term, and predicate term, respectively) would be:

4. All S are M
   All M are P
   So, all S are P

Every categorical syllogism has a subject term and a predicate term (the subject and the predicate of the conclusion), and a middle term, which is the term that appears in both premises.

Any argument with the form of (4) will be a valid argument as long as you substitute the same term for each occurrence of S, the same term for each occurrence of M, and the same term for each occurrence of P. So, for instance, (5) is also a valid argument, even though the terms substituted for S, M and P, respectively, are complete nonsense words:

5. All whizzles are gizzles.
   All gizzles are snizzles.
   So, all whizzles are snizzles.

Whatever a whizzle, gizzle, and snizzle are, if it's true that all whizzles are gizzles, and also true that all gizzles are snizzles, then it must be the

---

[2] A note about use, mention, and quotation in this book:

Philosophers distinguish between using a word and mentioning it by putting mentioned words in single quotes. For example,

1. I have a cat named Sunny Jim.

2. 'Cat' is a word with three letters.

In the former sentence, I use the word 'cat' and in the latter I mention it. This distinction is very important, and silly mistakes are sometimes made when philosophers are not careful about minding it. That said, whether I am using them or mentioning them, I do not put quotes around any symbols, single letters (either lower or upper case), or formulae. I use single quotes when I mention either names or incomplete phrases of natural language, and I use double quotes for full sentences. I don't think I've made any silly mistakes as a result, and the finished product, in my opinion, is a lot easier on the eyes than it would have been had I been stricter in my notation.

case that all whizzles are snizzles. Just as in (3) above, IF the premises are true, whizzles then have to be snizzles.

Indeed, (4) is a valid argument form even when an instance of it has premises and conclusion that are actually false. Consider (6):

6. All birds are reptiles.
   All reptiles are yellow.
   So, all birds are yellow.

In (6), neither of the premises are true, nor is the conclusion, and yet it is a valid argument. That's because the validity of this argument, like the validity of (3) and (5), doesn't depend in any way on the actual terms used, it only depends on the basic logical form as given in (4). Once again, if it's true that all birds are reptiles and that all reptiles are yellow, then it must be true that all birds are yellow. Of course neither of those premises is true, but IF they were, the truth of the conclusion would be guaranteed. So, even though the premises and conclusions of (6) are all false, it is a valid argument because it is an instance of a valid argument form. An argument is said to be *sound* if it is valid and has true premises. (6), therefore, is valid but not sound, and (3) is both valid and sound.

Not all deductive arguments are valid. The following is an example of an *invalid* categorical syllogism:

7. All artists are bakers.
   Some bakers are carpenters.
   So, some carpenters are artists.

What makes this invalid is that, unlike the arguments (3), (5) and (6) above, the truth of the conclusion is not guaranteed by the truth of the premises. To see this, imagine that in a small town there are only three artists, Gertrude, Herbert, and Ignacio, all of whom are also bakers. In this small town, however, there are two more bakers who are not artists, Julia and Kenneth, and let us suppose that of these five residents of this small town, only Julia is a carpenter. In this town, both of the premises are true: All artists are bakers (because Gertrude, Herbert and Ignacio are the only artists and they are all bakers), and some bakers are carpenters (because Julia is both a baker and a carpenter). Nevertheless, it's not true that some carpenters are artists because the only carpenter in this town is Julia and she's not one of the artists.

Here is a little diagram to further clarify the line of thought. In this diagram, circles represent each of the terms in argument (7), and lower case letters stand for the individuals discussed (g = Gertrude, h = Herbert, and so on). When an individual, like Gertrude, has more than one of the properties in question, we put the letter standing for the individual in the area of overlap between the circles in question.

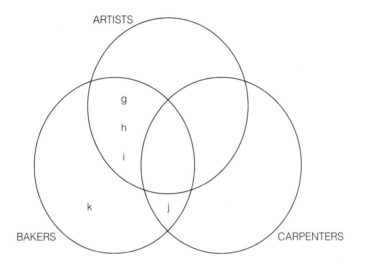

As this diagram makes clear, both of the premises of (7) are true, because all the artists (g, h, and i) are bakers and some baker (j) is a carpenter. Nevertheless, it's not true that some carpenters are artists, since no lower case letters are to be found in the overlap of the circles that represent carpenters and artists. Thus, the premises can be true even though the conclusion is false, and so this argument cannot be valid.

Like the valid arguments we considered above, the invalidity of (7) is also due to its form. The form of (7) is

8. All P are M
   Some M are S.
   So, some S are P.

Any argument with the form of (8) is an invalid argument, because the truth of the conclusion is not guaranteed by the truth of the premises for any argument with that form.

In total, Aristotle identified 24 valid argument forms, and numerous invalid ones. In addition, various relations were discerned between the sentence forms, and important logical notions were clearly defined and spelled out for categorical sentences.[3] For all of its successes, however, the modern logic that replaced Aristotelian logic is far more powerful and systematic in its treatment of important logical notions.

## III—MODERN LOGIC: FREGE'S INSIGHT

The logic that replaced Aristotolian logic began gaining momentum in the middle 1800's with the investigation of mathematicians like George Boole and Auguste DeMorgan, but it culminated at the end of the 19th century with the work of a number of mathematicians and philosophers throughout Europe and America. Though many contributed greatly to the developments in logic, chief among them was the German mathematician and logician, Gottlob Frege. Frege's primary goal was to develop a logic that would clarify the philosophical foundations of mathematics. The theory that resulted from his investigations produced a level of formalization that allowed a systematic treatment of many of the most fundamental logical notions.

Frege's contributions begin with the insight that each word or phrase in a language has a particular role to play in the sentences that it appears in. Some words, *names*, stand for particular individuals or objects. So, just as the name 'Gottlob Frege' stands for the man, Gottlob Frege, and 'Sunny Jim' stands for my cat, Sunny Jim, so too the word 'three' stands for the abstract object, the number three (if there is such a thing), and the word 'moon', stands for the concrete object, the moon. These naming words contrast with *predicates* and *relational phrases*, like '_____ is red' or '_____ is to the left of _____'. Predicate and relation phrases are essentially incomplete, which I've indicated by putting blanks where names for objects would go. These predicates and relational phrases stand for *concepts*, and these, too, are essentially incomplete. Just as incomplete predicates are made complete by names, so correspondingly, are concepts made complete by objects. When a predicate is

---

[3] For example, the notion of contradictory sentences was fully developed. Two sentences are contradictory if, when one is true the other must be false and vice versa. A and O sentences are contradictory, because when the subject and the predicate of an A and an O sentence are the same, if the A sentence is true then the O sentence must be false, and vice versa, as in "All whales are mammals" and "Some whales are not mammals." In this case, the truth of the A sentence guarantees the falsity of the O sentence.

completed by a name, a sentence is formed, and the sentence is said to be either true or false depending on whether the concept in question applies to the object in question.[4]

To illustrate this fundamental idea, consider what happens when we complete the predicate '_____ is red' with two different names, 'Elmo' and 'Big Bird'. The sentence that results when we complete the predicate is true just in case the object in question, as indicated by the name, can be said to belong to the group of things that are red. For the name 'Elmo' the completed sentence is, "Elmo is red", and this is true because Elmo, the puppet, is in fact, red. In the case of the name 'Big Bird', however, the completed sentence, "Big Bird is red" is false, because the puppet, Big Bird, is yellow, and therefore not found in the group of red things.

These might not seem like such grand observations. But the fact is that no one before Frege had really made this way of analyzing language so clear. And by making clear that each word or phrase had a particular function to play, Frege showed that certain logical and mathematical words played very similar, though importantly distinct, functions in a language. It was this move that allowed the full-blown development of mathematical logic and led to a complete systematization of many, if not all, of the most basic logical terms.

It will be easiest to explain this if I first introduce some Fregean terminology into the discussion. I noted above that predicate and relational phrases stand for incomplete concepts. For Frege, these concepts are also *functions*. The idea of a function is familiar to anyone who knows how to add. A function is just an operation that takes inputs and yields outputs according to certain specified rules. Addition is a function that takes numbers as inputs and yields new numbers as outputs. So, for the numbers 2 and 3, the function + yields the value 5, for the numbers 12 and 3, the function yields the value 15, and so on. Frege thought that '_____ is red' was a function as well, except that instead of taking numbers and assigning new numbers as values, functions like '_____ is red' take the names of objects like 'Elmo', and yield truth values. Returning to our examples above,

---

[4] Note, by the way, that Frege's use of 'predicate' differs from Aristotle's. For example, we saw above that according to Aristotelian logic the sentence "All whales are animals that nurse their young," has the predicate term 'animals that nurse their young'. According to Frege, however, that sentence actually contains three predicates: '_____ is a whale,' '_____ is an animal,' and '_____ is a nurser of its young.'

when the name 'Elmo' completes the predicate '_____ is red', the resulting sentence is true, while when the name 'Big Bird' completes the same predicate, the sentence is false:

| (Name) | (Predicate) | | (Truth value) |
|---|---|---|---|
| Elmo | is red. | = | True |
| Big Bird | is red. | = | False |

What distinguishes mathematical functions like + from functions like '_____ is red' is the kind of objects they take and the kind of values that they yield. Mathematical functions take numbers and yield other numbers,[5] whereas natural language predicates and relations take names and yield one of the two truth values, true or false. (Notice, so as to avoid any confusion, that some natural language functions, like '_____ is a number' can take number names as objects, but these yield truth values, not other numbers.)

In addition to mathematical functions which take numbers and yield new numbers, and natural language predicates which take names and yield truth values, Frege noticed that logical terms made up a third kind of function which take truth values and yield new truth values. The logical terms that Frege noticed included the ones we've already seen, like 'All _____ are _____' and 'Some _____ are _____' (as we will see in Chapter 5 one of Frege's most important legacies is his theory of these logical functions). In addition, building on the work of earlier mathematicians like DeMorgan and Boole, Frege explored logical functions that Aristotelian logic didn't address, like '_____ and _____,' as in the sentence "Elmo is red and Big Bird is red." These functions take sentences once they have been assigned a value of either true or false, and assign them new truth values according to particular rules. These distinctly logical functions, in other words, take complete declarative sentences with determinate truth values and yield new truth values according to certain specifiable rules.

What does it mean to take truth values and yield new truth values? Consider the '_____ and _____' sentence above, "Elmo is red and Big bird is red." This sentence (the technical term for it is a *conjunction*) is

---

[5] Strictly speaking, mathematical functions can take mathematical objects other than numbers as either input or output, but in my example I use only numbers. For ease of exposition, and so as to make the contrast between mathematical and other functions as stark as possible, I will speak of mathematical functions as taking numbers and yielding other numbers, as I have done here.

composed of two different complete declarative sentences (each of which is called a *conjunct*):

"Elmo is red."

"Big bird is red."

As we saw above, each of these sentences has its own truth value depending on whether or not the object referred to by the name in each sentence has the concept attributed to it by the predicate in each sentence. In this case, the first sentence is true and the second sentence is false. Is the conjunction as a whole true or false? Clearly, it is false, since it makes a claim that two things are true, and one of the things that it claims (that Big Bird is red) is not, in fact, true. The logical function '_____ and _____' takes the truth values of these constituent sentences and yields the new truth value, false. So, in just the way that the function + takes a number (or numbers), and adds them to yield a new number, the function '_____ and _____' takes the truth values of the sentences which it conjoins and assigns them a new truth value.

| (Truth Value) | | (Truth Value) | | (Truth Value) |
|---|---|---|---|---|
| True | and | False | = | False |
| (Elmo is red) | | (Big Bird is red) | | (Elmo is red and big bird is red.) |

Frege was very concerned about the distinction mentioned in the Introduction between the descriptive and the normative. When he was writing in the late 1800's, there were prominent theorists who had argued that logic should merely describe the laws of thought, i.e., how people actually did reason. Frege disagreed with these theorists, and argued that the focus of logic should be on the normative not the descriptive. Frege thought that logic's main job was to track truth, i.e., logic needed to guarantee that we could never go from true beliefs to false ones. He argued that the laws of thought might vary from person to person, but that only one logic would be the best at tracking truth. According to Frege, just as certain ways of using the function + are correct and other ways are not, so too, certain ways of using the function '_____ and _____' are correct while others are not.

One point that Frege made which is worth emphasizing is that logical functions are unique in that they are completely general, applying to any subject matter whatsoever. The best way to see what he meant by this is to consider the types of objects taken by each of the many kinds of functions that we've examined in this

**17**

section. + only applies to mathematical objects such as numbers. It makes no sense to say "Cat + Dog = Bird". '_____ is red' only applies to things that can be colored, but there are many things that we don't think of as being colored, such as numbers, ideas, and time periods, to name a few. It just doesn't make sense to say that the early 1920's were red, or 42 is a blue number, or that Frege's insight concerning the nature of logical functions is a very purple idea. On the other hand, the function '_____ and _____' can be used with any sentence that can be given a truth value, and we can write true or false sentences about virtually everything we think about. Here are just a few sentences to illustrate the many kinds of subjects about which we can form complete declarative sentences with truth values:

$1 + 2 = 3$

$4 - 3 = 2$

I have freckles.

Julie is married to Jim.

Quarks exist.

Cats are animals.

The three angles of a triangle add up to $180°$.

He hates war.

Dinosaurs were reptiles.

I hope the Independents will win in '08.

In the future, people will live to be 120.

When economic conditions are ripe, a revolution will occur.

There are eight planets in our solar system.

Notice that my list is made up of sentences that can have a truth value, not a list of true sentences. At least some of the sentences on my incomplete list are false. Notice too that some of the sentences may not have a clear truth value yet, such as "In the future, people will live to be 120," and "There are eight planets in our solar system," which is something that astronomers currently disagree about. What is important is that the sentence be truth evaluable, i.e., that it could be true or false, even if we don't know which it is.

Frege thought that logical functions were the most general of functions because their application is not limited to particular kinds of things, in the way that + and '_____ is red' are. Logical functions can apply to any domain of thought, because we can form sentences that can have truth values about every domain of thought. Logical functions, therefore, apply to anything and everything that we can think about, regardless of the area of inquiry. As long as the sentences in question are truth evaluable, even if we don't know their actual truth value, logical functions like '_____ and _____' can operate on them.

# 2

# An Overview
# of Classical Logic*

## I—TRUTH TABLES

The logic that Frege helped develop has come to be known as *classical logic*.[1] As we will see in later chapters, there are many alternatives to classical logic. But there is no denying that classical logic has dominated philosophical thinking for much of the 20th Century, and it is the theory most commonly taught in standard symbolic logic textbooks (at least in English speaking countries).

In the last chapter, I briefly discussed conjunction, the logical function best represented in English by the term 'and'. (I am dropping the convention from last chapter of making the incompleteness of functions explicit by using blanks where inputs should go, though all functions should still be understood to be incomplete in just the sense that I indicated.) 'And' and all the other logical functions that I'm

---

\* Readers who have already had a symbolic logic course are advised that they may safely skip this chapter, and readers who haven't are advised that this is intended merely as a very brief overview to introduce concepts and argument forms important for later discussions in the book. I have recommended some symbolic logic textbooks in the Further Readings.

[1] Classical logic actually differs from Frege's original formulation in a number of ways that need not concern us here, but Frege's work certainly contributed greatly to its development.

about to introduce, can be used with any one of the infinite possible declarative sentences that one can make in English, a tiny fraction of which I listed in the last chapter. So for instance, returning to my list and picking at random, I can form the following sentence:

I have freckles and he hates war.

As we saw, this conjunction is composed of two complete declarative sentences, the conjuncts. In this case, the conjuncts are "I have freckles" and "He hates war."

Let us suppose that it is true that I have freckles and also that it is true that he hates war. To know whether or not these sentences are true, of course, one would have to know who 'I' and 'he' refer to, but let us suppose that we do know this and that both sentences are true. Clearly, when both conjuncts are true, the entire conjunction is also true.

Even if both conjuncts are in fact true, notice that we could decide what truth value the whole conjunction should take if we didn't know that this were the case. Let's assume that each of the conjuncts, "I have freckles" and "He hates war" must be either true or false. In order to consider all the possible combinations of truth or falsity of the conjunction of the two sentences, therefore, we will have to consider four different possible truth value combinations of the two sentences. We can represent each possibility in the following table (where T stands for true and F stands for false):

|       | "I have freckles" | "He hates war" |
|-------|-------------------|----------------|
| i)    | T                 | T              |
| ii)   | T                 | F              |
| iii)  | F                 | T              |
| iv)   | F                 | F              |

We have just seen that a conjunction is true when both conjuncts are true, so row (i), where both the sentences in question are assigned a T should also be T. And we noticed in the last chapter that the conjunction "Elmo is red and Big Bird is red" was false, because the sentence "Big Bird is red" is false. That is, we noticed that a conjunction with a false conjunct is always false. Thus, (ii) and (iii) would both be rows where the conjunction gets an F. Finally, a conjunction where both conjuncts are false (for example, "Elmo is blue and Big Bird is blue") is also false, and so the whole conjunction should be assigned an F in row (iv). We can sum up these findings as follows:

CHAPTER 2

|      | "I have<br>freckles" | "He hates<br>war" | "I have freckles<br>and he hates war" |
|------|------|------|------|
| i)   | T    | T    | T    |
| ii)  | T    | F    | F    |
| iii) | F    | T    | F    |
| iv)  | F    | F    | F    |

What this *truth table*, as it is called, tells us is that this conjunction is true when both conjuncts are true, and false otherwise.

Notice that what I've said about the conjunctions "I have freckles and he hates war" and "Elmo is red and Big Bird is red" holds for any of the infinite possible English sentences that we can make. Take two more from my list in Chapter 1:

Cats are animals, and in the future, people will live to be 120.

This conjunction, too, will be true only when both declarative sentences, "Cats are animals" and "In the future, people will live to be 120," are true. And so, too, for any other conjunction of two complete declarative sentences. This is why Frege thought that logical functions were completely general. Logical functions apply to sentences regardless of what they actually say or what they are actually about. All that matters to the logical function that we've characterized here is the truth value of each conjunct. In other words, what logical functions like 'and' operate on is truth values and truth values alone. In technical terms, they are *truth-functions*.

Logicians represent the function 'and' with the symbol • (the *dot*—one of several symbols commonly used to represent 'and' in symbolic logic). And since, as we just saw, the actual content of individual sentences doesn't matter in assessing the possible truth values of a conjunction, we can use the letters p and q as *variables* for which any complete declarative sentence could be substituted. Variables allow us to characterize the possible truth values for complex sentences containing a • in a purely general way using a two-by-two matrix, as follows:

p • q

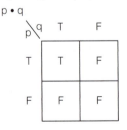

The matrix represents all the possible combinations of truth values of the constituent sentences of a conjunction. The horizontal truth values outside the box at the top are the possible truth values of q and the vertical truth values outside the box to the left are the possible truth values of p. The top left box (with the T) represents the truth value of a conjunction when both its conjuncts are true. All the other boxes have an F because in all the other boxes either p is false (as in the bottom left box) or q is false (as in the top right box) or both p and q are false (as in the bottom right box).

In addition to 'and,' classical logic also defines the logical functions that are supposed to be represented by the English logical terms 'or', 'if...then', 'if and only if', and 'not.' In what follows, I will introduce each of these logical functions, presenting its characteristic matrix in classical logic and briefly trying to motivate the reason for each truth value assignment. As with 'and,' I will use a standard logical symbol for each of the logical functions.

A sentence containing 'or' is a *disjunction*, and the sentences that make up its constituent parts are called its *disjuncts*. The symbol for 'or' is ∨ (the *wedge*), and the matrix that characterizes ∨ in classical logic is as follows:

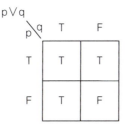

According to classical logic, a disjunction is false when both disjuncts are false, and true otherwise. To see why, consider the following example. Suppose that Jill meets a man named Bill at a work party, and says to her friend "Bill either works where I work or he came with someone who works where I work." Clearly, if neither disjunct is true, that is, it is not true that either "Bill works where Jill works" or "Bill came with someone who works where Jill works," then the entire disjunction is false. This is what is represented in the lower right hand box. Also, if Bill doesn't work for Jill's company, but came with someone who does, or if Bill works for Jill's company, but didn't come with someone who does, as is indicated by the upper right hand box and lower left hand box, respectively, then the disjunction is true. Intuitively, this is because, unlike a conjunctive sentence, someone who makes an 'or' statement is not committed to thinking that both of the declarative sentences in the disjunction are true. Lastly, the upper left box specifies that a disjunction is true when both disjuncts are true. In terms of our example, if it is true both that Bill is a fellow employee and that he has come with a fellow employee, Jill's disjunctive statement is clearly true.

This upper left hand box is the least intuitive value for a complex sentence containing the wedge. This is because, unlike the example of a disjunction that I have given, 'or' in natural language is frequently used in a way that would make an 'or' sentence false when both disjuncts are true. For example, if you order a dinner at a restaurant and the waiter tells you that you can have soup or salad with your dinner, he means you can have one or the other, but not both. These two senses of 'or' have different technical names. The first is the *inclusive* and the second is the *exclusive* sense of 'or.' Formally, the choice between these two characterizations is completely arbitrary since one can define either sense of 'or' in terms of the wedge and the other symbols of classical logic, and so whichever way one defines the wedge, the logic that results will still have the expressive power to encompass the remaining sense.

As I mentioned in the Introduction, a sentence with an 'if...then' structure is called a *conditional*. The 'if' part of a conditional is the *antecedent* and the 'then' part is the *consequent*. The symbol for 'if...then' is ⊃ (the *horseshoe*), and its matrix in classical logic is:

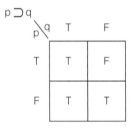

The matrix for the conditional in classical logic is perhaps the most controversial of all the logical functions, but it can be made intuitive by considering sentences such as "If you run a red light, then you have broken the law." If it's true that you have run a red light and it's true that you have broken the law, then the conditional as a whole is clearly true, as indicated in the upper left hand box. And if it's true that you have run a red light but false that you have broken the law (perhaps you are riding in an emergency vehicle), then the conditional as whole is clearly false, as in the upper right hand box. As for both the lower boxes, if you never run a red light, it makes some sense to think that the conditional as a whole is still true. In the lower left, it can be false that you run a red light but still be true that you have broken the law (perhaps you have committed some other traffic violation), but nevertheless the conditional is still true. After all, why should the fact that you haven't run a red light affect the legality of doing so? Similarly, if you haven't run a red light and you haven't broken the law, as in the lower right hand box, the sentence "If you run a red light then you have broken the law" is true, because it is still true that *if* you had run a red light, you would have broken the law. Summing up, a conditional in classical logic is false when its antecedent is true and its consequent is false, and it is true otherwise.

A sentence with an 'if and only if' in it is a *biconditional* (its name comes from the fact that it is equivalent to a conjunction of two conditionals). The symbol for 'if and only if' is $\equiv$ (the *triple bar*) and it is characterized in classical logic as follows:

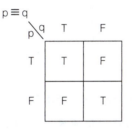

$p \equiv q$

An example of a biconditional in English is "Bush is president of the U.S. if and only if he received a majority of the electoral college votes." If it's true that Bush is president of the U.S. and if it is also true that Bush received a majority of the electoral college votes, then the statement as a whole is obviously true. Equally obvious, if one of these sentences is true and one of them is false (as in the lower left and the upper right hand boxes) then the biconditional is false. Lastly, the lower right hand box makes clear that if it's false that Bush is president and false that Bush received a majority of electoral college votes the biconditional sentence is still true. That is, it's still true that Bush would be president if and only if he gets a majority of electoral college votes, even if he is neither president nor the recipient of the majority of electoral college votes. The truth of a biconditional, in other words, depends on the two constituent sentences either both being true or both being false.

The last logical function that we will consider in this chapter is 'not'. (The remaining logical functions of classical logic will be introduced in Chapter 5.) Sentences containing this term are called *negations*. The symbol for negation is ~ (the *tilde*) and the matrix in classical logic looks as follows:

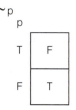

The values for a negation in classical logic are quite intuitive: if the sentence "2005 is the year of the tiger" is true, then its negation, "2005 is not the year of the tiger", is false. To make clearer that negations operate on whole sentences, it helps to think of 'not' as equivalent to 'it is not the case that', as in, "It is not the case that 2005 is the year of the tiger." And if it is false that 2005 is the year of the tiger, then it's true that it is not the case that 2005 is the year of the tiger.

## II—RULES OF INFERENCE AND VALID AND INVALID ARGUMENT FORMS

Classical logic can also be characterized by certain very general rules of inference. In an ordinary inference, recall, a person goes from some current beliefs to some new belief(s) by a chain of reasoning. For instance, returning to argument (2) from Chapter 1, Hannah infers from her two beliefs,

> Belief 1: Either my husband is at home or he has gone to the store.
>
> Belief 2: My husband is not at home.

to a third new belief:

> Belief 3: My husband has gone to the store.

Hannah's inference is an instance of an argument form known as *Disjunctive Syllogism* and it is just one of many argument forms that characterize classical logic. A *rule of inference* says how to go from one set of sentences to another, and can be seen as an idealization of our ordinary inferential practices. In the last section, I introduced some logical functions. Just as those functions operated on sentences regardless of their content, so too logical rules of inference are characterized purely generally.

Our Disjunctive Syllogism above contains two complete declarative sentences, "My husband is at home," and "My husband has gone to the store." Taking these sentences out, and replacing them with the variables p and q (for which, recall, any complete declarative sentence may be substituted), and preserving all the symbols for logical terms that we introduced above, we get an argument whose basic form looks like this:

Disjunctive (DS):    p ∨ q
Syllogism          ~ p
             So, q

Notice that the second premise gets represented as ~p. This is because 'not' in the sentence "My husband is not at home" is a logical function, and so it's important to represent it as part of the form of the argument.

Disjunctive Syllogism is one of many rules commonly used to define a system of *natural deduction* for classical logic. Natural deduction systems give us a method for characterizing good arguments in a way which is supposed to closely mimic how we actually reason. When we reason well, we can be seen as following certain idealized rules. A simple example might make this idea more concrete. Consider the following argument:

   1. If either Julie or Susan comes to the party, then Bill and Adam won't come. Julie is coming to the party. So Bill will not come.

This argument, I hope, seems intuitively valid in the sense that it should seem like the conclusion follows from the premises. We can demonstrate its validity by laying out the step-by-step way to go from the two premises to the conclusion via the rules of natural deduction (see box).

Classical logic can be defined many different ways. Not only are there different rules and combinations of rules, and so different systems of natural deduction, there are characterizations of classical logic that don't use rules exclusively (they also include axioms), and that use rules which don't seek to mimic natural reasoning patterns. What follows is an example of a few of the rules for one natural deduction system for classical logic. I am not giving a complete set of rules, only introducing the idea by focusing on rules that are particularly important to the discussions that follow. Each rule is accompantied by an instance of the argument form in question.

*Modus Ponens* (MP):    $p \supset q$

$p$

So, q

Example: If whales are mammals, then whales nurse their young.

Whales are mammals.

So, whales nurse their young.

*Modus Tollens* (MT):    $p \supset q$

$\sim q$

So, $\sim p$

Example: If John Kerry is president, then he got the majority of electoral votes in 2004.

It is not the case that John Kerry got the majority of electoral votes in 2004.

So, John Kerry is not president.

*Disjunctive* (DS):
*Syllogism*    $p \vee q$

$\sim p$

So, q

Example: Either my husband is at home or he's gone to the store.

He's not at home.

So, he's gone to the store.

| | |
|---|---|
| *Simplification* (Simp): | p • q |
| | So, p |
| | Example: Miami is in Florida and Pittsburgh is in Pennsylvania. |
| | So, Miami is in Florida. |
| *Conjunction* (Con): | p |
| | q |
| | So, p • q |
| | Example: Miami is in Florida. |
| | Pittsburgh is in Pennsylvania. |
| | So, Miami is in Florida and Pittsburgh is in Pennsylania. |
| *Addition* (Add): | p |
| | So, p ∨ q |
| | Example: Whales are mammals. |
| | So, either whales are mammals or birds are vertebrates. |

Note: many people find the rule of "Addition" particularly strange. What the rule allows one to do is to disjoin any sentence whatsoever to a sentence that has already been asserted. Below, I will show why this rule is justified.

In addition to these rules of inference, systems of natural deduction usually include both rules for more complex argument forms and also rules that make clear some common logical equivalences. An example of the former is *indirect proof*. Indirect proofs license the conclusion that the negation of a sentence, ~p, is true if a contradiction follows from the assumption that p. Simply put, this argument form says that if one can derive a contradiction from an assumption, then the negation of that assumption must be true. Here is an informal indirect proof (with a more formal example in Chapter 4) where the sentence substituted for p is itself negated (i.e., p = 2 is not the only even prime):

Suppose that 2 is not the only even prime. Then there is some other even number, n, that is prime. A number is prime if and only if it is only divisible by itself and 1. Even numbers are, by definition, divisible by 2. So, n is both prime and not prime. Therefore, it is not the case that 2 is not the only even prime.

*Equivalence rules* make clear how to rephrase sentences in a way that preserves their logical import. Each replacement rule allows one to go from one form of a sentence to a different, though *logically equivalent* sentence. For example, one equivalence rule of classical logic, known as *Double Negation*, states that p is equivalent to ~~p. Thus, the conclusion of the informal indirect proof, "It is not the case that 2 is not the only even prime" is equivalent to "Two is the only even prime," and so the latter conclusion also follows in classical logic from the indirect proof above. Here are two other sets of equivalencies (here symbolized ::) that will be useful to know for later examples. The first are known as *DeMorgan's Rules*:

~ (p ∨ q) :: (~p • ~q)
~ (p • q) :: (~p ∨ ~q)

According to the first of these, "It is not the case that either Kim or Dan will win the race" is equivalent to "It is not the case that Kim will win the race and it is not the case that Dan will win the race." The second set are called the *Distributive Rules*:

(p • (q ∨ r)) :: ((p • q) ∨ (p • r))
(p ∨ (q • r)) :: ((p ∨ q) • (p ∨ r))

An instance of the first rule makes "Jim turned left and he either went straight or he turned right" equivalent to "Either Jim turned left and went straight or he turned left and turned right."

You can prove the logical equivalence of each pair of sentences by using truth tables. For example, the truth table for the first of DeMorgan's Rules looks like this:

| 1 | 2 | 3 | 4 | 5 | 6 | 7 |
|---|---|---|---|---|---|---|
| p | q | p ∨ q | ~(p ∨ q) | ~p | ~q | ~p • ~q |
| T | T | T | F | F | F | F |
| T | F | T | F | F | T | F |
| F | T | T | F | T | F | F |
| F | F | F | T | T | T | T |

The main column for each sentence (4 and 7) has the same truth values, which means that the statements are logically indistinguishable. In essence, they have the same logical content.

In order to show how the conclusion in (1) follows from its premises by the rules of natural deduction, we first have to translate the whole argument into our symbolic language. There are four simple sentences (i.e., sentences that contain no logical terms), and we can symbolize each using an upper case letter as follows:

B = "Bill will come to the party."

S = "Susan comes to the party."

A = "Adam comes to the party."

J = "Julie comes to the party."

Given this, the conclusion (Bill will not come) can be symbolized ~B (because it is the denial of B). The second premise (Julie is coming to the party) can by symbolized simply by J. The first premise (If either Julie or Susan comes to the party, then Bill and Adam won't come) is complex, and is best symbolized as follows: (J ∨ S) ⊃ (~B • ~A). The parentheses are used to clarify the sentence's logical structure.[2] When translating from English to logical symbolization, one uses commas and phrases like 'either' and 'both' to help figure out where the parentheses go. In our first premise, the main operator is clearly supposed to be a conditional, as is indicated both by the presence of a comma before the consequent, and the use of the term 'either' to make clear that the disjunct that follows should be grouped together.

A *proof* of an argument makes each step from the premises to the conclusion explicit. In a proof, one numbers the lines and puts the justification for each line next to it. The only justifications allowed are that a line is a premise, or that it is derived from a previous line in the proof using one of the rules of the system, which is indicated by citing the line (or lines) and the rule used. Here is the proof of the argument above:

---

[2] J ∨ S ⊃ ~B • ~A is not only ill-formed and so unreadable, but it also is ambiguous, as one could place parentheses in different places to make it well formed. For example, we could make that sentence well formed in many different ways: J ∨ ((S ⊃ ~B) • ~A), ((J ∨ S) ⊃ ~B) • ~A, and J ∨ (S ⊃ (~B • ~A)), to name but a few. But each of these sentences says something different than the original. The first says "Either Jill will come to the party or, if Susan comes, then Bill won't come and Adam won't come." The second says, "If either Jill or Susan comes to the party then Bill won't come, and Adam won't come." The last one says "Either Jill will come to the party or, if Susan comes then both Bill won't come and Adam won't come."

1. $( J \lor S) \supset (\sim B \cdot \sim A)$     Premise
2. $J$     Premise
3. $J \lor S$     2, Addition
4. $\sim B \cdot \sim A$     1, 3, Modus ponens
5. $\sim B$     4, Simplification

All of the rules in a natural deduction system are valid rules of inference, and any argument that has the form of one of these rules is also valid in classical logic. In the previous chapter, I introduced the notion of validity, and explained the difference between valid and invalid argument forms in Aristotelian logic. In that discussion, I characterized validity purely intuitively, pointing out that valid argument forms guaranteed the truth of their conclusions whereas invalid argument forms did not. The characteristic matrices that we laid out in the last section provide another way of explaining validity and invalidity, one that is both clearer and more explanatory.

Let us use the tools of this chapter, then, and construct a truth table to show what it means for an argument, Disjunctive Syllogism, for example, to be valid.

DS)    $p \lor q$
      $\sim q$
      So, $p$

Recall from the first section of this chapter that there are four possible combinations of truth and falsity for two sentences. Here are the columns (which I will now number, for ease of discussion) representing those possibilities:

|      | 1 | 2 |
|------|---|---|
|      | p | q |
| i)   | T | T |
| ii)  | T | F |
| iii) | F | T |
| iv)  | F | F |

To see why DS is a valid argument form, we need to show that, for all these possible combinations of truth and falsity, the form DS will never take us from true premises to false conclusions. In order to show this, we need to determine the truth values for the premises, the first of which is $p \lor q$. We have already seen what the truth table for $\lor$ looks like, and we can add this column to our p and q columns above to get a table that looks like this:

|       | 1 | 2 | 3     |
|-------|---|---|-------|
|       | p | q | p ∨ q |
| i)    | T | T | T     |
| ii)   | T | F | T     |
| iii)  | F | T | T     |
| iv)   | F | F | F     |

The second premise of DS is ~q. To determine the possible values of this premise, we can consult our characteristic matrix for negation. What we see is that when a sentence (there indicated by the variable p) is true, ~p is false, and when p is false, ~p is true. This gives us a column for ~q that we can add to what we already have as follows:

|       | 1 | 2 | 3     | 4   |
|-------|---|---|-------|-----|
|       | p | q | p ∨ q | ~q  |
| i)    | T | T | T     | F   |
| ii)   | T | F | T     | T   |
| iii)  | F | T | T     | F   |
| iv)   | F | F | F     | T   |

In rows (i) and (iii), q is true, which is why on those rows, not-q is false. And on (ii) and (iv), q is false, which is why ~ q is true on those rows. The conclusion is just p itself, which is one of our original columns (column 1). If the conclusion here were complex instead of simple (i.e., if it had some logical terms in it), we would figure out its value in the same way that we figured out the values of the premises.

We can now demonstrate that DS will never take someone from true premises to a false conclusion. First we find the row (or rows) where both the premises (columns 3 and 4) are true. It's not enough that one premise be true, both have to be. The table that we have laid out to represent the possible combinations of truth and falsity in DS makes clear that only in row (ii) are both the premises true. Next, we check the truth value of the conclusion in that row. In row (ii), the conclusion, q, also is true. Therefore, disjunctive syllogism is a valid argument form because, when both the premises are true, the conclusion is also true.

In the list of natural deduction rules, I noted that many people find the rule of Addition to be particularly strange. This rule allows one to disjoin any sentence, q, to a sentence that has already been asserted, as follows:

p

So, p ∨ q

The truth table we just completed can also be used to show that this rule, too, is a valid rule of inference. On the truth table, it is clear that anytime p is true (column 1, rows i and iii), so is p ∨ q (column 3). That is why it preserves truth: if p is true, p ∨ q can't fail to be true as well.

Compare these valid rules of inference with the following invalid variant of the argument that we considered in Chapter 1:

2. Either my husband is at home or he's gone to the store. He is not at home. So I don't think he's gone to the store, either.

Because of its similarity to disjunctive syllogism, let us call it *Dysfunctional Syllogism*. The form of this argument is:

DysfS    p ∨ q

         ~p

         So, ~q

To see why this argument form is invalid, we figure out the truth values of both of the premises and the conclusion, just as we did with Disjunctive Syllogism (this time I won't go through all the steps). Here is the completed truth table:

|      | 1 | 2 | 3 | 4 | 5 |
|------|---|---|------|------|------|
|      | p | q | p ∨ q | ~p | ~q |
| i)   | T | T | T | F | F |
| ii)  | T | F | T | F | T |
| iii) | F | T | T | T | F |
| iv)  | F | F | F | T | T |

Following the same procedure as we did with DS, we find the row or rows in which both the premises (columns 3 and 4) get assigned a T, in this case, row (iii). The value of the conclusion (column 5) in row (iii) however, is F. In other words, DysfS does not guarantee that only true conclusions follow from true premises. DysfS, therefore, is invalid.

Recall that Frege thought that the job of logic was to make sure that we couldn't go from true beliefs to false ones. With this in mind, it is clear why DS and Add are better rules than DysfS. The valid rules guarantee that if my premises are true, then my conclusion will also be true, whereas invalid rules like DysfS cannot make this guarantee. The concept of a valid argument is tremendously important in logic. In classical logic, an argument is valid as long as it is an instance of one of the valid argument forms. All of the rules that define a system of natural deduction are valid argument forms.

# 3

# What is Truth?

## I—THE PROBLEM WITH TRUTH

In the first two chapters of this book the concept of truth has come up quite a bit (truth tables, truth preservation), and it is not unreasonable to want to know a little more about it. Most people have a fairly intuitive understanding of what truth is. Aristotle summed it up this way: "To say that that which is is not or that which is not is, is a falsehood; and to say that which is is and that which is not is not, is true."[1] On the face of it, this seems like a pretty good account of the matter. What makes the sentence "Snow is white" true is the fact that snow is white, and what makes the sentence "Grass is purple" false is the fact that grass isn't purple.

The problem is that, as it stands, the Aristotelian account may work well for sentences like those just considered, but the account will also make some sentences both true and false. Consider the following sentence, which I will call L because it is what is known as a *liar sentence*:

L) This sentence is false.

L is a sentence that attributes falsity to itself, which makes L's truth value very difficult to determine. If L is true then it is false (because it says that it is false) and if L is false then (because it says it's false) it's

---

[1] *Aristotle Metaphysics Books Γ, Δ, and E*, 2nd Edition, 1011b25 (1993) translated with notes by Kirwan, Christopher, NY, Oxford, Toronto: Oxford University Press.

true. Or, in Aristotle's terms, if L is true then what it says is the case, but in this particular instance, what it says is that L is false. Likewise, if L is False then what it says is not the case, but what L says is that it is false, and if that is not the case, then L is not false and must thereby be true.

The existence of sentences like L makes it very hard to be confident that Aristotle's account is all there is to truth. After all, in general things can't simultaneously have contradictory properties. For example, suppose that someone came up with a definition of 'cat' that made some creature both a cat and not a cat. Biologists would rightly question the coherence and usefulness of such a definition. In principle, the truth predicate should be no different. For this reason, even if the notion of truth is easily understood when it comes to sentences about the color of snow and grass, the fact that it can lead us so easily into contradictions is reason to be wary about whether our intuitive grasp of truth is good enough.

Since Aristotle's basic insight into the nature of truth seems to be on the right track in the vast majority of cases, the challenge is to come up with an account of truth that keeps what is right about it but eliminates the problematic cases like the liar sentence, L. The mathematician and logician Alfred Tarski came up with a theory of truth that did just that.

Tarski formalized Aristotle's definition with the following schema:

S is true if and only if p.

A *schema* is a pattern or template that can be used in many different instances or situations. An instance of this schema would be one in which S is a sentence in quotation marks (by putting it in quotation marks we are able to talk about it without using it ourselves), and p is that same sentence without quotation marks (so we can talk about the things meant by the sentence). Here are some instances of this schema:

"Snow is white" is true if and only if snow is white.

"Grass is green" is true if and only if grass is green.

"Bananas are yellow" is true if and only if bananas are yellow.

And so on. Aristotle's insight is preserved in each instance of this schema since, to take the first example, "Snow is white" is true when what it says is the case, and what it says is that snow is white.

To see how Tarski prevents sentences like L, consider what, in particular, has gone wrong in L. The main problem with L is that the truth predicate is being used to attribute a lack of truth to itself. This is what is known as a problem of self-reference. To rid the notion of truth of its paradoxical nature, therefore, Tarski argued that a truth predicate can never be allowed to refer to itself, as it does in L.

To fully explain Tarski's idea here, I have to introduce a bit of slightly technical terminology. Tarski distinguishes the *object language*, or the language being talked about, from the *meta-language*, which is the language being used to talk about the object-language.[2] Tarski's claim, in essence, is that in order to talk about what is true and false in some object language, one must use a meta-language. Self-reference is prevented because the truth predicate for any given object language is never a part of that object language, and so a sentence can never predicate truth (or the lack thereof) to itself.

An example will help to make this idea more concrete. Imagine that the English language lacked a truth predicate. According to Tarski, to talk about truth in English in a way that wouldn't lead us into any inconsistencies we would need to use a meta-language. This meta-language would be just like English except it would have the predicate 'true-in-English.' This predicate in the meta-language is what makes it possible to talk about the truth of the sentences of the object language, English. And since the T-schema, in some sense, defines truth, truth-in-English is just the instances of the true-in-English-schema, such as,

"Snow is white" is true-in-English if and only if snow is white.

"Rhinoceroses are dangerous" is true-in-English if and only if rhinoceroses are dangerous.

"Fish swim" is true-in-English if and only if fish swim,

If we could list every possible sentence of English, we could simply use that list to define truth-in-English.

Suppose, now, that we want to talk about truth-in-English, say because we want to know the truth conditions for the sentence "'Snow is white' is true-in-English". In this case, our object language is our former meta-language. That is, the language that we added the truth

---

[2] I noted in the Introduction that the ancient Greek word 'meta' literally means after, but the meaning has morphed several times since then. Today it is used in several differing contexts. In the current use, 'meta' means something like about or above. The meta-language allows us to talk about the object language without actually using it.

predicate to in our acceptance of all instances of the truth-in-English schema now becomes the language that we'll talk about, and so we'll need a new meta-language to talk about it. Let's call our former meta-language now turned object-language 'Trenglish' (for truth plus English). In order to talk about truth in Trenglish, we need another notion of truth, truth-in-Trenglish. Truth-in-Trenglish will be defined much like truth-in-English was defined, except the appropriate schema now is:

S is true-in-Trenglish if and only if p.

For instance,

"'Snow is white' is true-in-English" is true-in-Trenglish if and only if 'snow is white' is true-in-English.

"'Rhinoceroses are dangerous' is true-in-English" is true-in-Trenglish if and only if 'rhinoceroses are dangerous' is true-in-English.

"'Fish swim' is true-in-English" is true-in-Trenglish if and only if 'fish swim' is true-in-English,

and so on and so on. In this way, the truth predicate can never self-predicate, and so there will be no paradoxical self-reference. Sentences like L just can't arise on this theory of truth.

Note that according to Tarski's theory, we can never define a notion of truth independently of a language. In terms of our examples above, what we ended up defining was two notions of truth, 'true-in-English' and 'true-in-Trenglish.' We never defined 'true.' This is because, on Tarski's theory, there is not one truth predicate, there are as many truth predicates as there are languages. Truth, for Tarski, is always defined relative to a language.

Tarski's solution avoids liar sentences and thereby makes clear that our intuitive understanding of truth can be made respectable. Nevertheless, while virtually all philosophers agree that the T-schema is a defining feature of truth, many are critical of Tarski's many notions of truth. Among other things, these philosophers point out that truth doesn't seem like something that's relativized to a language. It seems more like there's one notion of truth, and that it applies to all languages at all times. In addition, it certainly looks, for all intents and purposes, like the truth predicate can be applied to itself, as in

T) T is true.

Advocates of a hierarchy of truths have to somehow explain why this sentence seems to make perfect sense to speakers of English.

## II—THREE THEORIES OF TRUTH

We have just canvassed one problem with our intuitive understanding of the notion of truth, and seen one possible solution to that problem. But a second difficulty confronts us. As correct as Aristotle's definition might sound, it is greatly lacking in details. There have been many suggestions as to how to best put a little flesh on Aristotle's basic insight. Which of the many ways of filling in the details on Aristotle's account of truth is the right one? In this section, I will briefly explain three of the most well-known accounts of truth, along with the problems associated with each.

### A. Correspondence Theories

*Correspondence theories of truth* are among the most widely advocated. Though distinct versions may differ in their details, according to theories in this tradition, a sentence is true in virtue of its ability to accurately represent or picture the world the way it is. These theories today are known as correspondence theories of truth because they make truth a matter of whether or not words in a sentence correspond to the world. Contemporary correspondence theories tend to regard truth as an objective relation obtaining between the world and the words we use to describe it, something like the relation between a map and the bit of the earth that the map is supposed to represent. According to these theories, truth is a property that some sentences have and others lack, whether or not we know which sentences have it and which don't.

Much of the recommendation for a theory like this comes from its intuitiveness. For example, the sentence, "A rhinoceros is in the room," will be true just in case there is a rhinoceros in the room in question. But though this way of thinking about truth is intuitive for simple sentences like these, it can become problematic pretty quickly. Take the subject of the current book, logical terms. How do sentences containing logical terms get pictured? For example, what does the sentence "It is not the case that there is a rhinoceros in the room," correspond to? Take a minute and try to draw a picture that corresponds to "It is not the case that there is a rhinoceros in the room."

The problem is that a picture of a room without a rhinoceros is not the same as a picture that corresponds to "It is not the case that there is a rhinoceros in the room." To properly represent "It is not the case that there is a rhinoceros in the room" one would need a picture that made clear that it was a rhinoceros that was missing. A picture of, say, an empty room leaves it unclear as to what, if anything, is missing, but the sentence "It is not the case that there is a rhinoceros in the room" isn't unclear about what's missing in the slightest.

In addition to difficulties like this, correspondence theories are bothersome to many philosophers because the notion of correspondence is a bit mysterious. The relation of correspondence, as I noted, is an objective one, but this objective correspondence seems to just add to the things needing explanation, rather than explaining the things to be explained. In answer to the question, "What is truth?," we are told by correspondence theorists that truth is a matter of objective correspondence, but what, on earth, is that? It seems that, rather than actually explaining what truth is, correspondence theories have just added another thing to the list in need of explanation.

Adding to the suspicion that objective correspondence isn't really playing a very central role in our account of truth is the following difficulty. Generally speaking, people are not very good at telling when their sentences have this objective correspondence relation to the world and when they don't. After all, the history of human thought is full of people believing sentences that were later understood to be false (e.g., "The earth is flat", "The sun goes around the earth."). Of course, people could be very bad at detecting when this objective relation of correspondence holds, even when it, in fact, does hold. By analogy, people are not very good detectors of the presence of ultraviolet wavelengths of light, either, and these wavelengths are certainly objectively out there. So my point is not that this consideration is decisive against the correspondence theories. But I do think it gives us a good reason to wonder how correspondence is supposed to help us to understand the concept of truth. After all, we invented machines that detect and record the presence of ultraviolet light, but a similar machine for detecting truth is not likely. At the very least, I think this should give us pause in our confidence that a property of correspondence is somehow essential to making sense of the notion of truth.

## B. Coherence Theories

There are two major rivals to the correspondence theory of truth. The first that we will examine are *coherence theories of truth*. As with correspondence theories, there are a number of different coherence theories which differ in their details. Coherence theorists of truth agree with correspondence theorists of truth that truth is a special and privileged property, but they disagree about what that property is. Coherence theories hold that truth is not a matter of correspondence between words in sentences and the world, but is, rather, a matter of overall coherence among many sentences. According to coherence theorists, the unit to be evaluated for truth is not single sentences (themselves broken down into clear correspondence relations between individual terms and things in the world), but rather, several sets of sentences or even entire theories. What makes a theory or set of sentences true is overall internal coherence, i.e, that it is consistent, that it draws conclusions according to accepted logical rules, and so on.

One major criticism of coherence theories is that they do not seem to require that the set of sentences in question in any way accurately represent the world that those sentences are supposed to be about. That is, if all that is important is internal coherence, then a set of sentences could be consistent with all the correct logical inferences made, but still not accurately represent the world. To see this, one need only consider the existence of conspiracy theories. Both the official report as to who shot John F. Kennedy (Oswald, acting on his own), and the conspiracy theory as to who shot Kennedy (Oswald, acting on the say-so of many high-level government officials) are consistent and internally coherent, and yet one of them, by necessity, can not be a correct account of the facts. For many, this fact about coherence theories makes them a poor choice for giving an account of truth, since intuitively, truth certainly includes the assumption that true sentences are accurate representations of the world.

One particular variant of a coherence theory comes from the American Pragmatists William James and John Dewey, and gives rise to a version of truth with its own name, the *pragmatic theory of truth*. According to James and Dewey, true theories are simply those that are instrumentally useful to us. If a theory fulfills our expectations and helps us to satisfy our goals, whatever these may be and however we may come to them, then that theory is true. This theory is a coherence theory since one of the expectations that we generally have for our total belief set is that it be coherent (i.e., consistent, and with all the proper entailments drawn).

Pragmatic theories of truth are often criticized for seeming to allow any sentence to be true, so long as that sentence is regarded as useful by the person who believes it. So, for example, what's to stop me from thinking that the sentence "I am queen of the world" is true, since my being queen would obviously be very useful to me? What stops me, according to this theory, is that truth is a social notion. What this means is that more than one person (the more the better) would have to find the belief useful, and in our example, it's hard to see how to make that belief at all useful to you or anyone else who might value not having to obey my orders. Perhaps more importantly, the pragmatists argued that one of the things we should value in our beliefs is their overall fit with the empirical evidence, and so in this way, they thought that what would be regarded as useful would be greatly constrained by the facts in the world. One would be hard pressed to simply make it true, i.e., useful, that drinking arsenic is good for one's health.

Even if the pragmatist can deal with some of the more obvious criticisms, the fact remains that some beliefs might come out true for a pragmatist which, strictly speaking, don't correspond to the way things are. It is possible on this understanding of truth that some belief might be tremendously useful, but still not be veridical, i.e., it might not correctly represent the world. And this is also true of coherence theories more generally. This remains the major drawback to any coherence theory of truth.

## C. Deflationary Theories

The last kind of theory of truth that we'll look at are *deflationary theories of truth*. Like correspondence and coherence theorists of truth, there are many variant deflationary theories of truth. What distinguishes them from correspondence and coherence theories of truth is that the deflationist doesn't think there is anything to truth at all. About all that can be said, in any systematic way about it, is given by Tarski's truth schema.

According to deflationism, the following two sentences mean the same thing:

It is true that there is a rhinoceros in the room.

There is a rhinoceros in the room.

That is, asserting a sentence and asserting its truth amount to the same thing, in terms of informational content. This is because truth is not a property at all, as it was for both correspondence and coherence theorists. In particular, for deflationists truth is nothing but a meta-linguistic device for talking about language. When I go to Jill's speech and report back that everything she said was true, I'm using a linguistic device to talk about Jill's sentences, without actually repeating each one. For deflationists, all of the instances of the truth schema do not add up to anything that can be theorized about. Rather, what makes "Snow is white" true is that snow is white, and what makes "Rhinoceroses are dangerous" true is that rhinoceroses are dangerous. Truth is not a property to be found in addition to what individually makes each sentence true, i.e., snow's being white and rhinos being dangerous.

Correspondence and coherence theorists have it that truth is some substantial property adhering to either sentences, or whole sets of sentences, respectively. (Correspondence and coherence theories are, you might guess, inflationary theories, since they inflate the truth predicate beyond its function as a device for talking about language.) But deflationists argue that when we attribute truth to a sentence, though it may look grammatically like we are predicating something of that sentence, the thing being predicated is not a property with any philosophically interesting attributes.

One of the main points in favor of deflationary theories is the dismal record of inflationary ones. The history of philosophy gives proof to the difficulty of giving more than a sketch of an account of either correspondence or coherence theories. Deflationism, in part, is driven by the thought that the continued failure of each suggested correspondence or coherence theory might be due to the fact that there's really nothing there that is amenable to systematic explanation.

Critics of deflationary theories argue that deflationism misses something fundamental and important about truth. Given that the truth of sentences about snow depends on snow and the truth of sentences about rhinos depends on rhinos, isn't it also clear that the truth of both sentences depends on the fact that some material object has some property attributed to it? And if there are generalizations like this to be made, even if there are places where the generalizations fail a bit and even if the generalizations are fairly general, then why not make them and try to figure out how they contribute to a sentence's truth or falsity?

## III—TRUTH AND LOGIC

Though my comments on truth and its nature have been very brief, they are sufficient for our purposes. In the first place, we now know that the concept of truth can be made consistent. Thus, we need not worry that our account of logic will be inherently flawed by its reliance on a notion of truth. In the second place, it turns out that no matter what theory of truth you favor, things like truth tables and truth preservation can be explained in terms of it. For example, if you think that correspondence theories are essentially right, then a valid argument is one in which if the premises correspond correctly to reality, the conclusion is guaranteed to correspond as well. If you think that true sentence sets are those that are most instrumentally useful, then valid arguments are going to guarantee that you don't go from useful to not useful sentences. Even a deflationary understanding is fine. Though deflationists deny that truth has any important or interesting intrinsic nature, they certainly can explain what it means to preserve truth. If the premises of an argument are true and the conclusion is "Snow is white", then snow is white. In short, no matter what you think about truth, you can define logical concepts in terms of that definition.

Of course, that doesn't mean that truth is completely unproblematic in the philosophy of logic. (Nothing is ever that easy in philosophy.) As we will see, some philosophers think that what you say about truth (and logic in turn) has big implications for metaphysics. But we can deal with this issue in Chapter 9. For now, talk of truth tables and truth preservation doesn't require us to commit to one theory of truth over another. When you see the words 'true' or 'truth', simply substitute your favorite theory and read on.

# 4

# Three Distinctions

## I—SYNTAX AND SEMANTICS

In this chapter, I will explain three distinctions that will be helpful for the discussions that follow. The first is between the syntax and the semantics of a language (either a natural language like English, or a formalized artificial language like classical logic). *Semantics* is the study of meaning and truth, whereas *syntax* is the study of structure or form. The best way to illustrate the difference between the two is by way of example.

Consider the following boxes:

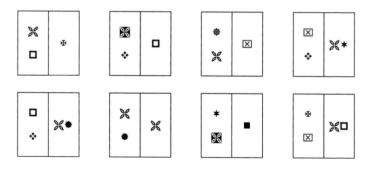

I'm going to ask you to answer five questions about these boxes. The questions will each consist of two symbols followed by a question mark. To find the correct answer, simply locate the box that has the two indicated symbols on its left hand side, and the right hand side of that same box will give you the right answer. Here goes:

1. ✴🕀?
2. ◻️❖?
3. 🕀❖?
4. ⊠❖?
5. ✵⊠?

The correct answers, of course, are:

1. ■
2. 🕸✴
3. ◻️
4. 🕸✴
5. 🕸◻️

When you answer these questions correctly, you are simply reading a series of marks, and then responding according to the instructions with the marks that are indicated by the relevant boxes. That is, you are seeing marks of various shapes and "responding" with other marks of various shapes. Your activity in this case is done purely by considering the physical form of the marks. This is what is meant by syntax. Syntax is concerned completely with the form of the questions and answers, and considers each simply as an assembly of marks (either auditory, if verbal, or written).

Semantics, on the other hand, is a way of spelling out the meaning or interpretation of these questions and answers. In semantics, languages are about something, and so they are understood primarily in terms of that something. Returning to the boxes above, and the questions I asked you, the following is a decoder key for the symbols:

🕸 = 1
🕀 = 2
✴ = 3
❖ = 4
■ = 5
◻️ = 6

✠ = 7

❀ = 8

☒ = 9

✱ = 0

Now, it should become clear that in each box, the symbols on the left are the numerals representing the two numbers to be added, and the symbol(s) on the right are the numerals representing their sum. Knowing this, you can understand what it is you were doing in answering the questions that I posed to you. If you go back and re-answer these questions, you are not merely correlating a series of marks with another set of marks. You are speaking and understanding and using a language. Your syntactic understanding has now been augmented, and it includes a semantic understanding as well, because you now understand the meaning of the symbols involved.

There are several important semantic notions, most notably meaning, truth and reference. Your ability to understand words in English is one that encompasses all of these semantic categories. For example, consider the English word 'cat.' You know what 'cat' means, you understand when it is true to say of an object that it is a cat, and you know that it refers to cats. The matrices and truth tables that we examined in Chapter 2 give the semantics for the logical functions that we examined there, but the semantics that it is concerned with is not nearly as rich as is your understanding of English terms. Truth table semantics are concerned only with truth, not with meaning or reference. On the face of it, leaving meaning and reference out of things might seem puzzling. After all, if we understood only that the following were true,

1. ✱ + ▨ = ■

2. ☐ + ❖ = ✄❀

3. ▨ + ❖ = ☐

4. ☒ + ❖ = ✄✱

5. ✠ + ☒ = ✄☐

then we wouldn't really understand these equations at all. They would just seem like a bunch of pretty symbols combined in a vaguely arithmetic way. Knowing whether or not a sentence is true or false seems a lot different than actually understanding that sentence and what that sentence is about.

In the next chapter, we will see that truth is not, in fact, enough. At the very least, some considerations of reference will be necessary in giving an adequate semantics for classical logic. In addition, in subsequent chapters we will explore proposed extensions of classical logic as well as alternatives to the classical understanding of the connectives, both of which challenge the adequacy of truth functional semantics.

For now, however, let me close this section by making clear why both syntax and semantics have been thought to be important. Roughly speaking, the syntax is supposed to determine the formal rules for the logical operations and the semantics is supposed to establish the adequacy of those rules by clarifying how those rules preserve truth. For example, in Chapter 2 we discussed the rule Disjunctive Syllogism. This rule's syntax tells us that when we have premises of a certain form we are entitled to a conclusion of a certain form. In symbolic terms, when we have premises of the form p ∨ q and ~p, we are also entitled to q. Truth table semantics then assures us that this rule is a good one by showing us in explicit terms how this rule preserves truth. Thus, the semantics helps explain why the syntactically defined rules are desirable to use. In combination, we get a very satisfactory explanation of what distinguishes good arguments from bad ones, and this, you may recall from the first chapter, is what logical investigations have always been about.

## II—FORM AND CONTENT

The second distinction to be explored in this chapter has already come up in connection with our discussion of logical form in Chapter 1. But I want to explain this distinction a little more fully and further clarify its importance. The form of an argument, recall, is its basic logical structure, replacing all non-logical terms with variables, and leaving the logical terms in their place. Content, on the other hand, is what the sentences of the argument are about.

Consider the following argument:

1. If Julie is going to Miami, then she is going to Florida.
   Julie is not going to Miami.
   Therefore, Julie is not going to Florida.

Now, let us suppose that in fact, Julie is going to New York City. In this case, the premises of this argument are true, and the conclusion is also true. So, in particular, it is true both that Julie is not going to either Miami or anywhere else in Florida, and that if Julie is going to Miami then she is going to Florida (because, of course, Miami is in Florida, and anyone who goes to Miami has to go to Florida as well). So, in this case, we have true premises and a true conclusion. Is (1) a valid argument?

The answer is no. To see why, let us test the form of this argument using the truth table method. The logical form of (1) is:

p ⊃ q

~p

So, ~q

In chapter 2, I made up Dysfunctional Syllogism myself,[1] but this invalid argument form is common enough to have a standard name: *Denying the Antecedent*. It is invalid for the same reasons that Dysfunctional Syllogism is invalid, namely, because it can take us from true premises to false conclusions.

|  | 1 | 2 | 3 | 4 | 5 |
|---|---|---|---|---|---|
|  | p | q | p ⊃ q | ~p | ~q |
| i) | T | T | T | F | F |
| ii) | T | F | F | F | T |
| iii) | F | T | T | T | F |
| iv) | F | F | T | T | T |

The premises for this argument form are given in columns 3 and 4, and the conclusion is column 5. In this argument form, there are two rows in which both the premises are true, rows (iii) and (iv). In row (iii) the conclusion is false, and in row (iv) the conclusion is true. Even though this argument form seems to satisfy what we want for a valid argument in one row, a conflicting row is enough to spoil its chances at validity. Validity is a kind of guarantee. If an

---

[1] The form of this argument, recall, is:

DysfS    p ∨ q

~p

So, ~q

argument form is valid, then it can't take us from true premises to false conclusions.

Just as with valid arguments, any argument that is an instance of an invalid argument form is a logically invalid argument. This is why (1) is invalid. But the truth table helps to make clear why, in spite of (1)'s invalidity, the premises and the conclusion can both, in fact, be true in Julie's case. In the truth table for Denying the Antecedent, row (iv) has true premises and a true conclusion. When you take into consideration the truth values of the sentences involved in Julie's case, (1) turns out to be an instance of row (iv).

Nevertheless, finding ourselves with a true conclusion is not the same as being guaranteed a true conclusion, given the truth of our premises. With Denying the Antecedent, when both premises are true there is a 50/50 chance that the conclusion is true (because half of those cases on the truth table have a true conclusion and half of them have a false conclusion). But with valid arguments forms, like Disjunctive Syllogism, when both of premises are true, the truth of the conclusion is guaranteed.

What this shows is that the truth of the conclusion in (1) is accidental from a logical point of view because, logically, the conclusion might have been false. For example, if Julie were going to Tampa it would have been false. In this case, both the premises would remain true, but the conclusion would be false because Tampa is in Florida.

Now let's consider a second argument.

2. This sweater is green.
   So, this sweater is not red.

Suppose that both the premise and the conclusion of this argument are true, which is to say that some particular sweater is green and is also not red. Is this argument valid? Well, the conclusion of (2) seems to follow from the truth of its premise. Put in slightly stronger terms, in (2), if the premise is true, the conclusion must also be true. After all, if something is green, it is guaranteed to not be simultaneously red as well.

Nevertheless, (2) is no more a logically valid argument than is (1). The logical form of (2) is just two different sentences, one a sentence without logical complexity (the premise), and one a negated sentence (the conclusion):

p
So ~q

**51**

Here is a truth table for this argument:

|      | p | q | ~q |
|------|---|---|----|
| i)   | T | T | F  |
| ii)  | T | F | T  |
| iii) | F | T | F  |
| iv)  | F | F | T  |

Just as with Denying the Antecedent, though there is one row where the premise (p) is true and the conclusion (~q ) is true (row (ii)), there is one row where the premise is true and the conclusion is false (row (i)). Remember, one possible combination of truth values where the premises are true and the conclusion is false is enough to make an argument invalid.

Even though (2) is just as logically invalid as (1), the truth of the conclusion in (2) is less accidental given the truth of the premises than was the case with (1). This is because in (2), the seeming necessity of the conclusion given the truth of the premise is not guaranteed by logic, but it is guaranteed by something, namely the meaning or content of the terms 'green' and 'red.' The conclusion follows from the premise because of a fact about colors, namely, if a thing is green, then it can't be red.

That the intuitive goodness of (2) depends on a fact about colors can be seen clearly by noting that there certainly are other instances of the logical form of (2) that don't seem intuitively valid at all. Consider:

3. Sam has blonde hair.
   So, Sam doesn't have freckles.

The difference between (2) and (3) is in the content of what the sentences are about, not in their logical form.

The status of (2) seems to lie somewhere between an invalid argument like (1) and a valid argument like Disjunctive Syllogism. That is, the truth of the conclusion is guaranteed by something given the truth of the premises, but the guarantee is not logical. When the truth of a conclusion is guaranteed by the truth of the premises for logical reasons the content of the sentences doesn't matter. Philosophers of logic sum up this fact about logical functions by saying that logic is *topic neutral*, which means that logical functions and rules of inference place no restrictions on the subject matter of the sentences that the functions/rules operate with. This topic neutrality is one aspect of the generality of logic that so impressed Frege.

(3) is a *counter-example* to the validity of (2) because it makes clear that an argument with the same form as (2) can have a true premise and a false conclusion. Providing counter-examples is one way of showing that an argument form is not a valid one. To show that some argument form is invalid by providing a counter-example to it, one simply replaces each variable in the argument with sentences that clearly make the premise(s) true, but the conclusion false. Consider the following invalid argument form, *Affirming the Consequent*:

    p ⊃ q

    q

    So, p

To prove this argument invalid by counter-example, we simply think of two sentences to substitute for p and q so that the premises of the argument are true but the conclusion is false. One counter-example (of many possible counter-examples) can be gotten by substituting the sentence "Miami is in Texas" for p, and the sentence "Miami is south of Detroit" for q:

    If Miami is in Texas, then Miami is south of Detroit.
    Miami is south of Detroit.
    So, Miami is in Texas.

Both of these premises are clearly true. It is certainly true that Miami is south of Detroit, and it is also true that, if Miami is in Texas, then Miami is south of Detroit. But it is clearly false that Miami is in Texas. Can you think of another counter-example to the argument form affirming the Consequent? How about a counter-example to the following:

    p ≡ q.

    ~p

    So, q

## III—LOGICAL CONSEQUENCE
## AND LOGICAL TRUTH

One thing that we might say about argument (2) from the last section is that the conclusion of (2) is a consequence of the truth of the premise, just not a logical consequence. This leads us to the final distinction that we will look at in this chapter, logical consequence and logical truth. These important notions are fundamental to making sense of the discussions that follow in this book.

An account of *logical consequence* says what follows logically from what and why. Put slightly differently, a proper analysis of the concept of logical consequence will be one that clarifies the relation 'logically follows from.' To see what this means and why it is important, I will introduce a silly example. Suppose we start out with the set of the following five sentences:

(i)   s

(ii)  ~q

(iii) s ⊃ r

(iv)  u ⊃ q

(v)   t ∨ q

Using the fragment of classical logic that I introduced in the box in Chapter 2, sentences 6-10 follow from these five sentences:

(vi)   r (by MP on i and iii)

(vii)  t (by DS on ii and v)

(viii) s • ~q (by Con on i and ii)

(ix)   s • ( t ∨ q) (by Con on i and v)

(x)    ~u (by MT on ii and iv)

The parenthetical remarks make clear why each sentence follows from the first set of five sentences. (vi) for example, follows by the rule Modus Ponens from sentences (i) and (iii). Clearly, there are many more sentences that follow from the first five sentences according to the rules I introduced in Chapter 2. For example, one could always conjoin sentences to other sentences in an infinite variety of ways (provided that repetition is allowed, so that, e.g., we could conjoin sentence (vi) to (vii), and then the resulting conjunction could be conjoined again with any other sentence, and so on). But this is enough to give the general picture.

Now, suppose that instead of Disjunctive Syllogism, our set of rules included Dysfunctional Syllogism. Then from our original five sentences, different sentences would follow. For example, instead of (vii) we would have:

vii')  ~t

The question is why should we think that (vii), and not (vii') logically follows from (i) through (v)? This question can be rephrased in terms of logical consequence. Why should we think that the correct account of logical consequence is given by the rules that include Disjunctive Syllogism instead of Dysfunctional Syllogism?

One possible answer to both ways of putting the question should be obvious. Dysfunctional Syllogism is an invalid argument form and, as such, it won't preserve truth, whereas Disjunctive Syllogism is valid. This answer appeals to the semantic properties of the divergent argument forms to clarify why one is preferable to another. But clearly more needs to be said. Among other things, truth preservation is not all that we want. If it were, then we should want to include arguments like (2) from last section in our account of logical consequence. In addition, we could certainly question why truth preservation is our primary desiderata.[2] An account of logical consequence, therefore, seeks to make clear what follows from what in a way that explains the proper scope of logic by taking into account all the aspects of logic that we have and will explore in this book.

What, then, is logical truth? *Logical truths* are sentences that are true simply in virtue of their logical form. One example of a logical truth in classical logic is the *law of non-contradiction*, $\sim (p \cdot \sim p)$ (not both p and not p, or colloquially, it can't be the case that a sentence and its negation are both true). This sentence form is a *tautology*, which means that no matter what the actual truth and falsity of the constituent sentence or sentences involved, the whole formula will always be true. Let's do a truth table for the law of non-contradiction. We need only two rows here because p is the only simple sentence whose possible truth values we have to take account of.

|  | 1 | 2 | 3 | 4 |
|---|---|---|---|---|
|  | p | $\sim p$ | $(p \cdot \sim p)$ | $\sim(p \cdot \sim p)$ |
| i) | T | F | F | T |
| ii) | F | T | F | T |

Recall from the matrix in Chapter 2 that a conjunction is true only when both conjuncts are true. That is, whenever either conjunct is false, the conjunction as a whole is false. The unnegated conjunction in this case (column 3) is a conjunction of a single formula and its

---

[2] For example, in Chapter 9 we will consider a non-classical logic where the semantics are given in terms of the provability of sentences, rather then their truth.

negation. Since when a sentence p is true, its negation is always false, and vice versa, a conjunction of a formula and its own negation will always have at least one false conjunct. Therefore, the conjunction itself will always be false. The negation of a formula that is always false is a formula that is always true.

Tautologies are true no matter what the actual facts of the world. Tautologies are true on every row of a truth table, for any possible combination of truth and falsity of their constituent parts. Correspondingly, *contradictions*, such as p • ~p are always false, no matter what the actual facts of the world. They are false on every row of the truth table.

Tautologies (and contradictions) are to be distinguished from *contingent* sentences, or sentences that are made true or false by the way the world is. Contingent sentences are true on some rows of their truth tables and false on others. These truths are said to be contingent because they might have been otherwise. For example, "Jennifer Fisher has a dog" is false, but it might have been otherwise. I might have a dog, and if I did have a dog, then the sentence would be true.

Logical truths like the law of non-contradiction are also *theorems* in classical logic. A theorem is a sentence that is provable using no assumptions or premises whatsoever. In Chapter 2, I briefly explained the idea of a natural deduction proof. In natural deduction proofs, one is given a set of starting sentences (the premises) and one can then derive a conclusion using logical rules. Theorems are sentences that are derivable no matter what one's assumptions or premises. That is, the rules themselves can generate the sentence in question, without needing any premises to start.

To illustrate, let's consider a different logical truth, p ∨ ~p, commonly called the *law of excluded middle* (or the *law of the excluded third*). This law says that every sentence is such that either it, or its negation, is true. The proof for p ∨ ~p doesn't begin with premises, but rather proceeds via indirect proof (briefly discussed in the box in Chapter 2). Indirect proofs are a common method in mathematics that we'll have more opportunity to examine in Chapter 9. In an indirect proof, one starts out assuming the negation of whatever sentence one wants to prove. If one can show that a contradiction follows, then one is entitled to assert the negation of the negation of that sentence, which in classical logic is equivalent to just the sentence itself. In other words, if a contradiction follows from ~p, then ~~p must be true. And since ~~p is equivalent to p in classical logic, if a contradiction follows from ~p, then p must be true.

The indirect proof for p ∨ ~p begins by assuming the negation of this formula, or ~(p ∨ ~p), and continues as follows:

1. ~(p ∨ ~p)          Assumption for indirect proof
2. ~p & ~~p           DeMorgan's Rules, 1
3. ~p & p             Double Negation, 2
4. ~~(p ∨ ~p)         Indirect proof, 1-3
5. So, p ∨ ~p         Double Negation, 4[3]

It is important to note that lines (2) and (3) only follow on the assumption in line (1). Natural deduction systems use various devices to indicate this logical dependence, though I have omitted doing so here.

Returning to our set of five sentences above, the fact that p ∨ ~p is a theorem means that we can always add it to that list of sentences, or any other list of sentences that are meant to obey the inference rules of classical logic. Theorems can always be asserted, no matter what our starting sentences are. This means that from two different sets of sentences like those above, both our sets will have as a consequence that p ∨ ~p. Since it is a theorem, it is always provable.

Historically, people have thought of logical laws as completely beyond doubt. They have been thought to be intuitively true in the sense that the truth is supposed to be obvious to anyone who understands the concepts in question, much like the axioms of Euclidean geometry. So, in the same way that it is obvious to anyone who cares to think about it that all right angles are equal, or that a straight line can be drawn through any two points, it is supposed to be obvious that either I have a cat named Sunny Jim or I don't have a cat named Sunny Jim, and that "I was born in Detroit" and "I wasn't born in Detroit" can't both be true.

In chapters 6 through 10 of this book, I will examine a number of logics that differ in various ways from classical logic. The notions of logical truth and logical consequence are indispensable tools for clarifying exactly how these logics are supposed to differ from classical logic. In some cases, the difference is easiest to see by noting how the logical truths of the various non-classical logics differ from those of classical logic. In others, the difference is best highlighted by considering the logical consequences of each rival logic, and comparing them to classical logical consequence. In some cases, a comparison on

---

[3] DeMorgan's Rules and the rule of Double Negation are two of the replacement rules that we met in the box in Chapter 2.

both accounts is most helpful. In every case, the important point will be to demonstrate how a rival logic differs from classical logic, in order to better compare the advantages and disadvantages associated with each logical system.

# 5

# Quantifiers and Identity

## I—QUANTIFIERS, VACUOUS NAMES, AND THE PROBLEM OF NON-BEING

We've seen how classical logic defines the logical symbols •, ∨, ⊃, ≡, and ~. These symbols are called *sentential or propositional connectives* because they connect whole sentences to each other. But we have not yet examined what is probably modern logic's biggest advance over Aristotelian logic, the Fregean treatment of the terms 'Some' and 'All.' This advance is why Frege is generally thought to be the greatest logician of modern times.

To see why we shouldn't leave our account of classical logical consequence as it stands, consider the following inference:

1. All humans are mortal.
   Socrates is human.
   So, Socrates is mortal.

This argument is intuitively valid. If the premises are true, then it just has to be true that Socrates is mortal. In fact, (1) is also logically valid, in the sense that what makes the conclusions follow from the premises doesn't depend on any facts in the world. However, the bit of classical logic that I've so far described can't adequately capture this validity. Since no English term standing for a sentential connective appears in this argument, its form is just three simple sentences, symbolized using variables:

p
q
So, r

CHAPTER 5

This argument form is not valid. The truth of the premises does not guarantee the truth of the conclusion. To see this, let us represent all the possible combinations of truth and falsity of the sentences involved. There are eight possibilities this time, because there are three simple sentences involved:

|       | p     | q     | r     |
|-------|-------|-------|-------|
| i)    | True  | True  | True  |
| ii)   | True  | True  | False |
| iii)  | True  | False | True  |
| iv)   | True  | False | False |
| v)    | False | True  | True  |
| vi)   | False | True  | False |
| vii)  | False | False | True  |
| viii) | False | False | False |

Since both the premises and the conclusion are all logically simple sentences, the base columns that represent all the possible combinations of truth values are also the columns that represent the premises and the conclusion. Rows (i) and (ii) are the only rows where both the premises (p and q) are true, and though r is true in row (i), it is false in row (ii), and so the truth of the premises is not guaranteed. To account for inferences like these, we have to add and formally explicate some new logical vocabulary.

Clearly, the validity of argument (1) above depends on the term 'all.' You will recall that we encountered this term in our discussion of Aristotelian logic, but we have not yet defined it in modern terms. 'Some' and 'all' are logical terms, but they are not like the connectives that we have so far studied. The connectives operate on the truth values of whole declarative sentences, as we have seen. So, for example, we have seen that 'or' is a connective that makes a false sentence when it is flanked by two false sentences, and a true sentence otherwise. 'Some' and 'all', on the other hand, are logical functions that operate on other functions, the ordinary predicates and relations like 'is red' and 'to the right of' that we briefly considered in Chapter 1. 'Some' and 'all' are *quantifiers*, because they indicate the quantity of things that have the predicates and relations in question.

The logic that we've looked at so far is called *sentential or propositional logic* because it operates on whole sentences or propositions.

60

Since the logical connectives functioned over whole sentences, all that we needed to know about those sentences was that they were complete and declarative. This is why we could symbolize them in previous chapters by the simple variables p and q. Adding the quantifiers to our logic means that we're going to have to formally capture more structure within a sentence than we've considered up until now. In particular, if 'all' and 'some' are functions over predicates, then we have to be able to express predicates and relations in our symbolic language, and we also need to be able to somehow express the names of the objects that complete these predicates and relations. For this reason, the logic with the quantifiers is called *relational predicate logic*.

To see how this works in general, consider the sentence "All things are self-identical." This sentence is going to be true just in case everything that exists is identical to itself. Since everything that exists is the same as itself (i.e., I am the same as myself, my filing cabinet is the same as itself, and so on), the predicate function 'is self-identical' gets assigned a true for every object that completes it (me, my filing cabinet, and so on, for everything that there is). That is, this 'all' sentence is true because the predicate 'is self-identical' is true of every object that there is. Contrast this with an 'all' sentence that is false, like "All things are human." The predicate in this case is 'is human,' and this function will be assigned a true every time it takes (is completed by) an object that is, in fact human. Since many things in the world are not human, like my filing cabinet for example, some sentences attributing humanness to some objects are false. This is why the 'all' sentence in this case is also false. So, 'all' is a function that takes another function, a predicate, and assigns a true just in case the predicate function assigns a true for every object, and it assigns a false just in case the predicate assigns a false for some object.

In relational predicate logic, predicates are symbolized with upper case letters. For example, we could use S to stand for 'is self-identical,' and H to stand for 'is human'. Among the objects that the predicate functions may be true or false of, we must distinguish specific objects, like me, my cat Sunny Jim, and the moon, from objects, in general. The former get indicated with lower case letters. For example, where j stands for me, the sentence that I am self-identical would be Sj and the sentence that I am human would be Hj. It is important to note that this new structure doesn't change anything vis-à-vis the logical connectives. Whereas before we would symbolize the sentences "I am human and I am self-identical" and "Sunny Jim is not human" by p•q and ~p, respectively,[1] these sentences would now be symbolized Hj•Sj, and ~Hs (where s stands for Sunny Jim).

What about objects in general, i.e, without being specific as to which objects we're talking about? To properly represent these we again use a lower case letter, but this time, the letter is understood to be a variable standing for any object whatsoever, in the same way that variables in algebra are understood to mean any number whatsoever. The convention is to use one of the last three letters of the alphabet. For example, Hx is 'x is human', where x could be any object whatsoever.

It is here that the quantifiers start doing their work by telling us how many x's we are talking about. If we are only talking about some of the x's, then we use the *existential quantifier*, ∃. (∃x)Hx means that something is human (∃x gets read "There is some x such that..." so that the whole sentence would be "There is some x such that x is human."). On the other hand, if we are talking about all of the x's, then we use the *universal quantifier*, ∀. (∀x)Hx means that everything is human (∀x gets read, "All objects x are such that..." so that the whole sentence would be "All objects x are such that x are human.").

I said that 'all' and 'some' are functions that take other functions as their objects, and we are now in a position to see just what I meant by this. Suppose that the only objects we're concerned to talk about are me, my cat Sunny Jim, Socrates, the moon, and the number 3. In logic, the objects that one wants to talk about are referred to as one's *domain of discourse*. In general, unless otherwise specified, the domain of discourse in logic includes everything there is, but in explaining how quantifiers are functions that operate on other functions, it will be helpful to limit our domain. "All things are self-identical" is true because everything in the domain has the property of being self-identical. Since every thing has this property, the sentence formed by predicating 'is self identical' of every object is correspondingly true. In graphic terms, the truth of each of these sentences (in the box) is what the 'all' sentence operates on:

---

[1] In many logic texts, p and q are used to stand for any sentence whatsoever, and specific sentences are supposed to be symbolized by upper case letters in propositional logic.

> Jennifer Fisher is self identical $=$ True
> Sunny Jim is self identical $=$ True
> Socrates is self identical $=$ True
> The moon is self identical $=$ True
> The number 3 is self-identical $=$ True

All x are such that x are self identical $=$ True

On the other hand "All things are human" will be false because not everything in the domain has the property of being human, and so not every sentence in the box is true:

> Jennifer Fisher is human $=$ True
> Sunny Jim is human $=$ False
> Socrates is human $=$ True
> The moon is human $=$ False
> The number 3 is human $=$ False

All x are such that x are human $=$ False

In essence, the function 'all' takes the truth values of other sentences and maps them onto new truth values, just like the logical connectives did. It's just that in the case of 'all', the truth values that must be taken into account are for sentences about every object in the domain: when every object in the domain has the property in question, and so every sentence with the predicate is true, 'all' sentences are true, and otherwise, they are false.

The story is similar for 'some,' except that what is required for the truth of a 'some' sentence is that some object in the domain have the property predicated of it (at least one, to be exact). So, for example, both of the boxes above also make clear that the following sentences are true: "Some x is such that x is self-identical" and "Some x is such that x is human." In both cases, since at least one object in the domain has the property in question, at least one sentence is true, and so it will be true to say "Something is self identical" and "Something is human." But let's try the sentence "Something is a fish." Our limited domain would now yield a false,

CHAPTER 5

because every sentence that predicates 'is a fish' to the objects in the domain is false:

> Jennifer Fisher is a fish = False
>
> Sunny Jim is a fish = False
>
> Socrates is a fish = False
>
> The moon is a fish = False
>
> The number 3 is a fish = False

Some x is such that x is a fish = False

Just like 'all,' 'some' takes the truth values of other sentences and maps them on to new truth values, and the truth values that must be taken into account are for sentences about every object in the domain. Unlike 'all,' though, a sentence containing 'some' will be true just in case one object in the domain has the property in question, and it will be false otherwise.

A slightly more complex example of how the function 'all' works comes from the first premise of argument (1) with which we started this chapter, "All humans are mortal." To see how 'all' works in this sentence, let us continue to limit ourselves to my domain of five objects. "All humans are mortal" is true if all the things in this domain that are human are also things that are mortal. We can sum up the facts with respect to humanness and mortality in this domain we are imagining in the following table, where an X in a column indicates that the object possesses the property.

|  | is human | is mortal |
| --- | --- | --- |
| Jennifer Fisher | X | X |
| Sunny Jim |  | X |
| Socrates | X | X |
| The moon |  |  |
| The number 3 |  |  |

What this table makes clear is that everything in this domain that is human is also mortal. Notice that one thing, Sunny Jim is not human, but he is mortal, and the moon and the number 3 are neither human nor mortal. So "All humans are mortal" is true in domains where some things are both human and mortal, some things are not human

64

but they are mortal, and some things are neither human nor mortal. The only thing that is ruled out by the truth of the sentence "All humans are mortal" is that there be a thing in the world which is human, but which is not mortal.

Recall from Chapter 2 that 'if... then' is the connective that gets a false when the antecedent (the if part) is true and the consequent (the then part) is false, but is true in every other case. This is just like the truth conditions for the objects in the domain with respect to the sentence "All humans are mortal." Our sentence is false in a world only if a thing is human, but not mortal. For this reason, 'all' sentences like this one (the A sentences that we encountered in our discussion of Aristotle) are understood to contain an implicit 'if... then.' This kind of 'all' sentence is true in a world just in case everything is such that if it has the first term, then it also has the second term. Symbolically, continuing to use H to represent the predicate 'is human' and using M to represent the predicate 'is mortal,' "All humans are mortal" looks like this:

$$(\forall x)(Hx \supset Mx)$$

The symbolic sentence says that all objects are such that if they are human, then they are mortal. Just as above, when our predicate was simple (i.e, 'is self identical,' 'is human') what makes "All humans are mortal" true is that for each thing in this domain, if it has the property of being human, it also has the property of being mortal, and so the sentence attributing this complex property (if human then mortal) is true. In terms of my prior graphics:

> If Jennifer Fisher is human then Jennifer Fisher is mortal=True
> If Sunny Jim is human then Sunny Jim is mortal = True
> If Socrates is human then Socrates is mortal = True
> If the moon is human then the moon is mortal = True
> If the number 3 is human then the number 3 is mortal = True

All x are such that if x is human then x is mortal = True

'All' is a function that takes the truth values of other completed functions and assigns a new truth value on that basis. In this particular case, the functions are the conditionally related functions 'is human' and 'is mortal,' and the objects that complete them are the five noted.

In this domain, it is clear why the intuitively valid argument at the outset of this section is also logically valid. The first premise says that everything in the domain is such that if it's human, then it's mortal. This means, essentially, that each of those five objects has that conditional property, if human then mortal. One of the things it is true of, of course, is Socrates, and indeed we see in the box that "If Socrates is human, then Socrates is mortal" is true. Since the truth of an 'all' sentence implicitly contains the truth of every sentence predicating the property in question of every object in the domain, the first premise of (1), $(\forall x)(Hx \supset Mx)$, thus allows us to infer each instance that makes it true. In terms of our argument, the relevant instance can therefore be inferred as a new premise, as follows:

All humans are mortal
If Socrates is human, then Socrates is mortal.
Socrates is human.
So, Socrates is mortal.

The first and third lines of this argument are still the premises of the original argument, and the second line is justified by the truth conditions for an 'all' sentence. The conclusion now follows in virtue of the inference rule, Modus Ponens.

In the real world, of course, there are many objects (maybe even infinitely many) and we couldn't possibly list each instance of this conditional property as we did in our domain of five objects. But that's okay because, as we have seen, 'all' means, simply, all the things in a domain. More particularly, what 'all' allows us to do is to refer to everything there is without actually knowing what there is. The truth of "All humans are mortal" is understood to imply that everything is such that if it is human then it is mortal, and this applies to the things we do know, but also to any things that we don't. Its truth is like a guarantee. Nothing in this world can be a human and not mortal.

I've just explained how 'all' works in terms of a few particular examples, but the rules for working with quantifiers are, like those for working with the connectives, fully general. Using the symbol $\Phi$ to stand for any predicate at all, and the letter a to stand for any individual in the world under considerations, we can generalize the quantifier rule that makes (1) logically valid in the following way.

$(\forall x) \Phi x$
So, $\Phi a$

Called the rule of *Universal Instantiation*, this rule allows one to infer an instance from a universal (all) sentence. Just like the rules for the sentential connectives that we saw in Chapter 2, this rule preserves truth. If it is true that all things are Φ then it is true that any random individual in the world, a, is also Φ (and note, Φ can be simple, like 'is human' or complex like 'if human then mortal'). Likewise, there is a purely general rule for 'some':

Φa

So, (∃x) Φx

Known as *Existential Generalization*, this rule says that as long as it is true that some thing in the domain has the predicate Φ, then we can always infer that there is some x such that x is Φ, or, more colloquially, that something is Φ.[2]

This formal understanding of the quantifiers helps clarify a very famous philosophical problem dating back to the time of Plato and Socrates, the *problem of non-being*. It is not unreasonable to think that what makes a sentence like "Kate drank a glass of water" true depends on whether or not Kate drank a glass of water. This has led some philosophers to propose that the meaning of a name like 'Kate,' is the person herself, Kate. But if we understand the meaning of names in this way, then a problem immediately arises. How would one go about denying the existence of fictional characters like Santa Claus? What we do in practice is utter a sentence like, "Santa Claus doesn't exist". But if the meaning of names is given by the objects named, then, since 'Santa Claus' is a name just like 'Kate,' it would seem that Santa Claus would have to exist in order for us to deny his existence. Something is clearly wrong.

One response to this difficulty came from the philosopher Alexius von Meinong, at the end of the 20th Century. The essence of Meinong's claim is that there are non-existent objects just as surely as there are existent ones. One reason for adopting a view like this is fairly straightforward, and can be gleaned from the brief motivation just given for the problem of non-being. People clearly can and do meaningfully deny the existence of things, but on the assumption that the meaning of a name is the thing named, this would only be possible if some names refer to non-existent things.

---

[2] There are other valid inference rules associated with both the universal and the existential quantifier, but since the other rules are more restricted, explaining them in the current context would take us too far afield.

Meinong's solution solves the problem, but in doing so, it obliges us to add an enormous number of entities to our ontologies (*ontology* is the study of what is). Just think about all the possible and impossible non-existent things that there are. There will have to be objects to satisfy every description that doesn't refer, like 'the golden mountain,' (Meinong's original concern, discussed in the next section), objects to satisfy every non-referring name, like 'Santa Claus,' and impossible objects, like square circles, to name but a few. Not only are there an extremely large number of non-existent things, but these things are also inaccessible to us in space and time. They are, after all, non-existent. Thus, Meinong's solution also raises questions about how we know what we know about these non-existents, and how we could be certain that the things we say about them are true. All in all, it's a solution that creates a lot of problems.

Fortunately, the mere addition of the quantifiers to our language allows us to solve the problem of non-being without resorting to Meinong's solution. Clearly, when we want to deny that something exists, what we are really doing is denying that there is anything that has all of the properties of that thing. In the case of Santa Claus, we are denying that there is a person who dresses up in a red suit delivering toys to good boys and girls on Christmas Eve. Thus, we can think of the name 'Santa Claus' as implicitly referring to the predicate, 'is a thing that dresses up in a red suit delivering toys to good boys and girls on Christmas Eve.' Using S to stand for this whole predicate, "Santa Claus exists" would be represented symbolically as follows:

$(\exists x)Sx$

This gets read "There is some object x such that x is a thing that dresses up in a red suit delivering toys to good boys and girls on Christmas Eve." This sentence will be true just in case there is at least one object and that object has that property. Since it is not true that there is any object in the domain with this property this sentence is false. We can now deny the existence of Santa Claus without being committed to there being a Santa Claus. "It is not the case that Santa Claus exists" would be symbolically represented as:

$\sim(\exists x)Sx$

This sentence will be true when it is not the case that there is at least one object that is a thing that dresses up in a red suit delivering toys to good boys and girls on Christmas Eve, and since $(\exists x)Sx$ was false, this sentence is true. To deny Santa Claus's existence, all that we are committed to is that there be a predicate 'is a thing that dresses up in a red suit delivering toys to good boys and girls on Christmas Eve.' which can take objects as values and yield new truth values.

On its surface, 'exists' is used as a predicate just like the ordinary predicates 'eats' and 'is a lion,' as in the sentences:

David eats.

Leo is a lion.

Santa Claus exists.

In spite of their grammatical similarity, however, Frege recognized that 'exists' is qualitatively different from these other predicates. Whereas 'eats' and 'is a lion' take objects as their values, 'exists' takes other predicates as its value. This difference can clearly be seen in the different logical symbolizations of these three sentences, which are respectively as follows:

Ed

Ll

$(\exists x)Sx$

What emerged was a solution to a long-standing philosophical conundrum, the problem of non-being. Being clearer about logic in this case allows us to see what's really going on when we either assert or deny a thing's existence.

## II—IDENTITY AND DEFINITE DESCRIPTIONS

We began the first section of this chapter by considering an intuitively valid argument that is not valid in sentential logic. It was for this reason that we added the quantifiers, thus giving us relational predicate logic. But as it stands, there are still intuitively valid arguments that even relational predicate logic cannot account for, such as the following:

2. Peter Parker is Spider Man.
   Spider Man is in love.
   So, Peter Parker is in love.

Clearly, if both of the premises in (2) are true, then Peter Parker just has to be in love. (2) is not only intuitively valid, it is also logically

Willhem Gottfried Leibniz (1646–1716) was a German philosopher, logician, mathematician, historian, and jurist, who left his mark on every area that he studied. He is widely regarded as the greatest logician to live between ancient and modern times. In addition to the law of identity that came to bear his name, he is also responsible for positing the *identity of indiscernibles*. According to this principle, if thing a has every property that thing b has, then a is identical to b.

Leibniz's Law holds true in many, many instances. However there are certain contexts where it seems to fail. For example:

Lois Lane believes Super Man can fly.

Super Man is Clark Kent.

So, Lois Lane believes that Clark Kent can fly.

Here the problem is that even though Clark Kent can fly (since he is Superman), Lois Lane doesn't believe this about Clark Kent because she doesn't believe that Super Man is the same person as Clark Kent. The failure of Leibniz's Law in cases like this has prompted some philosophers and logicians to try to come up with a logic for so-called belief contexts like Lois Lane's.

valid in the sense that the truth of the conclusion in (2) doesn't depend in any way on the content of the sentences involved. But to capture this logical validity, we must add one last symbol to our logic, $=$ (the *identity* symbol, to be understood as 'is identical with'). The resulting logical system, *relational predicate logic with identity*, represents the logical form of (2) as follows:

$p = s$

Ls

So, Lp

This is an instance of what is known as *Leibniz's Law*, according to which, identical objects have identical properties. This truism about everything can be expressed in a purely general way, as follows:

$a = b$

$\Phi a$

So, $\Phi b$

This says, in essence, that if two individuals, a and b, are identical, then if it is true of a that it has the predicate $\Phi$, it must be true of b that it also has the predicate $\Phi$.

In addition to allowing us to capture the validity of inferences like (2), the identity symbol allows us to clarify some logically important differences between superficially similar grammatical sentences. For example, I noted that Meinong argued in response to the problem of non-being that there must be a world of non-existent things. Meinong's original concern was with phrases like 'the golden mountain.' Phrases like this are what are called *definite descriptions*. Definite descriptions behave like Fregean names in the sense that they are meant to designate one particular thing. But grammatically they are more like predicates than names, as in "The next mountain is the golden mountain." Because they are meant to single out only one thing, however, they must be somehow different from other more ordinary predicates.

The philosopher Bertrand Russell wrote on many philosophical topics, from metaphysics and epistemology to social and political philosophy, and he is another of the primary contributors to the development of modern logic. One of the things that he is most famous for is his insistence that the grammatical form of a sentence may not be its logical form. The logical form of a sentence is the translation of that sentence into symbols, and Russell argued that to get the logic right in some cases one would have to go beyond the surface grammar of the sentence. In particular, Russell thought that the identity symbol is needed to adequately capture the uniqueness implied by sentences containing definite descriptions even though there is no indication in the surface grammar of definite descriptions that an identity between one thing and another is being asserted.

To see Russell's point, consider a different definite description, 'the author of *The Secrets of the Camera Obscura.*' This is a definite description because one and only one person, David Knowles, is the author of the novel *The Secrets of the Camera Obscura*. Now consider the two sentences, "David Knowles is the author of *The Secrets of the Camera Obscura,*" and "David Knowles is human." These sentences look grammatically similar (a predicate being attributed to a name). But whereas "David Knowles is the author of *The Secrets of the Camera Obscura,*" is true just in case only one person is the author of that book, "David Knowles is human," can be true even if there are other humans. Russell argued that we can capture the difference between these grammatically similar sentences by making clear that they have different logical forms. The logical form of "David Knowles is human" is straightforward:

Hd

According to Russell, however, the logical form of "David Knowles is the author of *The Secrets of the Camera Obscura*" (where A stands for 'is the author of *The Secrets of the Camera Obscura*') would be this:

Ad & (x)(Ax ⊃ x = d))

This says, "David Knowles is the author of *The Secrets of the Camera Obscura*, and every object, x, is such that if that object x is the author of *The Secrets of the Camera Obscura*, then x and David Knowles are identical." It's not pretty, but it better captures what is meant when we use definite descriptions, namely there is one and only one object that is their intended referent. And there is no way to capture this meaning except with =. To single out the uniqueness of the referent in this example we have to make clear that anything else that is the author of *The Secrets of the Camera Obscura* is actually identical with David Knowles.

Russell's move allows us to deal with the problem of non-refer-ring definite descriptions in exactly the same way that we dealt with the problem of non-referring names. For example, returning to 'the golden mountain" (symbolized M), when we say that the golden mountain doesn't exist, what we mean, logically, is this

~ (∃x)(Mx & (y)(My ⊃ x=y))

This says that it is not the case that there exists an x such that x is the golden mountain and for all y, if y is the golden mountain then x is identical with y, or colloquially, there is no unique object that is the golden mountain. Thus, adding the identity symbol to our logical language allows us to avoid Meinong's solution to the problem of non-being in the case of non-referring definite descriptions. Given the difficulties associated with Meinong's solution to this problem, this is a significant advantage to adding = to our list of standard logical symbols.

In both sections of this chapter, we have seen how adding certain symbols to our logic would allow us to account for more intuitively valid inferences. But in addition, we have seen how closer attention to the logical form of natural language also clarifies what's going wrong in the philosophical problem of non-being. Frege's original investigations into the foundations of mathematics lead to the development of a systematic way of representing how words (and the things that they refer to) form structured relations. Before long, the logic that resulted yielded a potent tool for philosophical analysis. Logical investigations, it would seem, bear fruit in many interesting and surprising ways.

# 6

# Modal Logic

## I—NECESSITY AND POSSIBILITY

The logical functions introduced in the previous chapters ($\cdot$, $\vee$, $\supset$, $\equiv$, $\sim$, $\exists$, $\forall$, and $=$) make up the core logical vocabulary of classical logic. In this chapter we will explore one possible way to further augment the account of classical logical consequence, and some of the philosophical questions that it raises.

The proposed extension adds symbols to stand for various *modalities*, or ways of qualifying the truth of a sentence. There are many different kinds of modalities. For example, the following are some sentences containing modal terms:

1. "It's necessary that a square has four sides"
2. "I know that fish swim"
3. "It rained yesterday"
4. "You ought not lie"

In each case, the truth or falsity of a sentence is being qualified in some way. The sentence in (1), "A square has four sides," is true in a particularly strong way, i.e., it is not possible for it to be false. (2)'s sentence, "Fish swim," is true in a way that is known by me. (3), "It is raining," (timeless) is true because it happened at some particular time. And (4)'s sentence, "Don't lie," is true in a way that entails a corresponding action on our part, as something that we ought or ought not to do

In the last chapter, I motivated the addition of the quantifiers and the identity symbol by noting that certain intuitively valid arguments contained logical functions that require us to extend our logic beyond the truth-functional connectives. A similar motivation could be given for adding modal terms as well. For example, the following intuitively valid argument contains modal terms:

It is necessary that vixens are female foxes.
So, vixens are female foxes.

*Modal logics* are the logics that attempt to formally capture the inferential connections in arguments containing modal terms. Though interest in modalities goes back to ancient times, it wasn't until this century that an adequate formal syntax and semantics were developed. Initially, this interest was spurred by a desire to give an account of necessity and possibility.

We use the words 'necessary' and 'possible' all the time. So, for example, though I have two children, it's possible that this might not have been the case. Or we might say that, necessarily, a square has four right angles. All English speakers understand both of these sentences. But what exactly do they mean? The first sentence means something like, I might have had no children, or one, or five. In essence, I seem to be saying that the world might have been different than it actually is. If something is necessary as in the second sentence, on the other hand, then the world couldn't have been any other way. No world can be a place where squares have more or less than four right angles since having four angles is part of what makes something a square. So, necessity and possibility have something to do with whether or not the world could have been different in some respect from how it actually is.

The standard way that this idea gets cashed out is due to Leibniz, who was the first to suggest that we understand necessity and possibility in terms of what philosophers call *possible worlds*. Possible worlds are worlds that might have been. The actual world, of course, is possible, and so too are many variations on the actual world, like the one we just considered in which I have either no children, or five children. But what is not possible, in any world, is that a square could have more or less than four angles. Necessarily, a square is a plane figure with four right angles and equal sides. To say that something is necessary, therefore, is to say that it is true in all possible worlds. And to say that something is possible is to say that it is true in at least one possible world.

We saw in Chapter 4 that semantics is the study of the interpreted side of a language, and we have already seen how truth table semantics clarifies propositional logic. For reasons that will become clear in section IV, however, to provide the same sort of clarification in the realm of modal logics we must introduce some new semantic apparatus. This new apparatus arrived in the latter half of the $20^{th}$ century when Leibniz's insight into necessity and possibility was given a more formal treatment called *possible world semantics.*

Let us imagine three possible worlds, and call the set of our worlds W. Mind you, there are an infinite number of possible worlds, but we'll restrict our attention to only three for purposes of explication. The value of any sentence, p, is now understood not simply to be true or false, but true or false at a world. This gets symbolized $v(p, w)$, where v means value of and w means a world, and so the symbolic sentence says the value of p at a world. Let us specify our three worlds as $w_1$, $w_2$, and $w_3$, and let p be the sentence "Jennifer Fisher has two children." Suppose that at world $w_1$ I have two children, at $w_2$ I have no children, and at $w_3$ I have five children. In this case, $v(p, w_1) = $ True, $v(p, w_2) = $ False, and $v(p, w_3) = $ False.

We can construct a logic for these possible worlds by making clear the rules that define various logical operations:

($\sim$)  $v(\sim A, w) = T$ if and only if $v(A, w) = F$. (i.e, the value of not-A at w is true if and only if the value of A at w is false.)

($\supset$)  $v(A \supset B, w) = T$ if and only if $v(A, w) = F$ or $v(B, w) = T$.

(&)  $v(A \cdot B, w) = T$ if and only if $v(A, w) = T$ and $v(B, w) = T$.

($\lor$)  $v(A \lor B, w) = T$ if and only if $v(A, w) = T$ or $v(B, w) = T$.

In addition, we can define the necessity operator (symbolized by a $\square$ and known as the *box*) as follows:

$v(\square A, w) = T$ if and only if for every world $w'$ in W, if $w$ R $w'$, then $v(A, w') = T$.

Possibility (symbolized $\lozenge$, and known as the *diamond*) is defined in terms of $\square$ and $\sim$ as follows: $\lozenge p = \sim\square\sim p$. This makes "It is possible that I might have become a chef" equivalent to "It is not necessary that I didn't become a chef." R in the definition for the $\square$ is a relationship that holds between worlds called the *accessibility relation.* In the next section, I'll explain what this relation is and how it works. For now, let me finish up my introduction to possible worlds by noting the notion of validity that emerges in modal logics.

Valid arguments are now going to be those arguments where, if the premises are true at certain possible worlds, then the conclusions will also be true at those same possible worlds. To see how this works, let's consider both a valid and an invalid argument with modal terms. First, the invalid one:

□ (p ⊃ q)

p

So, □ q

To see that this is invalid, it is sufficient to produce a counterexample to it, i.e., an instance of this argument form that has actually true premises at a world, but a false conclusion at that same world. Thus, consider the following instance of this argument:

Necessarily, if Jennifer Fisher has two children, then she has more than one child.

Jennifer Fisher has two children.

So, necessarily, Jennifer Fisher has more than one child.

Clearly, the first premise, "Necessarily, if Jennifer Fisher has two children, then she has more than one child," is true. It holds at all possible worlds because two is necessarily greater than one. The second premise is not necessary, but it is possible, which means that it will be true at some possible worlds, and false at others. Focusing only on the worlds where the second premise is true, however, the conclusion, "Necessarily, Jennifer Fisher has more than one child," is false. There certainly are possible worlds in which I have only one child, or no children, as I noted earlier. But in order for the conclusion to be true at the world where I do, in fact, have two children, the sentence "Jennifer Fisher has more than one child" has to be true at all possible worlds.

Now consider a valid argument form containing a modal term:

□ p

□ (p ⊃ q)

So, □ q

This argument can't fail to preserve truth. Consider one example of this argument:

Necessarily, even numbers greater than two are divisible by two.
Necessarily, if even numbers greater than two are divisible by
    two, then two is the only even prime.
Necessarily, so, two is the only even prime.

A little thought will reveal that each of the sentences substituted for p
and q in this argument must be true at every possible world. Hence,
the conclusion is also necessary, and so this argument preserves truth
at all possible worlds where the premises are true, which is to say, at
all possible worlds. And so too for any argument of this form. If it is
true that necessarily p and necessarily if p then q, then it must be the
case that necessarily q.

## II—OTHER MODALITIES

Though modal logics were originally developed for the terms 'necessary' and 'possible', their usefulness in formalizing other modalities
was quickly realized. In this section, I will explain the role of the
accessibility relation introduced in the last section by exploring some
of these other possible uses.

I noted in the rule for $\Box$ that all of the worlds in a set of
worlds W relate to each other by an accessibility relation. Accessibility is just what it sounds like. It represents our ability to access
one world from another. For all the w's in W, they may or may
not be accessible to each other in various ways. To illustrate, let us
consider three important ways that worlds might relate to or be
accessible to one another. The first is called *reflexivity*, and if the
relation R is reflexive, this means that each world is accessible to
itself. The second is called *symmetry*, and this means that if you can
access a world B, from a different world, A, then you can also
access A from B. The last is called *transitivity*, and this means that
if world A is accessible from world B, and B is accessible from
world C, then A is accessible from C. These three relations are
summed up as follows:

Reflexivity: for all w in W, wRw

Symmetry: for all $w_1$ and $w_2$ in W, if $w_1Rw_2$, then $w_2Rw_1$

Transitivity: for all $w_1$, $w_2$, and $w_3$ in W, if $w_1Rw_2$, and
    $w_2Rw_3$, then $w_1Rw_3$.

In all of my examples of necessity and impossibility thus far, I have used mathematical or geometrical sentences. This kind of necessity, usually called *logical necessity*, is very strong, and the accessibility relation is reflexive, symmetric, and transitive (among other things). One theorem in modal logics characterized by this kind of accessibility relation (of reflexivity in particular) is $\Box A \supset A$, or, colloquially, if A is necessary, then it is true.[1] This is fine when the $\Box$ is taken to mean 'it is logically necessary that,' because with logical necessity, if a sentence is necessary it must be true at all possible worlds, as we have seen.

But systems of modal logic can be used to clearly define all the different modalities that were mentioned in the sentences at the beginning of this chapter, and on some of these interpretations, $\Box A \supset A$ is more problematic. For example, in *deontic logics*, which are supposed to express the logic of moral and other obligations, the $\Box$ is understood to mean 'It ought to be the case that.' Given this, $\Box A \supset A$ (in deontic logics, this would be written 'OA $\supset$ A') is clearly too strong. After all, even if it ought to be the case that we don't commit genocide, it unfortunately doesn't follow that we don't commit genocide.

Fortunately, by playing with the rules that define the accessibility relation we can make different modal logics weaker than the one for logical necessity. This way, different modalities can be formalized using a modal logic of appropriate strength. With respect to the current example, an accessibility relation that is not reflexive will not have $\Box A \supset A$ as a theorem. This means, in particular, that we will not be committed to the obviously false sentence "We don't commit genocide" just because the sentence "We ought not commit genocide" is obviously true.

The transitivity of an accessibility relation can be similarly problematic. *Epistemic logics* are those that treat knowledge as a modality. In these, there is an operator K, which means 'it is known that.' Like the modal logic that governs logical necessity, epistemic logics are reflexive. The classical philosophical definition of knowledge is that knowledge is justified true belief. Given this, it is clear why the accessibility relation in these cases should be reflexive and hence why $\Box A \supset A$ holds. If it's known that

---

[1] A theorem, recall, is a sentence that is always provable. Any theorem in a system is also a logical truth of that system. To explain why this is a theorem in modal logics with a reflexive accessibility relation would require a fairly lengthy technical digression. Since the point of the current section is merely to familiarize the reader with the work that an accessibility relation can do, and to also introduce some of the many modal logics that are out there, I will not make this digression (and so too for the theorems associated with symmetrical and transitive accessibility relations that I discuss). I supply references in the Further Readings for the reader interested in pursuing this issue.

fish swim then fish swim, since for something to be known it must be true according to this classical understanding. 'It is known that' is not, however, transitive. This means that $\Box A \supset \Box\Box A$ will not be a theorem. People know all sorts of things that they are not consciously aware that they know, and hence they don't know that they know it. For example, a person might not think they know who the 35$^{th}$ vice president of the U.S. was, but give the right answer because they remembered it better than they thought from their high school history class. Arguably, this person knows who the 35$^{th}$ vice president was (since it is more than a lucky guess, it is a justified true belief), but wouldn't know that they knew it since they didn't believe that they were right, and hence didn't believe it.

*Temporal logics*, or logics of time sequences, nicely demonstrate why we might not want our accessibility relation to be symmetric. In temporal logics, the members of W are understood to be moments in time as opposed to possible worlds. Moments in time are ordered one after the other, and so they should not be regarded as symmetrical. If one moment is earlier than another, then that second moment is not earlier than the first. Modal logics with a symmetrical accessibility relation have as a theorem $A \supset \Box\Diamond A$. In temporal logics, therefore, the tensed version of $A \supset \Box\Diamond A$ is not a logical truth. In a future tense logic, the modal operator that corresponds to the $\Box$ is G, understood to mean, 'It will always be the case that,' and the modal operator that corresponds to $\Diamond$ is F, understood to mean 'it will at some time be the case that.' To see why $A \supset GFA$ fails, consider any contingent sentence, such as, "I am 38 years old." This sentence is true, but that doesn't mean that it always will be the case that it will at some time be the case that I am 38 years old, since there were many points in time when I wasn't 38 years old, and at those times, presumably, it wasn't guaranteed that I would survive this long.

There are many temporal or tense logics, and many, many more systems to capture all the other various modalities as well. But for the purposes of this book, I've said enough to allow us to consider some of the philosophical issues that crop up with the addition of modal logical terms.

## III—POSSIBLE WORLDS

The first point that needs to be addressed concerns the philosophical status of possible worlds. How should we think about the possible worlds that form the basis of the semantics of modal terms? There are two different kinds of responses that philosophers give to this question.

The first is usually called *modal realism*. According to modal realists, possible worlds really exist, just as surely as the actual world does. On this account, a statement of necessity would be true because it is true in all of those actually existing possible worlds. Possible worlds are not like distant planets that we might someday travel to, because they don't exist in our space and time (otherwise, they would be part of the actual world). Nevertheless, they exist in some space and time, and their existence helps us to sort out our modal intuitions.

The other main take on possible worlds is called *modal actualism*. According to this view, possible worlds exist as abstract objects and thus they are clearly distinguished from the actual world. There are various versions of modal actualism. In one, possible worlds are just re-combinations of actual things in the actual world. Clearly the things in the actual world could be rearranged in various ways, so that different sentences would be true or false. For example, it certainly seems possible that we could replace my cat with a dog. But we don't actually have to do the replacement. Each non-actual world is an abstract object that we access and understand in thought. Another variant of actualism has it that possible worlds are just sets of sentences.[2] The thought here is that any world (the actual one included) could in theory be completely described by all the sentences that were true and false of it. This would be a huge task, no doubt, but it could be done. The difference between the actual and possible worlds according to this account is that the actual world exists as a concrete object, whereas each possible world is simply the totality of all the sentences that describe it, and doesn't exist as a concrete entity.

To see the difference between modal realism and modal actualism (I'll focus on the recombination view for simplicity), lets explore an example. Suppose I wanted to assess the truth of the sentence: "It's possible that George Washington was not the 1st President of the U.S.A." According to modal realism, every thing in the actual world has some counterpart in some (though perhaps not all) of the possible worlds. So, for example, George Washington's counterparts will be those individuals who are not George Washington (there's only one

---

[2] This is the one place in this book where my preference for discussing sentences rather than propositions, mentioned in a footnote in Chapter 1, might cause problems. For reasons beyond the scope of this discussion, modal actualists define their possible but non-actual worlds as sets of propositions, not sentences. Propositions, recall, are just the timeless meaning of a sentence. I will stick with my terminology, but the reader should note that in this particular case, sentences might not be sufficient.

George Washington, and he lived in the actual world), but who are like George Washington in the important and relevant respects. For modal realists, the above sentence will be true just in case some counterpart of George Washington did not become the 1st President. This counterpart has to be similar enough to our George Washington so that we recognize him to be a reliable guide to truths about what is and is not possible concerning George Washington. For example, many find it plausible to think that George Washington's counterparts must, at the very least, be the son of the counterparts of the actual George Washington's parents, Augustine Washington and Mary Ball. It certainly seems possible that at least one of Washington's counterparts in some non-actual though existing possible world didn't become President. Perhaps his boat sank when he was crossing the Delaware, and he drowned. Thus, our sentence "It's possible that George Washington was not the 1st President of the U.S.A.," is true.

According to the modal actualists, on the other hand, the truth of this sentence is determined by possible recombinations of actual objects in various ways. So, by this theory, we consider the actual George Washington, and ask ourselves if there is any possible recombination of this world that would make *him* not become the 1st President. Clearly, we can make sense of the world being recombined in various ways so that Washington is never made president. To appeal to the possibility noted above, the world could be recombined in such a way that Washington's boat sank. Since in at least one of these abstract possible recombinations, Washington doesn't become president, the modal sentence is true.

One difficulty with modal realism is similar to the one I raised in the last chapter for Meinong's solution to the problem of non-being. Modal realism entails a lot of excess metaphysical baggage, requiring, as it does, that a potentially infinite number of worlds be added to our ontologies. However, this objection is not decisive, since there is considerable disagreement as to how parsimonious one's philosophical theories should be, and it is arguable that the benefits of possible world semantics outweigh their ontological excess. (Note that a defense of Meinong's world of the unreal is not quite as plausible. The quantifiers and identity symbol seem to solve the problem of non-being just as capably as Meinong did, but without the excess, whereas we cannot account for modal terms in a way that doesn't appeal in some way to possible worlds.)

Another difficulty for modal realism is that it's not clear how the view helps to explain our modal judgments. Why should concrete worlds that I can never access be regarded as reliable ways of assessing the truth or falsity of modal sentences? For example, suppose I want to know whether or not it is necessary that George Washington was male. How does modal realism help me here? I know that Washington has a counterpart on many of these spatio-temporally distinct other worlds, and I know that these counterparts will determine the truth or falsity of the sentence "It's possible that George Washington might have been female." But since I can't get to these possible worlds, and since they are completely distinct from my own, it's just not clear how they are of any help here.

Modal actualist theories, however, are not without their difficulties either. Recombining objects in the actual world to get a sense of possibilities is a very nice idea, except if I want to think about the possibility of something that doesn't exist in the actual world. How do I recombine the objects in the actual world to think about the possibility that Santa Claus might exist, for example? Should I take a hand from someone, and a nose from someone else? Or should I go down to the molecular level and just imagine all the molecules in the world being rearranged in a particular way? Must I really specify which other objects cease to exist in order to construct Santa Claus from these other objects' bits and pieces? Intuitive as it may be in general, the whole theory starts to look a little tenuous in the details.

Appealing to worlds as sets of sentences, however, also raises problems. To see what the main problem is, imagine a possible world in which it's true that if dogs are canines then dogs are social, and it's also true that dogs are canines. Clearly, in this world, it should also be true that dogs are social. But that is just to say that the sets of sentences that define the various possible worlds should obey logical rules. In and of itself this may be no big deal, but it certainly raises doubts about the cogency of using possible worlds to give the semantics of modal logical operators. After all, semantic accounts are supposed to explain how logical properties work in some deep and intuitive sense. If it turns out that we need to understand logic in order to understand logical properties, then its not clear how much explanatory power possible worlds will have. A standard example of a bad explanation in the philosophy of science literature is to explain why opium makes people sleepy by appealing to its dormitive properties. Since 'dormitive' means to make sleepy, this explanation hasn't really gotten at the deep underlying nature of things. Likewise, this criticism of modal actualism goes, possible worlds are supposed to explain in some deep underlying way the truth of modal and other logical claims. If it turns out that logic plays a role in determining the content of these possible worlds, then the explanation starts to look a little less informative.

Specific views about possible worlds aside, any appeal to possible worlds might be criticized for similar reasons. It's just not clear how explanatory appeal to possible worlds really is. Recall that possible worlds were first and foremost proposed to explain our judgments about modalities like necessity and possibility. But explaining 'it is possible that p' by saying that p is true in at least one possible world doesn't appear to get me very far. After all, if I really don't understand what possibility is, then appealing to possible worlds is not going to do me much good.

Another general criticism of the whole endeavor is that it implicitly endorses *essentialism*, the idea that everything has an essence or something that makes it what it is. This idea is familiar enough when we're talking squares and circles. It seems quite natural to say that a circle just couldn't have angles, for example, and so it doesn't sound strange to say that part of the essence of circularity is its lack of angularity. But many philosophers balk at this kind of talk when we apply it, as we've just done, to things like people. Talk of counterparts or rearrangements of actual objects, according to these objectors, involves a kind of superstitious belief in essences. Suppose that George Washington was necessarily male, for example. Why should we think this to be so? With circles, the answer is that they are well-defined by the axioms that make up the geometric system, and this is why their lack of angles is necessary. But there is no such corresponding answer about Washington that is uncontroversial in the way that the axiomatic definitions of a circle are.

In light of problems like these, some philosophers despair of ever giving an adequate account of modality. Many of these philosophers correspondingly object to the legitimacy of modal logic. The thought here is that logic is supposed to clarify fundamental notions like logical consequence and logical truth. If it turns out that explanations in modal logic require too many suspicious metaphysical or epistemological claims, then their usefulness in clarifying what are supposed to be more fundamental logical notions is seriously undermined.

## IV—BUT IS IT LOGIC?

In a very short and thought provoking little paper called "What is Logic?" the philosopher and logician Arthur Prior asks us to consider the difference between three groups of sentences.

A (1) If Polly is an animal, then Polly is an animal.

(2) If Polly is a feathered animal, then Polly is an animal.

(3) If all feathered animals breathe air then what does not breathe air is not a feathered animal.

B (1) If Polly is a feathered animal she breathes air.

(2) If Polly has feelings, I am obliged to treat her kindly.

(3) If Polly isn't my parrot, she's Peter's.

C (1) If there are parrots, there always will have been parrots.

(2) If I know that Polly breathes air, she does breathe air.

(3) If I am obliged to treat Polly kindly, then I am not obliged not to treat Polly kindly.

(4) If it is not possible for Polly not to be a parrot, then it is possible for her to be a parrot.[3]

He points out that most philosophers would readily accept that the sentences in group A are true in virtue of logic, and that those in group B are not. But with respect to group C, intuitions differ. All the sentences of group C, of course, contain modal terms. C(1) qualifies truth with respect to time, C(2) with respect to someone's knowledge, C(3) with respect to what someone is obliged to not do in light of his having an obligation, and C(4) with respect to the necessity or possibility of the truth of a sentence. The question, then, is why intuitions differ so much when it comes to modal logic. In this section, I will explain two of the issues that opponents of modal logic have raised.

The first issue that I will discuss is an elaboration of the criticism briefly mentioned at the end of the last section, that modalities and modal logics are philosophically suspect. To see what the complaint is, we must first note a very important difference between truth functional contexts and modal contexts. Recall that a truth function is one that assigns a value or true or false based on nothing but the truth values of its parts. For example, we can know the value of a disjunction as long as we know the truth values of its disjuncts. In a truth functional compound sentence, one can substitute any sentence for an original constituent sentence, and as long as the value of the substituted sentence and the original constituent are the same, the

---

[3] "What Is Logic?", Prior, Arthur (1976), in *Papers in Logic and Ethics*, eds. P.T. Geach and A.J.P. Kenny, Amherst: University of Massachusetts Press.

value of the truth-functional compound sentence will be unchanged. Continuing with disjunction, the value of the true compound sentence "The US is south of Canada, or Mexico is south of the US," will remain true for any true sentences that we choose to substitute for either disjunct. So, the following sentences are also all true: "The World Trade Center was destroyed on September 11, 2001, or Mexico is south of the US", "The US is south of Canada, or two plus two equals four," and "The World Trade Center was destroyed on September 11, 2001, or two plus two equals four."

A similar thing is true of the identity symbol, though it is not truth functional (a = b asserts a relation between objects in the domain, not sentences that are true or false). Given that two names and/or descriptions refer to the same object, and so the sentence that asserts their identity is true, one can substitute one name/description for the other in most sentences in which the name/description occurs, and the new sentence will retain its original value.[4] For example, given that George Washington was in fact the same person as the first president of the U.S., one can substitute the name for the description, and vice versa, and preserve the truth of the original sentence. Thus, "George Washington was the son of Augustine Washington and Mary Ball" is true, and it remains true when we substitute the description for the name, as in "The first president of the U.S. was the son of Augustine Washington and Mary Ball." Thus, for all of the logical functions that we've explored up until this chapter, substituting like values preserves truth, whether the values are truth values or objects in the domain.

But modal contexts do not tolerate this substitution of true sentence for true sentence (or false sentence for false sentence). The truth of the sentence "It is necessary that a square has four sides" is not preserved by substituting any true sentence whatsoever for the true sentence "A square has four sides." For example, "It is necessary that I have two children," is manifestly false, even though it is true that I have two children. Or consider the sentence "It is not possible that a circle has four sides." Substituting another false sentence for the false sentence "A circle has four sides," we get "It is not possible that Thomas Jefferson was the first President of the U.S.A." But whereas

---

[4] Why most? There are notable exceptions, such as when a name is being talked about qua word in a language (which philosophers indicate, as I noted in a footnote in Chapter 1, by putting the name in single quotes). For example, the sentence "'George Washington' has 16 letters in it" is true, but "'The first president of the U.S.' has 16 letter in it" is false. Another exception is in modal contexts, as I explain below.

"It is not possible that a circle has four sides" is true, "It is not possible that Thomas Jefferson was the first President of the U.S.A." is false. Jefferson, after all, was just as integral to the founding of the United States as was George Washington, if not more so.

In addition, modal contexts do not tolerate the substitution of one name/description for another name/description, even if the names/descriptions in question refer to the same thing. The clearest examples of this come from epistemic logics. It is certainly conceivable that "Jim knows that Muhammad Ali was a heavyweight champion" is true, while "Jim knows that Cassius Clay was a heavyweight champion" is false. After all, not everyone knows that Muhammad Ali's given name at birth was Cassius Clay.

Thus, it is clear that modal contexts differ from the contexts associated with the connectives, the quantifiers, and the identity symbol. Opponents of modal logics argue that this difference is significant because as we have seen, to give an adequate semantics for modal terms we must appeal to the idea of a sentence's truth conditions in all possible worlds. But according to these critics, semantic accounts that depend on a notion of truth conditions in all possible worlds are much more problematic than the notions of truth and reference appealed to in the semantics for the standard symbols of classical logic.

To get an idea of what the complaint here is, consider the difference between the truth of the sentences "John is a male and John is a teacher" and "Necessarily, John is a male." Arguably, the truth of the first sentence is very straightforward since all that it depends on is whether John is a male and John is a teacher. Thus, the truth conditions for "John is male and John is a teacher" are very clear-cut, as are the reference conditions of the name 'John.' But the truth of the second sentence is a far trickier matter. To his wife, necessarily John might be a male, while to the members of his glee club, necessarily he might be a good singer, while to his employer, necessarily he might be a conscientious worker. In each case, John's being necessarily one way or another is neither clear-cut nor independent of us and our interests in John.[5] Furthermore, whether or not some individual in another possible world is identifiable as John or one of his counterparts would seem to depend, at least in part, on what we think is most important about John. In short, the truth conditions for sentences about what is

---

[5] The sentence, "Necessarily 8 is greater than 7" might be an exception to this claim because its truth conditions do seem clear cut and interest free. Whether this is so is a subject of much debate, some of which I will introduce in the discussion in Chapter 9.

and isn't necessary are not as clearly defined as the truth conditions for sentences containing conjunctions.

Now, one might well wonder why any of this should matter, as far the legitimacy of modal logics go. After all, as we have seen, the job of logic isn't to tell us what is true or false, but to tell us what follows on the assumption that a particular sentence either is or isn't true. Though it may not always be easy to determine when some sentence is true or false necessarily, modal logics certainly clarify what follows in either case. For example, if "Necessarily, water is $H_2O$" is true, then it follows that water is $H_2O$ in all possible worlds, that it's not possible that water is not $H_2O$, that if Mary (or her counterpart) is drinking water then she (or her counterpart) is drinking $H_2O$, and so on. Since modal logics clearly do what we want a logic to do, why all the fuss?

Here's why. If the semantics of modal terms are as inherently problematic as the critics claim, then this prevents possible world semantics from doing what a semantics is supposed to do. As we saw in Chapter 4, logical languages are defined both in terms of their syntax and their semantics, and the semantics are supposed to clarify why the syntactic rules preserve truth. But if possible world truth conditions are as philosophically problematic as these critics claim them to be, then it's hard to see how they can provide a genuinely explanatory interpretation of the syntactic rules that define modal functions. In essence, the worry is that all of this semantic apparatus makes it appear as though modal notions have been clarified or explained when they have not.

Before I go on to mention a second problem raised against modal logics, I feel it is important to point something out in light of the criticism we've just explored. Though modalities may not be truth functional, they are similar to the standard logical terms of classical logic in other important ways. To name just one that we have discussed, there are no restrictions on the subject matter of the sentences that modal rules operate with, and so modal logics are topic neutral. In terms of the four sentences in group C above, each makes a claim about what follows from any sentence p, whatsoever; C(1) says that all sentences p are such that if they assert that there are x's, then there will always have been x's, C(2), that all sentences p are such that if I know p then p, C(3) that all sentences p are such that if I am obliged to p then I am not obliged to not p, and C(4) that all sentences p are such that if it is not possible that not p, then it is possible that p. As I noted in Chapter 4, this topic neutrality has long been thought to be a very important feature of logic and logic alone. Of course, topic neutrality is not the only quality that has been claimed to be somehow definitive of logical concepts, and different theories about what makes a logic a logic will give different results as far as modal logics go. Nevertheless, the fact that modal logics have this feature suggests that there may be something importantly logical about them, after all. At the very least, therefore, we should be clear that modal logics bear important similarities to and important differences from standard accounts of classical logic.

The second criticism that I will discuss is the one highlighted in Prior's paper, and it is perhaps one of the deepest difficulties raised against modal logics. As I noted before, Prior argues that philosophers are pretty unanimous in their judgments about the sentences in groups A and B. Those in A are logical and those in B are not. The reason for this is simple. All the sentences of group A are true in virtue of their logical form,[6] whereas those in group B are true in virtue of certain facts in the world. Thus, what's unclear about the modal sentences in C, according to Prior, is whether or not their truth depends on their logical form or on facts about the world. This problem with modal logics, therefore, is that they seem to blur the line between logical and non-logical consequence.

The problem is most stark in the case of temporal logics, but it holds for the other modalities in greater and lesser degrees. I noted in my brief discussion of temporal logics that time flows in one direction, and thus the accessibility relation for a temporal logic should not be symmetrical. But this directional asymmetry is a contingent fact about time. As philosophers of physics have long pointed out, the laws of physics work the same running forwards or backwards, and so there is a serious question about why time only seems to run in one direction. The reasons for the directionality of time aside, it is quite clear that temporal logics are structured to capture certain facts about the way time works. And the worry is, of course, that no matter how logical temporal logics appear to be (in the sense of being topic neutral, in the sense of stating clearly what follows from what given that a tensed sentence is true, and so on), at the end of the day the truth of sentences containing temporal operators depends more on the worldly fact that time goes in one direction than it does on logic.

---

[6] All are instances of tautologies: A(1) is an instance of $p \supset p$, A(2) is an instance of $(\forall x)((\phi x \ \& \ \psi x) \supset \phi x)$ and A(3) is an instance of $(\forall x)(\phi x \supset \psi x) \supset (\forall x) (\sim\!\psi x \supset \sim\!\phi x)$.

Let me conclude this section by making clear that Prior, himself, was not particularly bothered by this seeming intrusion of the world into the logical. He even goes so far as to suggest that, in principle, there might be a logic of biology, so that sentence B(1), "If Polly is a feathered animal she breathes air" could be a truth of logic. He is certainly skeptical of anyone ever really working out a biological logic, but his point is a philosophical one. According to Prior, the whole point of clarifying logical relations is to make clear that there is an underlying order to our thoughts about the world. Some aspects of this order are clearly more generally applicable than others, but at base the point of the ordering is very similar. We have seen how a well-constructed formal apparatus can do actual philosophical work, both by way of solving long-standing philosophical conundrums (such as the problem of non-being) and by clarifying previously murky concepts (such as the necessary and the possible). Prior's counsel, therefore, is to focus more on the potential rewards of formally representing this order, and less on the supposed problems with distinguishing the genuinely logical from the genuinely non-logical. Given the tremendous difficulty associated with actually distinguishing the two, this seems like wise counsel, indeed.

# 7

# Bivalence

## I—FATALISM AND FUTURE CONTINGENTS

We now have enough logical concepts at our disposal that we can start to evaluate the adequacy of classical logic as an account of logical consequence. As we will see in the next few chapters, classical logic has many critics, and virtually no assumption of this logic has gone unquestioned. In this chapter, we will begin by exploring a challenge to the semantics of classical logic. In particular, we will consider some arguments to the effect that sentences can be more than simply true or false.

The claim that sentences must be either true or false is called *bivalence* (literally, two valued). Challenges to bivalence go all the way back to ancient Greece. Aristotle thought that if bivalence was true, then the future could not be changed. The idea that there is no way for us to change the future is called *fatalism*. Fatalism presents big challenges to our conceptions of both how the world works and how we view ourselves as human beings. After all, if there is no changing the fact that tomorrow I will commit murder, then it hardly seems right to hold me responsible for doing so. If it was fated to be, I could not have chosen not to.

Aristotle's argument against bivalence was as follows. Consider the sentence "There will be a sea battle tomorrow." The natural thing to say about a sentence whose truth value can only be determined in the future (called a *future contingent*) is that we just don't know if there will be a sea battle tomorrow. There might be but there might not be as well. Now, if bivalence is true, and every sentence must be either true or false, then this sentence must also be either true or false. In particular, if it is true that there will be a sea battle tomorrow, then the sentence "There will be a sea battle tomorrow" is also true, and if it is false that there will be a sea battle tomorrow, then the sentence "There will be a sea battle tomorrow" is also false. But if the sentence about tomorrow must be either true or false today, then it seems like whatever is going to happen will happen no matter what we do. In other words, if "There will be a sea battle tomorrow" is true, then it would seem necessary that there will be a sea battle, and if it is false, then it would seem necessary that there won't be a sea battle. However, this conclusion just seems wrong. Whether or not there is a sea battle tomorrow is contingent (i.e., it could be true or it could be false), and depends on many factors such as the weather, the invading navy's timetable, the decisions of the commanders, and the like. Hence, bivalence must not be true.

At the outset, I should be clear that this argument is not a terribly good one. The problem with bivalence is supposed to be that it leads us to conclude that something contingent (i.e., it may or may not happen) is actually necessary (i.e, it necessarily will happen or it necessarily won't happen). But one of Aristotle's premises is ambiguous, and no matter how it's understood, the conclusion that a sea battle will either necessarily happen or necessarily not happen doesn't seem to follow. The premise in question is that if "There will be a sea battle tomorrow" is true now, then it must be the case (i.e., it is necessary), that there will be a sea battle tomorrow (and that if "There will be a sea battle tomorrow" is false, then it must be the case that there won't be a sea battle, though in what follows I'll focus only on the truth of this sentence for ease of exposition). Using S to stand for "There will be a sea battle tomorrow," this premise can be understood in either of the following two ways:

i) Necessarily, if S is true now, then it follows that S

or

ii) If S is true now, then S is true of necessity.

Read as in (i), the whole argument rests on a simple modal fallacy. (A *fallacy* is a mistake in reasoning.) Read as in (ii), Aristotle's argument is valid but the problem is that (ii) is completely implausible.

If Aristotle's argument is read with (i), then it is invalid. The form of this part of the argument would essentially be as follows:

$\Box\ (p \supset p)$

p

So, $\Box\ p$

This is a variant of the invalid modal argument that we discussed in the last chapter, replacing q from that argument with p itself.[1] If Aristotle's argument depends on reading the ambiguous premise as (i), then he can't validly establish that it is necessary that there will be a sea battle tomorrow. But if he can't establish this, then there is no difficulty for bivalence at all since the problem with bivalence was supposed to be that it would force us to conclude that a contingent sea battle would necessarily happen or necessarily not happen. If the argument depends on a premise like (i), it is clear that Aristotle can never establish this disjunction of necessities regarding the sea battle.

If, on the other hand, the argument is read with (ii), then Aristotle's argument is valid as it simply depends on an instance of Modus Ponens:

p

$p \supset \Box\ p$

So, $\Box\ p$

But if this is the correct reading of the ambiguous part of the argument, then the entire argument is not terribly convincing because this second reading of the premise in question is so implausible. Why should we think that if something is true now then it is true of necessity? All kinds of things are true now that are not true of necessity. For example, that I am sitting at my computer is

---

[1] A counter-example to this particular variant is not hard to find:

Jennifer Fisher has two children.
Necessarily, if Jennifer Fisher has two children then Jennifer Fisher has two children.
So, necessarily Jennifer Fisher has two children.

At some possible worlds it is true that I have two children and it is necessary at all possible worlds that if I have two children then I have two children. Focusing only on the worlds where it is true that I have two children, the conclusion is clearly false. As we saw in the last chapter, it is certainly possible that I have no children or any number of children other than two.

true now, that I am wearing blue jeans is true now, that I have two children is true now, but none of these things is true of necessity.

Even if Aristotle's argument is not a very good one, it raises the very important question of whether or not we must assume that every sentence is either true or false. In response to Aristotle's problem, the logician Jan Lukasiewicz proposed a three-valued logic that has come to be known as $L_3$.[2] In addition to the values true and false, Lukasiewicz argued that there is a third truth value, I, which means indeterminate or possible. The logical connectives in $L_3$ are characterized by the following matrices:

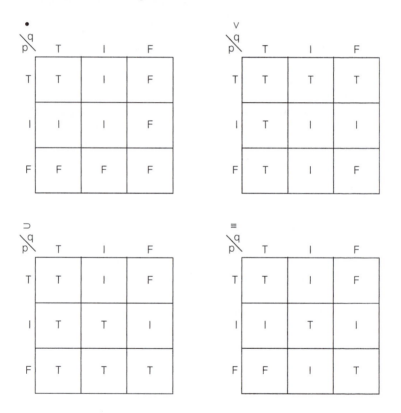

---

[2] There are a number of 3 valued logics, though I will not discuss any of the others here.

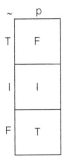

These matrices get read exactly like the two-valued ones. So, for example, to find the value of a conjunction whose first conjunct is true and whose second conjunct is indeterminate, one simply goes to the box in the matrix for the dot in $L_3$ where p gets a T and q gets an I, which is the second box on the top line. The value of a conjunction in this case is I.

A few things to notice. First, in $L_3$ when the values of both p and q are classical values (i.e., either true or false) the value of a compound sentence is the same as in classical logic. In this way, $L_3$ agrees with classical logic about the cases where sentences are either true or false. In addition, the general rules of thumb concerning truth and falsity also still hold, even with the addition of a third category. That is, a conjunction with a false conjunct is still false, even if the value of the second conjunct is indeterminate, and a disjunction with a true disjunct is still true, even if the value of the second disjunct is indeterminate. The divergence from classical logic comes to play only when the truth value of a sentence is indeterminate, and the classical value can't be assigned based on the value of the sentence that is known.

Second, in $L_3$ there will be very different logical truths. In particular, in $L_3$ neither the law of the excluded middle nor the law of non-contradiction will be tautologies. To see this, consider first the law of the excluded middle, p ∨ ~p (hereafter, abbreviated LEM). When the value of p is either true or false, the value of p ∨ ~p is true. This is because the negation of a classical value is itself a classical value, and disjunctions are indeterminate in $L_3$ only when one of the disjuncts is indeterminate. But when the value of p is indeterminate, its negation is also indeterminate, and the matrix for disjunction makes clear that a disjunction with two indeterminate disjuncts is itself indeterminate. So p ∨ ~p is not always true, hence it is not a logical truth in $L_3$. I'll leave it to the reader to figure out when the principle of non-contradiction ~(p • ~p) is not true, and hence why it is not a logical truth.

For this reason, $L_3$ is not a terribly good solution to the problem that concerned Aristotle, even though Lukasiewicz intended it that way. This is because Aristotle wanted to maintain LEM, which $L_3$ clearly does not do. But $L_3$ can easily be converted into a logic that denies bivalence but keeps LEM. The way to do this is with what is called a *supervaluational logic.*

The idea behind supervaluations is quite simple. A supervaluation assigns to compound sentences with indeterminate truth values whatever classical logic would assign to the compound, if there is a unique such value, and otherwise it assigns it no value. Returning to our sea battle, the value of the sea battle sentence, S, is presently indeterminate, which I'll write $v(S) = I$ (to be read, the value of S is indeterminate). Eventually, however, S will be either true or false. Specifically, when we know whether or not there is a sea battle (a fact that we'll know tomorrow), we will know the value of S (yesterday). A supervaluation, $v'$, is an assignment of values such that $v = v'$, except if $v(p) = I$ then $v'(p) =$ either T or F. So, if p were already true, then the supervaluation $v'$ would assign p a true, and if p were already false, it would assign it a false, but if p is indeterminate, it will assign it either a true or a false. Since $v(S) = I$, $v'(S) =$ either T or F. Either way, however, $v'$ will make (S ∨ ~S) a tautology, since, as we saw, $L_3$ assigns classical values whenever the simple sentences take classical values. And since what we've said about S is true of any future contingent, LEM still holds. So, LEM would still be a logical truth, because no matter what the value of p turns out to be, p ∨ ~p will be true. Hence, even though Bivalence doesn't hold, LEM does.

Aristotle's argument highlights an important issue. The logic that we choose might make a real difference to a lot of the other ways that we think about our world. Lets look at another challenge to bivalence that is based on a better argument.

## II—VAGUENESS

Bivalence requires that every sentence be either true or false, but some sentences don't seem to clearly be either true or false, and so the challenges that we are currently considering ask whether or not bivalence is at fault. We've just seen that future contingents are one class of sentences which bivalence doesn't clearly accommodate. Another class is sentences containing vague terms.

A *vague* term is one that doesn't have clear truth conditions in every case. 'Bald', for example, is a term that is clearly true of some people, clearly false of others, and not clearly either true or false for many. Many terms of natural language have some degree of vagueness.[3] Certainly most adjectives (red, large, angry, beautiful) are vague, but so are many nouns and verbs. Though it is clear that Mt. Everest is a mountain, and equally clear that an anthill is not, there are a lot of large mounds of land where we're just not sure, and so the noun 'mountain' has a certain amount of vagueness to it. Likewise, though preparing a four course meal from scratch should definitely count as cooking, and going out to dinner should definitely not, it is not at all clear whether opening a can of chili and heating it up on the stove is a case of cooking or not, and so the verb 'to cook' is vague as well. Indeed, there may be some very important ethical issues that hinge, at least in part, on vague language. When is a person a person? Many people think that a zygote is not a person, and most think that a newborn baby is, but there are a lot of in-between stages, and people notoriously disagree about those.

One possible response to the pervasiveness of vagueness in ordinary language is to think that with many vague terms there is some kind of clear-cut criterion, even if that criterion is not always easily applied. So, for example, I noted that 'red' is a vague term, but redness is well defined scientifically as being light waves between a certain length. Just because our eyes can't always discern when a particular color is between those wave lengths (as in the case of very reddish oranges, say), doesn't mean that 'red' is vague, in the sense that it has no clear truth conditions. So, according to this response, the reason why we aren't always sure of the application conditions for vague terms is that we are frequently unable to discern the relevant differences where they exist.

One problem with this response is that color terms are probably unusual in being so well defined. What could possibly serve as a clear

---

[3] Vague terms come in at least two different kinds: those whose constituent parts come in discrete packets and those that don't. Examples of the former kind of vague terms are 'bald,' 'rich,' and 'red' (the discrete packets being the number of hairs, pennies, and wavelengths of light, respectively). Examples of the latter kind of vague term are 'beautiful,' 'boring,' and 'nice' (since whatever it is that determines if a thing is beautiful, boring or nice is not anything like units of beauty, boredom or niceness). In my discussion, I will focus only on the former. In doing this, I already make the problem of vagueness easier to solve logically than it would otherwise be. Clearly different possible solutions would have to be considered for the non-discrete vague terms.

criterion for terms like 'large' or 'to cook'? (And this is to say nothing of the difficulty with taking this line for the vague terms whose constituent parts don't come in discrete units (see fn 1 of this chapter).) But putting this issue to the side, this response is problematic in light of what is known as the ancient *paradox of the heap*.

Suppose that I have one grain of sand. Clearly, one grain of sand does not make a heap of sand. So the sentence "One grain of sand is a heap of sand" is false. Now, suppose I add one grain of sand to the first. No one would want to say that I now have a heap of sand, so the sentence "Two grains of sand is a heap of sand" is still false. In fact, in general, it seems true to say that if n grains of sand are not a heap of sand (for any number n), then the addition of one grain of sand won't make the difference between a heap and a non-heap. Specifically, if "n grains of sand are a heap of sand" is false, then "n+1 grains of sand are a heap of sand" ought to be false as well. But now, suppose that I keep adding grains of sand until I have 1,000,000 grains of sand. We would then have a long argument like this:

| | |
|---|---|
| 1. | "One grain of sand is a heap of sand" is false. |
| 2. | If "One grain of sand is a heap of sand" is false, then "Two grains of sand is a heap of sand" is false. |
| 3. | "Two grains of sand of sand is a head of sand" is false. |
| 4. | If "Two grains of sand is a heap of sand" is false, then "Three grains of sand is a heap of sand" is false. |
| | . |
| | . |
| | . |
| 1,000,000. | If "999,999 grains of sand is a heap of sand" is false, then "1,000,000 grains of sand is a heap of sand" is false. |
| 1,000,001. | So, "1,000,000 grains of sand is a heap of sand" is false. |

This argument is called a *sorites* argument. A sorites is a series of arguments strung together. This argument seems to take us from true premises to a false conclusion. Yet, it is not clear which premise we should reject, and the reasoning seems to be beyond reproach. It is just a bunch of strung together instances of Modus Ponens, after all, and Modus Ponens is certainly a valid argument form. In other words, what is so puzzling about this argument is that the conclusion is false, but the premises seem correct, and the reasoning seems correct as well. This is why this argument is paradoxical.

This sorites argument makes clear exactly why the response to the problem of vagueness that we first considered is problematic. That response seems to require that one grain of sand does make the difference between some pile's being a heap or not (or that one hair makes a difference between someone's being bald or not, or that one penny makes the difference between someone's being rich or not, and so on). Intuitively, however, this just isn't so.

Unlike Aristotle's challenge to bivalence, the problem of vague terms is not based on problematic reasoning. If bivalence is true, then sentences containing vague terms must be either true or false. But this not only goes against common usage, it also implies that there are definite criteria and cut-off points that determine the correctness of applying each and every vague term. An advocate of classical logic might well bite this bullet, and just insist that in spite of its odd appearance, this is, in fact, the case. That is, this advocate might just say that there is a definite criterion for each vague term, and so one grain of sand (or one hair or one penny) does make the difference. But many have thought that this is just too counter-intuitive, and so they have proposed non-classical logics as a solution.

One proposed solution is a supervaluational logic like the one we examined in connection with future contingents. In the case of future contingents and the case of sentences containing vague language, the supervaluational approach begins with the assumption that some sentences are neither clearly true nor clearly false, and so can get a value of indeterminate. Unlike future contingents, however, the truth value of sentences with vague language are not clarified in time, so when applied to vagueness, what gets supervaluated are what are called precisifications of the language. A *precisification* of a term is a way of making the applications for that term more precise without actually specifying strict criteria. Different people might well have different precisifications for each vague term, but all the precisifications, presumably, will have certain things in common. For example, every precisification of tallness will have it that if one thing is taller than a second thing, and that second thing is taller than a third thing, then the third thing is taller than the first thing. (Tallness, in other words, is transitive.)

This solution has the advantage that logical truths like LEM and the law of non-contradiction will still be logically true. One quality that surely all precisifications will have is that, no matter how a term gets made more precise, it won't be the case that it both does and doesn't apply. For example, it won't be the case that some one pile of sand is both a heap and not a heap. In addition, it should be the case that a pile of sand either is or isn't a heap, no matter how the term 'heap' is made more precise. So, though a sentence like "500 grains of sand is a heap of sand," may be indeterminate in a supervaluational logic, LEM and the principle of non-contradiction are still logical truths. This is because in every precisification of the term 'heap', "Either 500 grains of sand is a heap of sand or its not the case that 500 grains of sand is a heap of sand," and "It is not the case that 500 grains of sand is a heap of sand and 500 grains of sand is not a heap of sand," are both true.

However, this supervaluational solution has the distinct disadvantage that it doesn't clearly solve the problem. In fact, in a sense, it creates more problems just like the original. The problem of vagueness, assuming bivalence, is that there are grey areas where we just aren't sure whether a sentence with a vague term is either true or false. But surely there is also a grey area between truth and indeterminacy and falsehood and indeterminacy. That is, just as we might be unsure whether "Dick Cheney is bald" is true or false, we might be equally unsure whether that same sentence is indeterminate or true. In going from two values to three values, supervaluational semantics just doubles the possibility for grey areas.

With this in mind, another solution is a many-valued *fuzzy logic* that allows objects to have properties in greater and lesser degrees. Thus far, we have only looked at a three valued logic, but in principle, we can define logics that have any number of values, even an infinite number. The procedure for turning a three valued logic like $L_3$ into a many valued logic is quite general. Truth values are given in terms of fractions (or decimals) ranging from 0 (or falsity) to 1 (or truth). Whatever the number of truth values, n, the range of values can be defined as follows:

$n-1/n-1$, $n-2/n-1$, ... $2/n-1$, $1/n-1$, $0/n-1$.

So, $L_3$ has truth values

1, 1/2, 0

and $L_4$ (a four-valued logic) has truth values

1, 2/3, 1/3, 0.

$L_{10}$ has truth values

1, 8/9, 7/9, 6/9 (2/3), 5/9, 4/9, 3/9 (1/3), 2/9, 1/9, 0.

In each n-valued logic, one can define the connectives as follows (where $|p|$ means the value of p):

$|\sim p\ | = 1 - |p|$

$|p \lor q| = \max \{|p|, |q|\}$ (Note: max $\{\ldots\}$ means the maximum of the set, and min. $\{\ldots\}$ means the minimum of the set. This rule and the next mean simply that one should take the value of the connective in question to be the minimum/maximum of the two options given between the set brackets $\{\}$.)

$|p \cdot q| = \min \{|p|, |q|\}$

$|\ p \supset q\ | = \min. \{1, (1 - |p|) + |q|\ \}$ [or equivalently: $p \supset q = 1$, if $|p| \leq |q|$, $(1 - |p|) + |q|$ otherwise]

$|p \equiv q| = 1 - ||p|-|q||$

Here are some examples to make these various notions clearer. In the four valued logic $L_4$, if p = 2/3, then $\sim$p = 1/3, since the value of a negation is given by the formula $1 - |p|$ (1 minus the value of p), and 1 - 2/3 = 1/3. In the 10 valued logic $L_{10}$, if p = 5/9, then $\sim$p = 4/9, and so on. In $L_4$, a disjunction of two sentences, p and q, where $|p| = 2/3$ and $|q| = 1/3$ would be 2/3, since that is the maximum of the two values. And in a 10 valued logic, a conjunction with two sentences p and q, where $|p| = 1/9$ and $|q| = 7/9$ would be 1/9, since that is the minimum of the two values being conjoined. The value of a conditional $p \supset q$ is the minimum of the two options, either 1, or $(1 - |p|) + |q|$. So, a conditional in $L_4$, where the antecedent $|p| = 2/3$ and the consequent $|q| = 1/3$, would have the value 2/3, because $(1 - |p|) = 1/3$, and 1/3 + 1/3 = 2/3, and 2/3 is the minimum of 1 and 2/3. And in a 10 valued logic, a conditional with antecedent $|p| = 1/9$ and consequent $|q| = 7/9$ would be 1, since $(1 - |p|) + |q| = 15/9$, or 1 1/3, and 1 is the minimum of these two values.

One quick point, and then we'll return to the issue of vagueness and get clearer about how a fuzzy logic is supposed to help. Notice that classical logic is just the two-valued instance of one of these many valued Lukasiewicz logics. The values as given by the formula above are 1 and 0, and the connectives are clearly defined by these formula. So, if $|p| = 1$ (true), then $|\sim p| = 0$ (false), since 1 - 1 = 0, and if $|p| = 0$, then $|\sim p| = 1$. In addition, a conjunction with one false conjunct will always be false, since the value of that false conjunct will be 0, and 0 will always be the minimum of the two numbers in the set. Likewise, a disjunction with a true disjunct will always be true, since the value of the true disjunct will be 1, and that will always be the maximum. A conditional will be false when the antecedent, p, is true ($|p| = 1$) and the consequent, q, is false ($|q| = 0$), since $(1 - |p|) + |q| = 0$, and it will be false otherwise (I leave it to the reader to work this, and the truth table for the biconditional, out).

So, how does this help with vagueness? We saw that at least one problem with supervaluational logics as a response to the problem of vagueness is that supervaluations just seem to make more grey areas. What these many valued logics make possible, however, is a logic whose values coincide with vague predicates. Fuzzy logics are logics that, using formal apparatus like the one we've just examined, allow there to be varying degrees of a thing's satisfying a certain vague term. For example, suppose that 0 grains of sand is definitely not a heap, so the sentence "0 grains of sand is a heap of sand" would get the value 0, and that 1,000,000 grains of sand is definitely a heap, so that "1,000,000 grains of sand is a heap of sand" would get the value 1. We could then construct a 1,000,000-valued logic that would allow our intuitions concerning the amount of heapness in a given pile of sand to vary exactly with the amount of sand ("499,972 grains of sand is a heap of sand" would get a value of 499,972/999,999). If we interpret 1 as true and 0 as false, we have a logic that allows for varying degrees of truth for sentences containing vague terms. There certainly would be no problem with grey areas since each grain of sand would have its own corresponding fuzzy truth value.

In addition to actually solving the problem of vague terms (unlike supervaluational logics) this suggestion has a certain naturalness to it. We do seem to think in terms of things being somewhat true, very true, a little untrue, and so on. "Dick Cheney is bald" is somewhat true, and "Bill Gates is rich" is definitely true, while "Madonna is old" is not altogether false, and "Mt. Everest is tiny" is definitely false. Nevertheless, there are a lot of problems with fuzzy logics.

Even though there is a certain naturalness to the idea that truth comes in degrees, we generally don't distinguish degrees of truth quite as fine-grained as a 1,000,000 valued logic would have us do. Worse still, the logic leads to some pretty counter-intuitive results. In the first place, we have already seen that LEM and the law of non-contradiction are not logical truths in $L_3$. Nor are they logical truths in any multi-valued variant of $L_3$. So, Dick Cheney is bald and Dick Cheney is not bald will get a value of more than 0, which means that the contradiction is not definitely false.

This will strike a lot of people as a pretty odd result. Another oddity can be brought out in the following way. Take two people, John and Bill, and lets suppose that Bill is hairier than John. Suppose that "Bill is bald" gets a 5/10 (1/2), and "John is bald" gets a 6/10 (3/5). This would mean that "John is not bald" gets 4/10 (2/5) and "Bill is not bald" gets a 5/10 (1/2). What would the conjunction "John is not bald and Bill is bald" get? Since conjunctions are assigned whichever is the minimum value of their conjuncts, this conjunction would get a 4/10 (2/5). But that seems wrong. After all, we know that Bill is hairier than John, but on this construal, the conjunction that asserts both that John is not bald and that Bill is bald, though perhaps somewhat false, is also almost half-true.

Thus, neither of the solutions to the problem of vagueness that we have considered is without its problems. But then again, solutions that keep classical logic are also problematic. One such solution is to simply ignore the problematic class of sentences entirely. According to this response vagueness is a problem with natural language, not logic, and sentences with vague terms are actually ill-formed or not meaningful in some way. This solution emphasizes that logic operates best on languages, like mathematical ones, where every term is clearly defined and where issues of vagueness can't arise.

There is both a descriptive and a normative reason to take this response seriously. On the descriptive side, logicians and philosophers have always been concerned to capture the structure of mathematical reasoning, and this concern continues to this day. The justification for this focus is normative. Mathematicians, at least in part, are in the business of proving theorems in the various branches of mathematics. These proofs have required mathematicians to carefully define all their terms and to pay close attention to the reasons they give for going from a premise to a conclusion. Given that the questions we're asking in this book are supposed to be normative, it makes sense that logicians would study fields whose practitioners take extra care to reason well, and for whom the difference between good and bad reasoning is of the utmost importance.

That said, there still is a problem with simply dismissing the existence of vagueness in the way currently under consideration. For one thing, sentences with vague terms do seem to be perfectly meaningful and well-formed to us, and so it's hard to see why we should think that these sentences are somehow less meaningful or clear than their more rigorously defined mathematical relatives. In spite of the vagueness of the term, "Bill Gates is rich" seems about as clear to me as does your average mathematical equation.

The main problem with this response, though, is that it seems to entail that logic is not useful for studying patterns of reasoning in natural language. But that just seems wrong. Even if it is true that natural languages are not as well behaved as the more artificially constructible languages of arithmetic, that doesn't mean that logic doesn't or shouldn't apply to them. As we have seen, logic seems to be readily applicable and even useful in discussing many instances of reasoning in natural language. Indeed, even arguments with vague terms seem to be ones that can be assessed logically. For example, the following is a good argument:

> Either Bill Gates is rich or Bill Gates is not rich.
> It is not the case that Bill Gates is not rich.
> So, Bill Gates is rich.

And this argument is a bad one:

> If Marv Alpert is bald, then Dick Cheney is bald.
> If Dick Cheney is bald, then Al Roker is bald.
> So, it's not the case that if Marv Alpert is bald, then Al Roker is bald.

In other words, in spite of the difficulties of always being clear about the proper application conditions of a vague term, it certainly seems for all intents and purposes that logic can be used in assessing at least some arguments containing vague terms.

One other solution is still available to the classical logician. Earlier I noted that advocates of classical logic can bite the bullet and keep bivalence, but only at the cost of needing to say that there are clear cut-offs and definite criteria for the application of vague terms. In terms of the above sorites argument, this would be tantamount to saying that at some n, the conditional "If n grains of sand is not a heap of sand, then n+1 grains of sand is not a heap of sand," will actually be false. For example, the conditional "If 500,000 grains of sand is not a heap of sand, then 500,001 grains of sand is not a heap of sand," will be false (or if not this number, then some number). This seems pretty strange, as the original intuition is a fairly strong one. How can one tiny grain of sand make the difference between heapness and non-heapness?

Another problem concerns the fact that even if we embrace the falsity of one of those sorites sentences, we need to ask how speakers of a language know which one is the false one. After all, no one ever taught me the specific number of hairs on a head that constituted baldness versus hirsuteness, and yet I feel pretty confident that I use these terms properly. One such view has it that these cut-offs and criteria do, in fact, exist, it's just that we don't know them. This view regards vagueness as an epistemic problem. (Epistemology, recall, is the philosophical study of knowledge). This view strikes many as wildly implausible. How could we manage to communicate so effectively, and do so much with language, if we don't even know the application conditions of the words that we use? Though some defenders of classical logic are willing to bite this bullet, they have to have pretty strong teeth to do so.

So we are left with a difficult problem with no clear-cut solution. This is frequently the case in philosophy in general, but perhaps even more so in the philosophy of logic. In trying to figure out which logic is correct, we will frequently find ourselves balancing the advantages and disadvantages of the various proposed logics, with no clear winner emerging. The reasons for this will become clearer as we consider more and more non-classical logics and the issues they raise.

# 8

## The Conditional

### I—THE PROBLEMATIC MATERIAL CONDITIONAL

Of all the logical connectives, the conditional is expected to account for the most varied natural language phenomena. To name just a few, we use the conditional to indicate cause and effect relationships ("If I drop this cup on the ground, it will break"), rules ("If you run in the halls, you will be sent to the principal's office"), logical entailments ("If it is true that the bread is moldy and the butter is rancid, then it is true that the bread is moldy"), and *counterfactuals*, which are sentences that say what follows if we assume something contrary to the facts in the antecedent ("If I had jumped off the observation deck of the Empire State Building, I would have died"). How can one little symbol, the horseshoe, possibly account for so many different uses?

The answer is, most likely it can't. For this reason, many philosophers guard against any direct understanding of cause and effect in terms of the conditional, logical entailment is given a different meta-logical symbol to make sure the two notions aren't confused, and there is a veritable cottage industry of logicians and philosophers trying to make sense of counterfactuals. Nevertheless, there is no denying that 'if...then' does a lot of varied work for us, and giving a proper account of the conditional has proven particularly difficult.

The conditional in classical logic is called the *material conditional*. In Chapter 2, we saw that the material conditional seems to make sense for examples like "If you run a red light, then you break the law." Even granting this, though, there is no doubt that the material conditional has some wildly counter-intuitive logical consequences.

The material conditional, recall, is false only when the antecedent is true and the consequent is false. This means that a material conditional is true whenever its antecedent is false or its consequent is true. You can check this on the truth table on the next page. The antecedent is false in rows (iii) and (iv), and the consequent is true in rows (i) and (iii), and in both rows, the conditional gets a true. So, in more concrete terms, the sentence, "If pigs fly, then the moon is blue" will be true. If you're like most people, this will not sound at all right.

Even more troubling, the following conditional is also true: "If pigs fly, then the moon is not blue." Thus, both conditionals are true since they both have the same false antecedent, and yet they seem to be saying that contradictory things follow from the assumption of that antecedent. Intuitively, though, if either of these sentences is true then only one of them should be true. After all, at least part of the point of a using a conditional in natural language is to allow us to consider what would follow from something's being the case. If contradictory things can be said to truthfully follow from some assumptions, then it's not clear how the conditional can be helpful to us in any way. To put the point in terms of a less frivolous example, it seems like only one of the following conditionals should be true: i) If there are no trees in the park then there isn't any shade. ii) If there are no trees in the park then there is plenty of shade. Assuming that there actually are trees in the park in question, both of these sentences are true. Intuitively, however, (i) is true and (ii) is false.

We can sum up the problems with the material conditional by noting that the following are classically valid arguments (the abbreviations stand for problematic material conditional argument 1 and 2):

PMC1)        ~p
             So, p ⊃ q

and

PMC2)        q
             So, p ⊃ q

The validity of both of these arguments can be seen with the following truth table:

|      | p | q | ~p | p ⊃ q |
|------|---|---|----|-------|
| i)   | T | T | F  | T     |
| ii)  | T | F | F  | F     |
| iii) | F | T | T  | T     |
| iv)  | F | F | T  | T     |

Clearly, when ~p is true (rows (iii) and (iv)), the conclusion is also true, and so PMC1 is valid. Likewise, when q is true (rows (i) and (iii)), the conclusion is true, and so PMC2 is valid.

One reason for the counter-intuitive consequences of the material conditional is the assumption of bivalence. If every sentence has to be either true or false, then so does every sentence that results from combining simple sentences according to logical functions. So, in particular, there are only three other possibilities as far as what to say about a conditional with a false antecedent (or a true consequent), and none of the other options are any good. The three other possibilities are:

| 1. | p | q | p ⊃ q |
|----|---|---|-------|
|    | T | T | T     |
|    | T | F | F     |
|    | F | T | T     |
|    | F | F | F     |

| 2. | p | q | p ⊃ q |
|----|---|---|-------|
|    | T | T | T     |
|    | T | F | F     |
|    | F | T | F     |
|    | F | F | T     |

| 3. | p | q | p ⊃ q |
|----|---|---|-------|
|    | T | T | T     |
|    | T | F | F     |
|    | F | T | F     |
|    | F | F | F     |

The problem with (1) is that the column under p ⊃ q is the same as the column under q. In other words, if we adopted (1) as the correct truth table, we would be saying in essence that conditionals are logically the same as their consequents. In the case of our original example of a conditional, this would be tantamount to saying that logically speaking,

"If you run a red light then you break the law" is the same as saying "You break the law." But these statements clearly make very different kinds of claims about the world. At the very least, given the importance of a conditional in many inferences in natural language, we should want a formal means of distinguishing conditionals from their consequents. Suggestion (1), therefore, is not adequate for making this distinction.

Similar considerations cast doubt on (2). (2) would make "if . . . then" sentences equivalent to a biconditional. But "If you run a red light then you break the law" is logically not the same as "You run a red light if and only if you break the law." The latter says that breaking the law and running red lights is one and the same thing. If "You run a red light if and only if you break the law" were true, nothing other than running a red light would be illegal. But, "If you run a red light then you break the law" leaves room for the possibility that there might be other things one could do to break the law. Given this, truth table (2) above is a better representation of the "if and only if" sentence. (2) indicates that the whole sentence is false only when p and q get different truth values. In other words, (2) captures the truth values for a sentence that makes breaking the law and running a red light one and the same thing.

(3), on the other hand, would make the conditional equivalent to a conjunction. It is true that some conjunctions in English clearly have an "iffy" feel to them, such as, "He fell down and skinned his knee." However, even if this is true of some conjunctions, it is certainly not true of all of them. For this reason, it is important for us to be able to distinguish the logical roles played by typical conjunctions from the logical roles played by typical conditionals. In addition, in terms of the example that I've been appealing to, "If you run a red light, then you break the law" is clearly true even if neither "You run a red light," or "You break the law" is true, and so (3) is just not a good account for current purposes. What all of this suggests is that as long as we are committed to bivalence, the material conditional is probably the best of all the possible options.

Is there anything to be said in defense of the material conditional? The philosopher Paul Grice argued that there are rules that govern conversation that go beyond the merely logical. According to Grice, it is these other kind of rules, not the logical rules, that account for the counter-intuitiveness of the truth table for the material conditional.

Conversations are governed by all kinds of tacit assumed rules that ordinary speakers come to understand in the course of learning to speak a language conversationally. So, for instance, if someone asks me how I liked the movie that I saw over the weekend, and I respond, "The opening credits were good," the implication is that I didn't like the movie. After all, if I did, I would have said so. According to Grice, tacit rules explain both my response and the fact that English speakers understand its implications. In this particular case, one of these tacit rules is that speakers should only assert what they believe to be true and justified, and another rule is that speakers should assert as much as they can. Both of these rules give rise to my responding in the most honest way possible, given that I didn't really like the movie. Of course, neither I nor the person I'm conversing with ever made these rules explicit, nor did we ever explicitly learn them. But people do pick up these norms of proper conversation, and Grice is right to point out that they play an important role in the ordinary give and take of everyday discussions.

The two operative rules in the little imagined exchange above are also relevant to our discussion of the conditional. According to Grice, the problem with conditionals like "If pigs fly then the moon is blue," is not logical. Rather, it is that asserting a conditional like this would defy one or the other of these conversational rules.

To see why, first note that in classical logic, the material conditional is logically equivalent to a disjunction with a negated disjunct. So, "If it rains then you should bring your umbrella" is equivalent to "Either it isn't raining or you should bring your umbrella." We can prove that these sentences are logically equivalent by noting that the truth tables for each sentence form is identical:

| p | q | ~p | p ⊃ q | ~p ∨ q |
|---|---|----|-------|--------|
| T | T | F | T | T |
| T | F | F | F | F |
| F | T | T | T | T |
| F | F | T | T | T |

According to the rule that says that speakers should only assert what they believe to be true and justified, speakers should only assert a disjunction if they think it is justified to do so. This means that we should only assert a disjunction, according to Grice, when we're not sure which disjunct is the case. For example, suppose I respond to someone's query, "Where's Sheila?" by saying "She's either in the conference room or at lunch." Suppose further that I know that she's at lunch. In this case, the disjunctive answer is misleading. By the rules of conversation that I considered above, I should assert as much as possible of what I know to be true and justified. Given this, my disjunctive assertion gets read as an assertion that one or the other disjunct is true but I don't know which. If I know that she's at lunch, it doesn't matter that what I said is still truth-functionally true, what matters is that I knew which disjunct was true but still asserted a disjunction. Since in this example I do know which is true, asserting the disjunction gives the wrong impression about what I do and do not know.

In the same way, Grice argued that asserting the problematic conditional, "If pigs fly then the moon is blue," is equivalent to asserting a disjunction when one knows precisely which disjunct is true. The disjunctive equivalent of the conditional is "Either pigs don't fly or the moon is blue." This disjunction is true since a disjunction with a true disjunct is always true. However, the disjunction is not one that we should assert if Grice's rules about conversational etiquette are followed. Assuming that I know that pigs don't fly, asserting this sentence would be just like my assertion above about Sheila's whereabouts. In both cases, one disjunct is known to be true and yet a disjunction is nevertheless asserted.

This defense of classical logic thus assigns the blame for the problematic inferences not to the logic of the situation but to the underlying rules of ordinary conversation. In essence, the claim is that a material conditional with a false antecedent is true, as classical logic says it is. Nevertheless, many instances of material conditionals with false antecedents and true consequents are not generally assertible in ordinary conversational contexts since asserting them would go against the rules of conversation. In particular, the assertion "If pigs fly then the moon is blue," is equivalent to a disjunction "Either pigs don't fly or the moon is blue." To assert this disjunction, however, would be highly misleading in most ordinary conversational contexts since everyone knows that pigs don't fly.

## II—CONDITIONAL LOGICS AND POSSIBLE WORLDS

Let us suppose that Grice is correct about these conversational demands. One still might object that this solution doesn't really address the problem with the material conditional as an account of 'if...then'. Many believe that we use 'if...then' to construct sentences that assert some sort of a connection between the antecedent and the consequent. So, for example, I might say to my children, "If you work hard, you can be anything you want to be," and what sounds right about this is that hard work is supposed to be somehow connected (even if only ideally) to a person's achieving their goals.

The material conditional just doesn't make this requirement. As we have seen, "If pigs fly then the moon is blue" is true in classical logic, but there is no plausible connection to be made between pigs and their flying abilities and the color of the moon. Thus, even if Grice's explanation can account for why people have such strong intuitions against the material conditional, it still doesn't really capture the correct account of English 'if... then' sentences.

The main response to this difficulty has been to try to capture in a formal way this intuitive idea of there being an important connection between antecedent and consequent. There have been many suggestions as to how to best do this. *Conditional logics* are logics that attempt to give an account of the conditional that more naturally accords with its uses in natural languages, and, at the very least, is not subject to the paradoxes of the material conditional. In this section, I will focus on one kind of conditional logic, according to which conditionals are to be assessed in terms of possible worlds and the similarity relations between those possible worlds.

To see how possible worlds can help us to assess the proper relation between antecedent and consequent, let us consider another problematic argument that is classically valid:

1. If I go to San Francisco this summer, I will see my brother. So, if I go to San Francisco this summer, and my brother moves to New Mexico before I visit, I will see my brother.

This argument doesn't sound like it should be valid, but it is in classical logic. The form of (1) is

PMC3)     $p \supset q$
          So, $(p \cdot r) \supset q$

Here is a truth table for this argument form:

|       | p | q | r | $p \supset q$ | $p \cdot r$ | $(p \cdot r) \supset q$ |
|-------|---|---|---|------|------|------|
| i.    | T | T | T | T | T | T |
| ii.   | T | T | F | T | F | T |
| iii.  | T | F | T | F | T | F |
| iv.   | T | F | F | F | F | T |
| v.    | F | T | T | T | F | T |
| vi.   | F | T | F | T | F | T |
| vii.  | F | F | T | T | F | T |
| viii. | F | F | F | T | F | T |

The premise (p ⊃ q) is true in every row except row (iii) and (iv), and the conclusion is always true when the premise is. Thus, this argument clearly preserves truth and so is valid in classical logic.

The problem that argument (1) helps to highlight is that a conditional is only true on certain assumptions. In this case, I'll only see my brother in San Francisco when I visit on the assumption that he doesn't move to New Mexico before I get there. These assumptions are generally implied by the context in which a conditional is uttered, and they are not usually explicitly stated. Most importantly, the assumptions implicit in conditional sentences seem to affect their logical behavior. Argument (1) really doesn't seem like it should be valid, because one of the implicit assumptions in the premise is denied in the conclusion.

One possible way of dealing with this difficulty with implicit assumptions might be to appeal to the distinction between logical form and grammatical form. If we make the logical form of the premise of (1) clearer by conjoining not-r (it is not the case that my brother moves to New Mexico before I visit) to the antecedent, we completely avoid the problem. The form of (1) would then be

(p • ~ r) ⊃ q
So, (p • r) ⊃ q

and this argument, as you can check, is now invalid:

|  | p | q | r | (p • ~r) | (p • ~r) ⊃ q | p • r | (p • r) ⊃ q |
|---|---|---|---|---|---|---|---|
| i. | T | T | T | F | T | T | T |
| ii. | T | T | F | T | T | F | T |
| iii. | T | F | T | F | T | T | F |
| iv. | T | F | F | T | F | F | T |
| v. | F | T | T | F | T | F | T |
| vi. | F | T | F | F | T | F | T |
| vii. | F | F | T | F | T | F | T |
| viii. | F | F | F | F | T | F | T |

The problem with this suggestion is that there are way too many assumptions that are implied by the truth of the conditional sentence: my brother isn't abducted by aliens, my brother doesn't move to New York, my brother doesn't join a crazy cult that won't allow him to see his family, and so on. It's really not possible to conjoin the negation of every possible assumption to the antecedent. Given the difficulty (perhaps impossibility) of thinking of every conceivable assumption involved in the truth of a conditional, this solution seems unlikely to be workable in practice. What the failure of this sugges-tion makes clear is that we need some device for indicating that whatever the assumptions are, they are part of the truth conditions for the conditional as a whole. According to advocates of conditional logics, possible worlds like those that we discussed in Chapter 6 are just that device.

Recall that we can understand necessity and possibility in terms of possible worlds as follows: a necessary sentence is one that is true at every possible world and a possible sentence is a sentence that is true at some possible world. To see how possible worlds might be helpful, let's consider the conditional that we have been focusing on, "If I go to San Francisco this summer, then I will see my brother." Intuitively, the truth of this sentence comes down to the sentence's being true at all possible worlds where, if the antecedent is true and its assumptions are satisfied (all of them, whatever exactly they are), the consequent is also true. In some possible worlds my brother moves to New Mexico, so that assumption is not satisfied. In other possible worlds, my brother is abducted by aliens, so that assumption is not satisfied. Because the assumptions are not satisfied at these possible worlds, we shouldn't even consider them in assessing the truth of the condi-tional. The only time that a conditional will be false will be if there is a world where the antecedent is true, all of the assumptions hold, and the consequent is false. In terms of this example, imagine a possible world where I go to San Francisco this summer, North Korea reunites with South Korea, and I don't see my brother when I'm in San Francisco. This would tell me that the conditional we are con-sidering is false. After all, the separate status of North and South Korea is not one of the assumptions implicit in the original conditional, and so the fact that the antecedent is true and the consequent is false at this world demonstrates that the original conditional as a whole is false.

In conditional logics, accessibility between worlds is based on a similarity relation. Worlds are accessible to each other in virtue of their overall similarity in the particular respects relevant to the condi-tional at hand. The truth of a conditional in the actual world is then given by the truth value of the consequent at the closest similar world or worlds where the antecedent is true and the assumptions implicit in the antecedent also hold. If the consequent in this world or worlds is false, then the conditional as a whole is false, and if the consequent is true, then the conditional as a whole is true. In terms of my example above, if the world where North and South Korea reunite is the closest similar world to the actual one, it would be relevant to the truth of the conditional, and that is precisely what would make the conditional as a whole false.

Of course, saying that a possible world is similar to ours and specifying exactly what makes one world more similar to ours than another are two different tasks. A major source of disagreement among advocates of conditional logics concerns what the correct account of similarity is. In the previous paragraph, for example, I explained the view in terms of the closest similar world or worlds. According to one of the two main accounts of the similarity relation, there is one closest similar world, whereas according to the other, there may be more than one world similar enough to be relevant to the truth of the conditional. Both accounts have advantages and disadvantages, and so the challenge is to come up with rules to define the similarity relation that explain away the problematic uses of the conditional without creating more problems than they're designed to fix. This is not a criticism of the view, mind you. Rather, it is just to point out that there is considerable disagreement as to the proper details, and currently, no account clearly fixes the problems with the conditional in a way that is itself problem free.

Conditional logics (no matter what the details of the similarity relation) give a very satisfying answer as to what's gone wrong with PMC 3. How do they address PMC 1 and PMC 2? PMC 1 is easy to reject now, because the only worlds that I need to take into consideration in assessing the truth of a conditional are the closest similar worlds where the antecedent is true. But the premise of PMC 1 is the denial of the antecedent. Thus, there can be no close enough similar worlds where the premise is true and the conditional in the conclusion is also true. PMC 2 is also no longer valid. There may be no closest similar world in which the consequent is true and the premise and all its assumptions also hold. In terms of my example, it is certainly possible that I see my brother this summer in all the closest similar worlds to the actual world, but that I don't go to San Francisco at all. Rather, my brother visits me. Thus, PMC 2 is no longer guaranteed to preserve truth.

In spite of the fact that many of the problematic classically valid arguments are no longer valid in conditional logics, there is still some question as to whether or not these logics really capture the intuitive connection between antecedent and consequent. This is because a conditional with a true antecedent and a true consequent will automatically be true in conditional logics. According to both accounts of the similarity relation mentioned above, what makes a conditional true is the truth of the consequent at the closest similar worlds where the antecedent is true. But suppose that my brother moves to New Mexico after all, and that he comes to visit me before I go to San Francisco this summer. Our original conditional "If I go to San Francisco this summer, then I will see my brother" will still be true because the antecedent is true and the consequent is true. Indeed, bizarre conditionals like "If fish swim then Earth is the third planet from the sun" will be true, simply because both the antecedent and consequent of this conditional are both true. This suggests that though conditional logics go a long way toward explaining what the connection between antecedent and consequent might be, they still haven't really nailed it down completely.

One important thing to note about the conditional in conditional logics is that it is no longer truth functional. To assess the truth or falsity of a conditional, we now need to consider other possible worlds and their relative similarity to each other. Just as with the modalities that we examined in Chapter 6, to judge whether or not some conditional sentence is true or false we will have to think about more than the truth values of the sentences involved. In terms of the example that I have used in this section, we have to consider my brother and how different he and/or his circumstances might be in order for a world to be similar enough to be relevant to the truth of the conditional premise "If I go to San Francisco this summer, I will see my brother." Whether this should count against the view is a question that I will consider in the next section.

## III—RELEVANCE LOGIC

Possible worlds are one way to clarify the idea that there is some sort of intuitive connection between antecedents and consequents. Another is with a kind of logic called a *relevance logic* (in some parts of the world, they are called *relevant logics*). Relevance logics are multi-valued logics that accomplish a similar thing as the conditional logics that we just discussed but by different means. In essence, relevance logics are motivated by a desire to make the conditional more intuitive by requiring a connection of relevance between antecedent and consequent.

There are many relevance logics, and they are technically quite complex, but the basic idea can be made relatively simple by example. According to one of the more intuitive accounts of the semantics for relevance logics, the truth conditions for conditionals are given not by a similarity relation between possible worlds but by something like the flow of information.[1] More particularly, a conditional will be true when the flow of information is such that a conditional is the device that helps information to flow from the antecedent to the consequent.

Take my advice to my children, "If you work hard, then you can be anything that you want to be." To evaluate this sentence's truth or falsity, we need to consider how information flows from situation to situation, where a situation is something like a partially described possible world. To explore my conditional advice to my children, we need three different situations, we'll call them x, y, and z. x is the situation in which the conditional is true, y is the situation in which the antecedent is true, and z is the situation in which the consequent is true. The conditional x will be true just in case it is the thing that carries the information from y to z. More concretely, when my children work hard (y), it is the truth of the conditional (x) that makes it the case that they can be anything they want to be (z). The situation in x (that those who work hard can be what they want to be) is what makes it the case that both situations in y and z (my children's working hard and their having become what they want to be, respectively) are connected.

A conditional could fail to be true for one of two reasons on this account. Either my children do work hard (y) but they don't succeed at being anything they want to be (not z), or both the situations in y and z are the case, but the conditional in x wasn't the connection between both situations. The first of these would make the conditional false. In this case, my children work hard (y) but fail at being anything they want to be (z), and so the situation in x fails to connect what happens in y with what happens in z. In the second case, we would have to suppose that my children work hard, and are able to be what they want to be, but these two situations are just luck. Here, the truth of the conditional will not be the reason for these two situations occurring, and so the

---

[1] I focus on the flow of information semantics for their non-technical intuitiveness, but the reader should note that the adequacy of this semantics for relevance logics is still very much under discussion.

conditional would be neither true nor false. The point is that the truth of the conditional needs to somehow be the reason why the consequent is true when the antecedent is true. A conditional is doing its proper work when the antecedent is relevant to the consequent in such a way that the truth of the antecedent is somehow responsible for the truth of the consequent. This is just what a relevance logic does.

Like conditional logics, relevance logics like the one sketched here do not give a truth functional account of the conditional. If a conditional in relevance logic has a true antecedent and a true consequent, one cannot just substitute any other true sentences in either place and be guaranteed to retain the truth value of the original. Earlier, in my discussion of modal logics in Chapter 6, I pointed out that modal operators are not truth functional either, and we explored a little both how this difference from the more standard logical operators manifested itself and some of the reasons why this difference might be worrisome enough for philosophers to reject modal logics. For philosophers of this ilk, a similar point could be made about the non-classical accounts of the conditional offered in this chapter.

Nevertheless, one might take the considerations of this chapter in a slightly different light. Stopping to think about it for a second, if the problem with the material conditional is that the antecedent is not required to be related to the consequent in any way, shape or form, then any real solution is going to have to address what the proper relation between antecedent and consequent ought to be. On the face of it, it is pretty hard to imagine our ever clarifying this relation in a way that defines that relation purely in terms of the truth or falsity of the sentences in the antecedent and the consequent. Given this, one might see this whole chapter as a challenge to the desirability of defining logical terms truth functionally where possible, and the attendant requirement that logical contexts must be contexts in which one can always substitute sentences of like value for sentences of like value. Unlike modal operators, no one thinks that one can properly characterize a logic without a conditional, and so if a proper account of the conditional requires us to abandon truth functionality, then maybe logical functions just aren't necessarily truth functional after all. Before we go abandoning this ideal completely, however, it is worth considering what many believe to be a serious drawback of relevance logics.

# IV—RELEVANCE LOGICS AND THE
# FAILURE OF DISJUNCTIVE SYLLOGISM

One important argument form that is no longer valid in relevance logics is Disjunctive Syllogism. Because of this, the classically valid argument known as *ex contradictione quod libetum* (from contradictions come anything you like, or more colloquially, anything follows from a contradiction) will no longer be valid, either. I will end this chapter by briefly discussing the invalidity of these two argument forms in relevance logics.

In Chapter 1, I noted that Disjunctive Syllogism is one argument form that intuitively seems to be a very good one, and in Chapter 2 we saw that it is, in fact, valid in classical logic. But even though this argument form is intuitively valid in the vast majority of cases, it licenses an extremely unintuitive consequence in classical logic, namely that anything follows from a contradiction. So, for example, the following argument is valid in classical logic:

I have two brothers.
I don't have two brothers.
So, pigs fly.

The form of this argument is:

p
~p
So, q

In classical logic, in other words, any sentence whatsoever follows from a sentence and its negation. Another more colorful expression for this is that classical contradictions are *explosive*. A set of sentences that contain a contradiction explodes in the sense that any and every sentence will then be a consequence of that set.

The reason that this is a valid argument in classical logic can be seen in two different ways. First of all, if you do a truth table for this inference, it looks like this:

|      | p | q | ~p |
|------|---|---|-----|
| i)   | T | T | F |
| ii)  | T | F | F |
| iii) | F | T | T |
| iv)  | F | F | T |

Because there is no line in which both the premises are true, this argument is what is called vacuously or trivially valid. It guarantees that you can only go from true premises to a true conclusion by guaranteeing that you can never have simultaneously true premises. (Indeed, one aspect of the paradoxes of the material conditional which I didn't bring out at the time is that any argument with contradictory premises will always be valid in classical logic.)

The way one gets to the conclusion using the rules of natural deduction is via Disjunctive Syllogism and the principle Addition:

| | | |
|---|---|---|
| 1. | p | premise |
| 2. | ~p | premise |
| 3. | p ∨ q | 1, Addition |
| 4. | So, q | 2, 3 Disjunctive Syllogism |

It is because Disjunctive Syllogism is not a valid argument form in relevance logics that these logics are not explosive.

Now, for some people, the failure of Disjunctive Syllogism is reason enough to reject relevance logics. After all, returning to the first argument from Chapter 1, if Hannah's husband is either at the store or at home, and he's not at the store, then how could he not be at home? It just seems like this argument is good, and so any logic that doesn't make this argument valid just has to be wrong.

In response to this, an advocate of relevance logics says two things. First of all, even if Disjunctive Syllogism is completely intuitive in arguments like Hannah's, there clearly are cases where it doesn't look right at all. Disjunctive Syllogism is arguably much less intuitive whenever it is used to derive any q from a contradiction. Feeling right in one (or even many) instances, doesn't change the fact that a rule might feel dead wrong in others. And where it does feel so wrong, this seems like that should be a pretty good reason to question whether or not the rule is a good one, even in the instances where it feels right. This, in fact, is exactly the line of reasoning at the beginning of this chapter. The material conditional seems fine for conditionals like "If you run a red light, then you break the law," but it doesn't seem right at all for a lot of other cases, and thus it was deemed worthwhile to see if we might do better.

Second, the instances where Disjunctive Syllogism seems correct are those where the sentences in questions are consistent. It is only when we have inconsistent sentences that this rule seems to steer us in the wrong direction. With this in mind, we can still maintain that Disjunctive Syllogism is correct to use in many, perhaps most instances.

In particular, it is perfectly fine to use Disjunctive Syllogism when the sentences involved are free from contradictions. Since sentences about people's whereabouts are consistent, as are (hopefully) the vast majority of sentences about the vast majority of things, Disjunctive Syllogism is perfectly okay to use in Hannah's intuitively valid argument about her husband's whereabouts, and many others, even if it is not, strictly speaking, valid. It is worth spelling this second response out in a little more detail, though to do so will require a brief digression.

In Chapter 7 we looked at a logic called $L_3$ that had three possible truth values, T, I, and F. There, recall, we took I to mean indeterminate. In light of the subjects of Chapter 7 (both the problem of future contingents and the problem of vague language), one natural way to interpret this I is to think of it as meaning neither true nor false. In logic, we indicate this by saying that future contingents and sentences with vague language are both instances where there are supposed *truth-value gaps*, i.e., sentences that don't clearly have a value of either true or false.

Another way we could interpret I in $L_3$, however, is as a *truth-value glut*, i.e., both true and false. I'll have a much fuller discussion of possible cases of truth value gluts in the next chapter, but for now, we can get the gist of what this might mean by considering the following theological difficulty:

If God is omnipotent, then God can do anything. So God should be able to make a mountain that He can't destroy. But if God can make a mountain that he can't destroy, then God isn't omnipotent (since if He was, He should presumably have the power to destroy whatever He wishes). So, if God is omnipotent, then God shouldn't be able to make a mountain that He can't destroy.

Whatever one wants to say about this as a theological conundrum, the sentence "God can make a mountain that He can't destroy" is a good candidate for a sentence that is both true and false. After all, God's omnipotence implies that this sentence is true and also that this sentence is false. In our current terminology, this sentence appears to have a truth value glut.

If we understand I as a truth value glut, then we have to also reconsider what we mean by a valid argument. For example, consider the following argument:

God can make a mountain that He can't destroy.
God is the creator of the universe.

So, the creator of the universe can make a mountain that He can't destroy.

Assuming that the first premise really is both true and false, and so it takes the value I in whatever the logic is in question, we would want to make sure that what was true in that premise gets preserved in good arguments. In other words, given that we want valid inferences to preserve truth, valid arguments would be arguments that whenever the premises were either T or I (since I is both true and false), the conclusion is also either T or I. The values that one wants preserved in valid inference are called the *designated values*. In classical logical (and in $L_3$ and its multi-valued variants), the designated value is true.

Returning to the main thread of the discussion, we can now see how to make sense of the relevance logician's claim that one need only restrict Disjunctive Syllogism in contradictory contexts. The following is an example of a four-valued matrix for ∨ and ~ in a relevance logic.

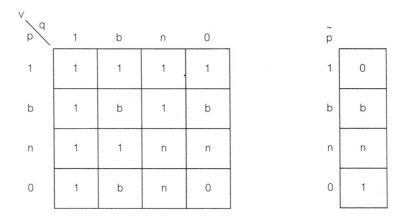

Here, b stands for a truth value glut (both true and false) and n stands for a truth value gap (neither true nor false). 1 and 0 now stand for true and true only, and false and false only, respectively. The designated values are true only and both true and false (i.e, 1 and b), so these are the values that need to be preserved in valid inference. With this in mind, consider the following (now 16 row) truth table for disjunctive syllogism:

|       | p | q | ~p | p ∨ q |
|-------|---|---|----|-------|
| i)    | 1 | 1 | 0  | 1 |
| ii)   | 1 | b | 0  | 1 |
| iii)  | 1 | n | 0  | 1 |
| iv)   | 1 | 0 | 0  | 1 |
| v)    | b | 1 | b  | 1 |
| vi)   | b | b | b  | b |
| vii)  | b | n | b  | 1 |
| viii) | b | 0 | b  | b |
| ix)   | n | 1 | n  | 1 |
| x)    | n | b | n  | 1 |
| xi)   | n | n | n  | n |
| xii)  | n | 0 | n  | n |
| xiii) | 0 | 1 | 1  | 1 |
| xiv)  | 0 | b | 1  | b |
| xv)   | 0 | n | 1  | n |
| xvi)  | 0 | 0 | 1  | 0 |

The rows where ~p, and p ∨ q both get designated values are rows (v), (vi), (vii), (viii). (xiii) and (xiv). But in rows (vii) and (viii), the conclusion, q, does not have a designated value. In (vii) it takes an n and in (viii) it takes a 0. So clearly this inference is invalid.

This truth table makes clear that the second response of the relevance logician is correct. The problem with Disjunctive Syllogism occurs when p takes a glutty truth value. (Of course, in some of the cases where p takes a glutty truth value, Disjunctive Syllogism does preserve designated values, but such is the way when dealing with truth value gluts!) Only then will this rule take one from designated values to non-designated values. In all the other cases, Disjunctive Syllogism is valid. So, Disjunctive Syllogism is okay to use when we know that our beliefs about a particular area of discourse are consistent.

One problem with this response is that many invalid argument forms are such that, in some cases, they seem to preserve truth. For example, we saw in Chapter 4 that the argument

If Julie is going to Miami, then she is going to Florida.
Julie is not going to Miami.
Therefore, Julie is not going to Florida.

seemed to "work" since Julie was in fact going to New York City. And yet, as we also saw, this argument is an instance of an invalid argument form, Denying the Antecedent. So if we accept the relevance logician's response in the case of Disjunctive Syllogism, what's to stop us from making a similar argument with respect to denying the antecedent, and to say that in cases like Julie's above, we should think of Denying the Antecedent as good even though it is not, strictly speaking, valid?

An advocate of relevance logics might respond that one difference between the case where Denying the Antecedent works in classical logic and the cases where Disjunctive Syllogism works in the four-valued relevance logic that we've just looked at is that former rule works in classical logic only when one is lucky. Though the premises and the conclusion in the argument are both, in fact, true, it is just luck that makes it that way. It has nothing to do logic. In the case of Disjunctive Syllogism in relevance logics, on the other hand, there seems to be something more principled at work. When one's beliefs are inconsistent, Disjunctive Syllogism won't work, but when they aren't, it will do just fine. In one sense, the cases where Disjunctive Syllogism works have nothing to do with logic (since, strictly speaking, this argument form is invalid in relevance logic), but in another sense, they do, since the criterion for when it works and when it doesn't is itself a logical criterion (i.e., it doesn't work when there are premises with the form p and ~p).

Still, though we know that our theological sentences are glutty, and though there may be other examples where we are aware that we believe inconsistent sentences, the fact remains that we are not always aware when a set of sentences is inconsistent. This might well give one pause in accepting at least the second half of the relevance logician's response to the problem of the intuitive validity of Disjunctive Syllogism. After all, if we feel licensed in using this rule in cases where we believe wrongly that the premises in question are consistent, then we might, unbeknownst to us, be taking ourselves from designated to non-designated values. How much of a problem this really is, I will leave for the reader to ponder.

# 9

## Two Logical Truths

### I—INTUITIONISM, REALISM, AND THE LAW OF THE EXCLUDED MIDDLE

The non-classical logic known as *intuitionism* began in the world of mathematics. Part of the original motivation for this view came from a metaphysical concern. The standard view of most working mathematicians is that mathematics is a matter of discovery. Just as, say, paleontologists make discoveries about dinosaurs that lived long ago, mathematicians make discoveries about mathematical objects. Of course, mathematical objects are very different than ancient dinosaur bones. In philosophical lingo, the latter are what are known as *concrete objects*, and the former are known as *abstract objects*. Abstract objects are like concrete objects in that they exist independently of human thought. Unlike concrete objects, however, abstract objects don't exist in space and time.

The idea that there is a world of mathematical objects which is independent of humans and their ways of thinking, but which is accessible to humans through the exercise of reason, is known as *Platonism*. The name comes from Plato, who thought that the world of concrete objects could never be the source of knowledge and that real knowledge could only be attained by considering abstract objects. Another name for this view is *mathematical realism*. According to this view, the world of mathematical objects is real (though abstract), and mathematical knowledge is a matter of discovery, not creation.

Mathematical realism is generally a little puzzling to those who haven't studied a lot of philosophy or done a lot of mathematics. One quick way to make the view more plausible is to ask yourself this: would $2 + 2 = 4$ still be true in a world where there were no humans or other sentient beings? Of course, I don't mean whether or not those symbols would still stand for what we take them to stand for. Clearly, in a world without humans or other sentient beings, those symbols would mean nothing at all. Rather, I mean whether or not two things, when added to two things, would make four things, whether or not humans were there to count them. Hopefully you answered yes to this question (pretty much everyone does). But if that's the case, then mathematical truths must be independent of us. According to the realist, this in turn is best explained by the fact that mathematical objects themselves don't depend on us for their existence. After all, it is because dinosaurs didn't depend on us for their existence that truths about dinosaurs are independent of us.[1]

Against mathematical realism, there is a view called *constructivism*. According to the constructivist, mathematical objects, and hence the truths about them, are constructed by the operations of human thought. Mathematics is not a matter of discovery, but of creation. Of course, we are not free to create mathematical objects any way that we please. We can't, for example, make it the case that $2 + 2 = 5$. That's because our constructs are constrained by the rules of mathematics, which in turn are governed by reason, and an arithmetic in which $2 + 2 = 5$ would be inconsistent with those rules.

These two views concerning the metaphysics of mathematics historically led to very different views about logic as well. One of the main differences is that realists accept that law of the excluded middle (LEM) is a logical truth, while constructivists don't. Intuitionist logic is a multi-valued logic (in fact, it's an infinite valued logic) in which LEM is not a logical truth. Mind you, this doesn't mean that the negation of LEM ($\sim(p \lor \sim p)$) is a logical truth either. According to intuitionists, $p \lor \sim p$ is true in some cases and false or neither true nor false in others, thus neither LEM nor its negation is a theorem. This is important to point out because, as we saw in the classical proof

---

[1] This argument is certainly not definitive in favor of realism, as there are other metaphysical views in the philosophy of mathematics that can account for the intuition that mathematical truth is independent of us in this way with out appeal to mathematical realism. Nevertheless, the argument does at least make clear that mathematical realism is not crazy.

of LEM in Chapter 4, a contradiction follows from the negation of LEM, and though there are other classical logical truths in addition to LEM which are not theorems of intuitionist logic, the law of non-contradiction is a theorem in both logics. For an intuitionist, if it can be proven that a contradiction follows from a sentence, p, then the negation of that sentence must be true. Since a contradiction follows from ~(p ∨ ~p), ~~ (p ∨ ~p) is a theorem in intuitionist logic. Thus, we have it that in intuitionism neither LEM nor its negation is a logical truth, but the negation of the negation of LEM is.

Another difference in logics between the two views is that a realist accepts proofs by *reductio ad absurdum* and a constructivist finds this form of proof illegitimate. To prove a sentence, p, by reductio, one assumes ~p and then shows that a contradiction follows from that assumption. Proofs by reductio are similar to the indirect proofs that we first met in Chapter 2, and in classical logic the two forms of proof are equivalent, but they are not quite the same. In particular, in an indirect proof, if a contradiction follows from an assumption, then the negation of that assumption must be true. So, from p and a contradiction, one can derive ~p, and from ~p and a contradiction, one can derive ~~p (as in my example in Chapter 2), and so on. In reductio proofs, by contrast, if a contradiction follows from the negation of a sentence, then the sentence itself must be true (so, from ~p and a contradiction, one can derive p directly). Though the difference between these two forms of proof might seem small, it is an important one, and the two forms of proof are not equivalent in intuitionist logic. As I just noted, if it can be proven that a contradiction follows from an assumption in intuitionist logic, then the negation of that assumption must be true. This shows that intuitionists accept the legitimacy of indirect proofs in spite of rejecting the legitimacy of proofs by reductio.

To see why the intuitionist accepts one but not the other, we need to better understand how the meanings of the logical connectives in intuitionist logic differs from the meanings of their classical counterparts. In classical logic the connectives are taken to operate on the truth values of sentences. According to intuitionists, on the other hand, the connectives operate on proofs. So, in intuitionist logic, the negation of a sentence, not p, means it has been proven that a proof of p can't be given, or put slightly differently, it has been proven that there is no proof of p. The other connectives are understood as follows. A conditional, if p then q, is understood to mean that any proof of p is also a proof of q, p and q means there is a proof of p and a proof of q, and p or q means that either there is a proof that p or there is a proof that q.

This difference in the meaning of the connectives helps explain how it is that ~~(p ∨ ~p) is a theorem of intuitionism whereas p ∨ ~p is not. Classically, a sentence is equivalent to its double negation (p is logically the same as ~~p). This makes sense if you think of a negation sign as operating on a truth value in a bivalent logic. If a sentence is not true, then it must be false, and when this truth value is in turn negated, the resulting value must be true. This means that the inference from p ∨ ~p to ~~(p ∨ ~p) is valid, as is the inference from ~~(p ∨ ~p) to p ∨ ~p. In intuitionist logic, however, this equivalence doesn't hold. Though intuitionists allow the inference from p ∨ ~p to ~~(p ∨ ~p), they do not allow it the other way. This also makes sense, given that the things negated in intuitionistic logic are not truth values but actual mathematical proofs. Proving that there is no proof that there is no proof of some sentence is not the same thing as giving a proof of that sentence. Thus, an intuitionist can show that there is no proof that there is no proof of LEM because the negation (read: the proof that there is no proof) of LEM entails a contradiction. But this is not the same thing as proving LEM. This in turn further clarifies why indirect proofs are legitimate for intuitionists while reductio proofs are not. Intuitionists claim that in order to know that some sentence, p, is true, you must prove p directly. For an intuitionist, therefore, a proof that a contradiction follows from a sentence ~p is good enough to establish that ~~p, but that is not the same as proving that p. If the assumption ~p entails a contradiction, then one can establish ~~p by indirect proof, but one needs reductio (powered by LEM and the equivalence of p and ~~p) to go from that same assumption and contradiction to arrive at the conclusion p.

It is safe to say that intuitionists are a minority among mathematicians. Numbers aside, intuitionism was also widely criticized for its reliance on a notion of proof and provability that was never made philosophically clear or mathematically acceptable. For these reasons, it is likely that if the only arguments for intuitionism came from considerations from the world of mathematics, the view would not be much discussed today. However, the philosopher Michael Dummett favors intuitionist logic for different sorts of reasons. His arguments have been found to be much more plausible than those of the early mathematical intuitionists, and it is largely because of his philosophical writing that intuitionist logic still occasions as much debate as it does.

Unlike early intuitionists, who thought that intuitionism should be the logic for mathematical reasoning alone, Dummett argues that intuitionism is the right logic for all reasoning, not just mathematical reasoning. When a revision of logic is recommended for only one particular domain, the recommendation to revise is *local*, and when the revision is recommended for all uses of logical terms it is said to be *global*. Dummett's recommendation, therefore, is for a global revision of logic.

Dummett's arguments against classical logic depend on considerations from the philosophy of language. According to Dummett, linguistic meaning is given by assertability conditions. For example, to know the meaning of the word 'green' is just to know when a thing can be asserted to be green and when it can't. This rules out our attaching a meaning to any word that goes beyond its conditions for assertion. In the case of 'green', for example, it rules out our arguing that being blessed by an invisible goddess is part of the meaning of the word 'green'. After all, we can't ever know when a thing has been blessed by an invisible goddess. For this reason, it makes no sense to think that part of the meaning of 'green' is to have this blessing. How could we ever have learned to use the term if its meaning was in part determined by factors that are inaccessible to us? This is a silly example, but it illustrates Dummett's fundamental point. One can't postulate some mysterious meanings for words that don't ever connect, in practice or in principle, with their actual application conditions.

These constraints on meaning, according to Dummett, give rise to a substantial philosophical challenge to the correctness of LEM. To see why, let us consider one of Dummett's examples. Jones is a man who died quietly of old age in his sleep after living a safe and comfortable life, having never faced any danger at all. If LEM is a logical truth, then we would have to say that the sentence, "Either Jones was brave, or Jones was not brave," is an instance of a logical truth. But given that what makes a person brave is their actually doing something courageous, and that what makes a person not brave is their actually doing something cowardly, it just doesn't seem right to say that Jones was either one or the other. Nothing in the assertability conditions of the word 'brave' actually specify what to say in a situation like Jones'. In fact, as far as our understanding of 'brave' goes, the right thing to say here seems to be that Jones was neither brave nor not brave. There just isn't a fact of the matter. If this is true, then LEM is not a logical truth. If the assertability conditions for 'brave' don't make clear whether or not we should judge Jones to be brave, then it is neither assertable that "Jones was brave" nor assertable that "Jones was not brave." And since one can't make a meaningful disjunction out of sentences that aren't assertable, their disjunction shouldn't be assertable either.

Suppose we just insisted that LEM is a logical truth, and so either Jones was brave or Jones was not brave. According to Dummett, this entails a metaphysical realism that is philosophically unjustified. To see why, let us return to the issue of realism. Recall that realists about a particular realm think that the objects and/or properties in that realm exist whether or not humans know of them. As I noted above, realism is quite plausible about things like dinosaurs. Dinosaur bones were fossilized long before humans came on the scene, and their existence doesn't seem to depend in any way on us and what we know. In particular, there is presumably some reason why the dinosaurs suddenly disappeared whether we know that reason or not. Now there is much disagreement among paleontologists about why the dinosaurs died out, and there are several theories as to the reasons for their extinction. Perhaps the most well-known of these theories postulates that there was massive climate change as a result of some cataclysmic event, like a giant meteor. We don't need to discuss the pros and cons of this theory. The point that is important in the current context is that whatever happened to the dinosaurs did so regardless of what we think to be the case. With respect to the reasons for their extinction, either it was a giant meteor that was ultimately responsible for their mass extinction, or it wasn't, whatever we think about it.

Now consider the sentence, "Either a giant meteor was responsible for the mass extinction of the dinosaurs, or it isn't the case that a giant meteor was responsible for the mass extinction of the dinosaurs." For Dummett, what would make this sentence assertable is the fact that the assertability conditions for "A giant meteor was responsible for the mass extinction of the dinosaurs" and "It is not the case that a giant meteor was responsible for the mass extinction of the dinosaurs," are clear-cut. Even if we don't in fact know which sentence is true, the meaning of the terms in the sentences in question are such that we can understand what the correct context of assertion would be in either case, and hence we can clearly understand their disjunction as well.

With this in mind, what is wrong with the suggestion that we just stipulate the truth of "Either Jones was brave or Jones was not brave," is that in this case the assertability conditions for the disjunction can not be made similarly clear. Realism is a plausible metaphysical view for dinosaurs and perhaps many other things that humans think about. But in some contexts realism is unjustified and, according to Dummett, unjustifiable. What would make it plausible in the realms where it is plausible is that the sentences in question have assertality conditions such that the meaning of both a sentence and its negation are completely clear. But since some sentences don't have assertability conditions that are this clear cut, realism is not a plausible metaphysical view for every domain.

Now, a lot of people don't buy Dummett's arguments about bravery, and it is worth pointing out that he does give other examples (some mathematical sentences, and future contingents, for example). For our purposes we needn't spend time defending or explicating Dummett's particular examples, as this argument is merely a springboard for discussing issues in the philosophy of logic. The important point that Dummett is making (whether you agree with him about the specific cases or not), is that LEM seems to fail in some cases because of considerations stemming from a theory of meaning. What Dummett has made clear is that insistence on the truth of LEM rules out the possibility of this kind of failure, and so entails realism about all the properties and objects that we form sentences about. Even if one is inclined to be a realist about everything, it is hard to see why the logic we use ought to be the determiner. Logic is supposed to formalize how we ought to reason, but whether or not we should be realists is not a logical matter but a philosophical one.

We can sum up Dummett's argument in the following way. A plausible theory of meaning about the word 'brave' puts pressure on the idea that either the sentence "Jones was brave" or its negation is clearly assertable. This shows that some instances of LEM are not genuinely assertable. However, if classical logic is the correct logic for us to be using, then every instance of LEM is assertable. As we saw in Chapter 4, logical truths are theorems and can always be proven, no matter what, because they can be proven using the rules of logic alone. If classical logic is the correct account of logical consequence, therefore, we can't deny realism. But realism is a substantial philosophical thesis, and it shouldn't be presupposed by one's logic. Only when we have independent reasons for adopting realism about a particular area of discourse should we be realists. At the very least, we shouldn't have it forced on us by our logic.

# II—PARACONSISTENT LOGICS, DIALETHEISM, AND THE PRINCIPLE OF NON-CONTRADICTION

In the previous chapter, we informally explored a class of logics known as relevance logics. Relevance logics, as I noted, are not explosive, which means that they do not license us to conclude anything and everything from a contradiction. Logics where contradictions are not explosive are called *paraconsistent logics*, so relevance logics are also paraconsistent logics. In recent years, some paraconsistent logicians have argued for a thesis known as *dialetheism*. According to dialetheists, there are true contradictions. This view is extremely controversial, but largely due to the work of the philosopher and logician Graham Priest, the view is now being discussed more and more.

The reason for the controversy is many-fold, but we can start to get an idea of the resistance to dialetheism by the following analogy. In ethics, there are many topics that are controversial in the sense that a lot of people disagree about them. Among them (in the U.S. at least), are abortion, capital punishment and the legalization of recreational drugs like marijuana. There are also, however, topics in ethics about which there is almost universal agreement, such as that genocide is wrong, that murder (defined as the unprovoked taking of an innocent life) is wrong, and that charity is a good thing.

Arguably, these fairly uncontroversial topics form a kind of bedrock that makes reasoned discussion of the more controversial issues possible. For example, people disagree about whether or not abortion is a form of murder. But to the extent that people can and do reasonably discuss the issue, one bedrock principle that all participants in a discussion would seem to have to agree on is that murder is wrong. After all, if one doesn't agree that murder is wrong, then there's hardly any point in debating the finer point of whether or not abortion is wrong as well. Those who oppose abortion oppose it because they think that it is the unprovoked taking of an innocent life, and so if someone thinks that it is perfectly okay to take an innocent life without provocation, they just can't be a party to the abortion debate.

Returning to logic, many have felt that the law of non-contradiction (LNC) is a bedrock principle similar to the view that murder is wrong. In the first place, it is just undeniable that our intuitions are overwhelmingly in favor of it (in the same way that our intuitions are just overwhelmingly against genocide). It just doesn't seem possible, for example, for "Sunny Jim is an orange cat," and "It's not the case that Sunny Jim is an orange cat" to both be true.

Secondly, LNC seems to be a bedrock principle that makes discussion of other logical principles possible. Consider some logical principle about which there is controversy, say LEM. How could we even begin to discuss this principle if we disagreed about LNC? After all, if there are true contradictions, then it seems as though it could be true both that LEM is a logical truth and that LEM is not a logical truth. Our intuitive understanding of the term 'not' just doesn't seem to allow both p and not-p to be true, and in order to disagree about whether or *not* LEM is a logical truth, we need to agree about what 'not' means. So, in much the same way that we can't discuss abortion with those who don't agree that murder is wrong, it is hard to see how we can discuss much of anything at all with those who believe that there are true contradictions.

This view was summed up very nicely by the philosopher David Lewis. Lewis, it should be pointed out, was not generally afraid of defending very controversial philosophical positions. He is perhaps the most well-known advocate of modal realism, the view briefly discussed in Chapter 6 which posits the actual existence of possible worlds. Lewis was asked to contribute to a recent volume discussing the law of non-contradiction, and with characteristic elegance, he declined as follows:

> I'm sorry; I decline to contribute to your proposed book about the 'debate' over the law of non-contradiction. My feeling is that since this debate instantly reaches deadlock, there's really nothing much to say about it. To conduct a debate, one needs common ground; principles in dispute cannot of course fairly be used as common ground; and in this case, the principles 'not' in dispute are so very much less certain than non-contradiction itself that it matters little whether or not a successful defence of non-contradiction could be based on them. (Lewis, 1999)[2]

So what can we say in favor of dialetheism? The first point to make is that intuitions change. Returning to the ethics case, many people once had the intuition that slavery was okay, and most people don't now. What changes intuitions is an interesting and difficult question, but it seems that over time, the few who argue for what were once

---

[2] *The Law of Non-Contradiction: New Philosophical Essays*, eds., Priest, G., Beall, J.C., and Armour-Gard, B., (2004), NY, Oxford: Clarendon Press

controversial views begin to prevail, and as more and more people become convinced of the view, it is no longer regarded as controversial. Indeed, in the case of slavery, it is arguable that the wrongness of that practice has gone from being highly controversial to one of those ethical bedrock views about which we don't tolerate disagreement, and all in the relatively short span of about 200 years.

At least part of what makes controversial views gain acceptance is persuasive arguments in their favor. The second thing to look at, therefore, is some of the arguments in favor of dialetheism. In the last chapter, when I discussed the possibility of truth value gluts, I used a theological example, "God can make a mountain that he can't destroy." If the only good examples of true contradictions were theological, dialetheism probably wouldn't get off the ground. This is because when it comes to religion and the supernatural, many people are content to note that the workings of a deity are mysterious, and that we, with our finite minds, couldn't possibly understand the world in the way that God does. Though it might sound contradictory to us that God can make a mountain that He can't destroy, it is surely not a contradiction to God, who can make sense of things that we cannot. In other words, if the only examples of true contradictions that the dialetheist could point to were theological, we could explain the contradictory appearance as merely apparent, and thus dodge having to say that it is both true and false that God can make a mountain that He can't destroy.

Priest, not surprisingly, gives other examples of true contradictions. Imagine what would happen if some benighted legislature passed the following two laws:

1. No aborigine shall have the right to vote.
2. All property holders shall have the right to vote.

Suppose that after the passage of these two laws, some aborigine comes to own property. It seems, given both of these laws, that it is both true and false that this aborigine has the right to vote.

Now some might argue that this contradiction can be explained away (is merely apparent), every bit as much as the theological one, and better yet, in a way that even our finite minds can understand. For example, many countries have laws that account for possibilities like this by various means. Perhaps they determine that the last law to be passed always takes precedence, or that constitutional principles always take precedence over laws passed by a legislature. But surely this is insufficient. It is at least possible, for example, that both (1) and (2) above were passed in the same bill (some kind of a voting rights bill) and that there are no precedent setting constitutional principles in the case at hand. This possibility, it is argued, is sufficient to show that there might be true contradictions, even if no contradiction like this ever actually happened.

Another example of a true contradiction that Priest points to is the liar sentence. We saw in Chapter 3 that a sentence that attributes falsehood to itself presents a problem. It seems as though it is true if it is false and false if it is true. Tarski's solution to the paradox, recall, involves relativizing truth to a language and restricting its applicability so that no truth predicate can be applied to itself. But many other solutions have been offered as well. Some philosophers, for example, have argued that these sentences are neither true nor false, but are examples of what we earlier called truth value gaps. Others have appealed to complicated set-theoretic machinery. The problem is that all of these solutions have rather major problems of their own. According to Priest, in fact, the problems that each has are so great that the least problematic solution is to accept liar sentences at face value. They are, in fact, both true and false.

This illustrates a point that I made earlier in our discussion of vagueness. In the philosophy of logic, questions that get raised rarely have perfect answers. Most solutions to problems of the sort that we are considering in this book are going to have their own drawbacks, and so most arguments either for classical logic or for some non-classical logic tend to be of the variety "the advantages of logic X outweigh the disadvantages of logic Y". Priest's argument that liar sentences are both true and false is quite explicitly of this kind. Since the other known solutions to the liar paradox (whether they retain classical logic or argue for truth value gaps or whatever) all have big problems of their own, his dialetheist solution is argued to be preferable.

The final ingredient in changing intuitions is to convince opponents of controversial views that their fears about what would happen if the controversial view were accepted are unfounded. Here, too, Priest has presented some very powerful points. Perhaps the most important one speaks to the issue I raised earlier concerning the difficulty of speaking reasonably with someone with whom one has really bedrock disagreements. Just because dialetheists argue that there are some true contradictions doesn't mean that they think that all contradictions are true. In fact, the set of potentially true contradictions is extremely limited, and the vast majority of contradictions would be regarded as illegitimate by dialetheists. In particular, I don't think that any dialetheist would argue that "Sunny Jim is an orange

The famous mathematician Kurt Gödel immigrated to the United States shortly before WWII. When he was studying for his citizenship test, he became alarmed because he thought he had discovered a contradiction in the U.S. constitution. When he raised this issue with friends, they encouraged him not to bring it up at the hearing for his citizenship application, as they were certain that this would only increase his chances of being seen as a subversive and thereby denied citizenship.

No one is exactly sure what contradiction he thought he discovered. Some think that it might have been a problem of self-reference, since the U.S. constitution seems to permit its own amendment in a way that is paradoxical. In particular, Article V allows that, with three exceptions, articles in the constitution can themselves be amended or repealed with the proper 2/3 majority of the states agreement. But Article V is not itself one of the exceptions, and so presumably Article V can itself be amended. But this looks a little like a self-referential paradox. It would seem that in amending that article we would also make it illegitimate to amend that article.

Gödel, by the way, after demonstrating a sufficient understanding of the issues that he was queried about, raised his worry about the contradictory nature of the U.S. Constitution, in spite of his friends' warnings to the contrary. The presiding judge, apparently, invited Gödel into his chambers, where they are said to have had a very lengthy and interesting discussion of the issue.

cat" is both true and false, a fact takes much of the wind out of the sails of those who oppose dialetheism.

Nevertheless, many people feel that even if dialetheists aren't committed to the truth of every contradiction, even one true contradiction is too much. This, I think, is what Lewis is saying in his letter. That a contradiction can't be true is just too much of a bedrock principle. So no matter what the problems are with the other solutions to the liar paradox, that a contradiction can't be true will always be more certain for Lewis than any other issue involved with these possible solutions.

Another difficulty for the dialetheist is one we've already discussed. Paraconsistent logics, we saw in the Chapter 9, don't make Disjunctive Syllogism a valid inference form, and this is problematic for all the reasons indicated in our discussion in that chapter. Though addressing this concern is certainly no small task, I think it is safe to say that the biggest challenge to dialetheists at this stage is that intuitions about bedrock principles are not easily dislodged.

## III—HOW TRUE ARE LOGICAL TRUTHS?

In Chapter 7 we saw that neither LEM nor LNC were tautologies in $L_3$, and so the certainty of logical truths was already a bit shaky, even before we considered the arguments of the intuitionists and the dialetheists. Having finally engaged in a full discussion of at least some of the philosophical motivations one might have for actually rejecting one of these logical truths, it is time to return to the issue of the status of logical truths.

We know that logical truths are supposed to be those rare complex sentences that are always true, no matter what their simple constituents are about. In modal terms, they are supposed to be true in all possible worlds. But, focusing on LEM for ease of discussion, if one defines the logical connectives intuitionistically rather than classically, LEM will not be true in all possible worlds. In other words, whether or not something is a logical truth is entirely dependent on what logic one adopts to govern inferences.

Does this make logical truths less special, to put it plainly? In one sense yes, and in another sense no. The good news first. Logical truths still have a special status within a logic. They are still the sentences that are guaranteed to be true, no matter what the content or the value of their constituents, and this is still a pretty unusual thing, if you think about it. Within a well-defined relation of logical consequence, the logical truths are those that can always be asserted, always be proven, and always be relied upon. But, for all that, there is also a sense in which they are not as certain as philosophers once thought they were. At the very least, what counts as a logical truth depends entirely on which rules of logic are the right rules to use. Assuming that only one account of logical consequence can be correct, this means that we might be wrong about which logical truths really are true.

What's more, it is very difficult to even discuss the legitimacy of a logical truth, since the disagreements in these cases tend to be so bedrock. As we have seen in this chapter, our intuitions about logical truth are frequently inextricably linked to other philosophical issues, which means that we cannot assess the correctness of a logical truth in purely logical terms. To put it somewhat paradoxically, the truth of a logical truth is just not an easy thing to establish.

# 10

## Quantum Logic

### I—PHYSICS AND QUANTUM MECHANICS

The last non-classical logic that we will consider in this book is *quantum logic*. Quantum logic was proposed as a solution to certain longstanding interpretive difficulties in quantum mechanics. Though quantum logic has very few advocates among contemporary philosophers, the philosophical issues raised by quantum logic are very rich and interesting, which is why it is worth discussing in this book.

Theoretical physics, at least since Gallileo and Newton, attempts to describe the workings of the physical world in ever more accurate mathematical terms. Before quantum mechanics and relativity theory Newtonian physics reigned supreme. This latter theory made several implicit assumptions about the underlying nature of objects in the physical world. Among these assumptions are the following:

1. there is an objective world out there existing independently of humans and their interests,
2. the things in this world are knowable in principle in a determinate way,

Both of these assumptions seem true of the ordinary objects that populate our lives (things like tables, chairs, moons, suns, stars—philosophers call these objects *medium-sized objects* to distinguish them from the very small objects that quantum mechanics deal with and the very large objects like black holes that astrophysicists think about). Thus, Newtonian physics made a certain intuitive sense even to those who couldn't understand the complex mathematics behind it. The essential difficulty with quantum mechanics is that neither of these assumptions seems to hold, and so, whether or not you understand the math, the world of quantum particles presents some peculiar interpretive challenges.

Assumption (1): there is an objective world out there existing independently of humans and their interests. In our discussion of intuitionism we talked a little bit about realism. Among the objects for which realism is a plausible theory (like tables and chairs), it would seem reasonable to say that our observation of these objects doesn't fundamentally alter either them or their properties. This fundamental principle, however, is challenged by quantum mechanics. In quantum mechanics the state of a system is represented by mathematical functions, which track the wave like statistical probabilities of a particle's having some particular value (its position or momentum, for example). These mathematical functions are aptly called wave functions. When we observe the system, say by actually making a measurement, our measurement determines the values in question at one particular place and a time. According to quantum mechanics, the state prior to our measurement just is all of its statistical probabilities, and so our observation actually changes the system. In particular, our observation changes it from the wave function that represents all of the many possibilities to the one actuality. Our measurements, in other words, interfere with the quantum system under investigation in such a way that we make it a different system than it was prior to our observations.

This difficulty was made clear early on by the physicist Erwin Schrödinger in a very famous thought experiment involving a cat. Schrödinger asked us to imagine a box containing the following items: a cat, a glass vial of poison gas, a piece of radioactive matter, and radiation detector hooked up to a device that will break the vial if it detects a radioactive particle and leave the vial undisturbed otherwise. Suppose that the radioactive material has a 50/50 chance of decaying, and hence releasing a radioactive particle within a certain set amount of time. According to quantum mechanics, when the time is up, the state of the box is represented by the statistical probabilities of all its possible states, which in this simplified case is either decay or no decay. This means that before we look in the box, the state of the box is one of both decay and no decay (since those are the two equiprobable possibilities). Because of our experimental set-up, however, this means that the cat inside is both dead and alive. After all, if the matter has decayed, then the radiation detector would have broken the poison gas vial, and if the matter hasn't decayed, then the vial would still be intact. Once we open the lid and look in, of course, we interfere with the system and at this point, both the material and the cat will be definitely one or the other (either decayed or not decayed in the case of the material and either dead or alive in the case of the cat). But until the system is observed, there is no escaping the conclusion that the cat is both dead and alive.[1]

Next comes assumption (2): the things in this world are knowable in principle in a determinate way. One consequence of Newtonian physics is that the world behaves in completely predictable and determinable ways. So predictable is the Newtonian world of objects that if it were possible to know the complete state of every object in the universe in its total detail at one point in time, then in theory one would be able to figure out the entire future and the entire past of the universe. The model that is often used to describe this is of billiard balls. If you knew exactly how hard one ball was hit, and in exactly what direction, and you knew the exact locations of the other balls on the table and the exact nature of the surface of the billiard table, you would be able to predict exactly where it would send any other ball that it hit, and also exactly where it would subsequently come to a stop. This is just what professional pool players learn to do with long hours of practice.

The world of very small things, however, is irreducibly random. Returning to Schrodinger's cat experiment, to say that a piece of radioactive material has a 50/50 chance of decaying is to say that one or the other will happen, but that there is no predicting which. This indeterminacy is not a matter of us and our ignorance. Even if we could know everything there is to know about the state of the material in question, we still would not be able to calculate whether it would decay or not. Even God could not know, and God presumably knows everything about everything. Indeed, Albert Einstein rejected the randomness of quantum mechanics, famously saying "God does not play dice."

Let me finish up this section with a brief description of one of the most famous experiments in quantum mechanics. The

---

[1] On some interpretations, the cat would be neither alive nor dead until we look in the box, but this is not much less strange than the cat's being both alive and dead, if you think about it. So, however one interprets the state of the box prior to our checking the box's contents, quantum mechanics is counter-intuitive at best.

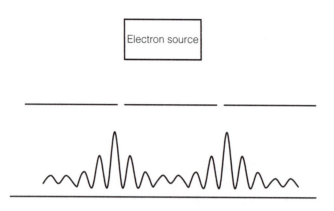

**FIGURE 10.1** An interference wave pattern when both holes are simultaneously open.

experiment is called the *two-hole experiment* (it is also called the *two slit experiment*), and it embodies what is known as *particle-wave duality*. This is the idea that subatomic particles behave in both a wave-like and a particle-like fashion. According to the physicist Richard Feynman, particle-wave duality lies at the root of all the mysteries of the micro-world.

In this experiment, there is a filament that spews electrons one at a time towards a screen with two holes equidistant from the electron source. Both holes can be opened and closed at the experimenter's will. Behind the screen is a plate that is sensitized to record the places where the electrons hit when they get through the screen via hole 1 or 2. When 1 and 2 are both open, there will be what is called an *interference pattern* on the plate (see figure 10.1). There will be peaks right behind each of the open holes, with troughs to either side of these large peaks, and then somewhat smaller peaks to either side of each trough, and smaller troughs again, and so on. An interference pattern is exactly what we'd expect to find if electrons behaved more like waves. If we did this experiment with water, we would find a pattern much like this on the sensitized plates, with the peaks representing the highest point of the successive waves as they hit the plate and the troughs representing the lowest point of the waves.

Now, suppose that we conduct the experiment so that only one hole at a time is open. When hole 2 is closed, the pattern on the detector plate is an *additive pattern*, having one large peak that sharply tapers off on either end. Let's call the additive pattern that we get one

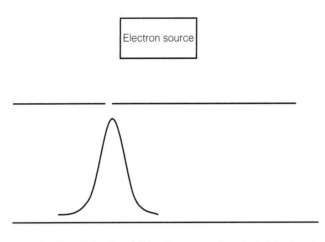

**FIGURE 10.2** An additive 1-pattern when hole 2 is closed.

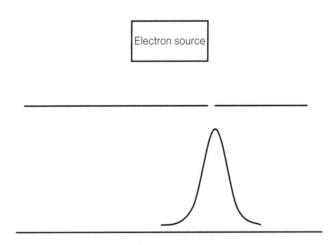

**FIGURE 10.3** An additive 2-pattern when hole 1 is closed.

hole 2 is closed the '1-pattern' (since its made by leaving hole 1 open) (see figure 10.2). If we then close the first hole and leave the second one open, we will get a similar additive pattern, which we can call the '2-pattern' (see figure 10.3). Now, suppose that we superimpose the 1-pattern on the 2-pattern. The resulting pattern will look like

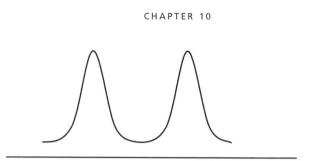

**FIGURE 10.4** The 1-pattern superimposed on the 2-pattern.

figure 10.4. These additive patterns are exactly what we'd expect to find if electrons were more like discrete particles. If we did these experiments with billiard balls, we would find the patterns on the plates to be similar.

The problem, at its heart, is that the patterns in figures 10.1 and 10.4 are each simply a representation of a series of electrons traveling one at a time through either hole 1 or hole 2 and registering on a sensitized plate. Nevertheless, these patterns are very different from each other. Intuitively, it should not make a difference to the pattern that emerges on the sensitized plate whether both holes remain open the whole time or whether one or the other hole is always closed. After all, if we did a similar experiment with billiard balls the pattern would look like the one in figure 10.4, whether both holes were open simultaneously or not. And likewise, if we did an experiment like this with water, the pattern would look similar to the one in figure 10.1 whether both holes were open at the same time or not. The difficulty is to explain why it is that the patterns are so very different in the quantum case.

## II—QUANTUM LOGIC

There are many interpretations of the strange results that we've just considered. One suggestion, first made in 1936 by the mathematicians G. Birkhoff and J. Von Neumann, and later taken up most famously by a philosopher named Hilary Putnam, is to change the laws of logic so as to limit the validity the distributive rules.[2] I briefly discussed the distributive rules in the box in Chapter 2. They are two classical

---

[2] By 'quantum logic' I will mean this one particular non-classical logic, but note that a number of non-classical logics have been proposed as solutions to these so-called quantum mechanical anomalies.

logical equivalences, which means the formulas on either side of :: are logically equivalent to each other in classical logic:

$(p \cdot (q \vee r)) :: ((p \cdot q) \vee (p \cdot r))$

$(p \vee (q \cdot r)) :: ((p \vee q) \cdot (p \vee r))$

We will spend the remainder of this chapter looking at the idea that we should change our logic in response to the interpretive difficulties of quantum mechanics.

Putnam's argument for revising our logic in light of the peculiarities of quantum mechanics was essentially that limiting the validity of the distributive rules would undermine the reasoning that lead to the false conclusions. The distributive rules make the following inferences valid:

D1)     $(p \cdot (q \vee r))$
        So, $((p \cdot q) \vee (p \cdot r))$

D2)     $(p \vee (q \cdot r))$
        So, $((p \vee q) \cdot (p \vee r))$

D3)     $((p \cdot q) \vee (p \cdot r))$
        So, $(p \cdot (q \vee r))$

D4)     $((p \vee q) \cdot (p \vee r))$
        So, $(p \vee (q \cdot r))$

According to Putnam, an idealization of physicists' reasoning shows that all of the anomalous results discussed in the first section depend, in some way, on an instance of the distributive rules.

Focusing on the two-hole experiment, Putnam argued that one must use a distributive rule to get from the sentences that describe the experimental set-up to the conclusion that the two-patterns ought to be the same. Putnam argued that limiting the validity of the distributive rules would disallow the inference to the falsified predictions of quantum mechanical experiments. To see why, let's focus on the two-hole experiment, only suppose that we were doing the two-hole experiment with billiard balls.

If you had to figure out what the probability was of a ball hitting some particular area, say right behind hole 1, when both holes were open, the following seems pretty reasonable. Figure out what the probability is of a ball hitting that region when only hole 1 is open, and what the probability is of its hitting that region when only hole 2 is open, and divide the resulting sum by 1/2. Probabilities are measured on a scale ranging from 1, which is definite, to 0, which is impossible. For simplicity, let's assume that each ball always goes through a hole, so it never hits the edge of the hole and gets deflected off. Given this assumption, the chance of a ball hitting right behind hole 1 when only hole 1 is open is 1, i.e., it is certain, and the probability of it hitting right behind hole 1 when only hole 2 is open is 0, i.e., it can't happen. The sum of these two probabilities is 1, and half of 1 is 1/2. Thus, the probability that any ball will hit right behind hole 1 when both holes are open is 1/2 of what it is when you add the probabilities of its hitting right behind hole 1 when only one hole at a time is open.

This little informal argument, however, depends on an instance of the distributive laws. To see this, I need to briefly explain the idea of conditional probability. Formally, the probability that one thing, a, will happen given that another thing b happens, is symbolized P (a | b), and the formula for figuring out conditional probabilities is:

$$\text{Conditional Probability: } P\,(B\,|\,A) = \frac{P(A \;\&\; B)}{P(A)}$$

This probably (no pun intended) looks quite daunting, but the idea is actually very intuitive, and can be made clear by considering a simple example. The probability of flipping a coin and getting heads (indicated by H), given that a previous flip was tails (indicated by T) would be:

$$P\,(H \mid T) = \frac{P(H \bullet T)}{P(T)} = \frac{1/2 + 1/2}{1/2} = \frac{.25}{.5} = .5$$

Of course, the probability that it will be tails, given that the first flip was tails, is also .5, but this is because the probability of getting heads or tails on a fair coin is always .5, no matter what the previous throws have been. (To think otherwise is what is known as the Gambler's Fallacy.)

Now, the conditional probability of a ball hitting right behind hole 1 (call this area r) given that it has gone through either hole 1 or hole 2 ($h_1$ or $h_2$ respectively) is:

$$\text{1. } P\,(r \mid h_1 \lor h_2) = \frac{P[r \bullet (h_1 \lor h_2)]}{P(h_1 \lor h_2)}$$

The distributive law D1 allows us to expand the right hand side to

$$\text{2. } \frac{P[r \bullet (h_1 \lor h_2)]}{P(h_1 \lor h_2)} = \frac{P[(r \bullet h_1) \lor (r \bullet h_2)]}{P(h_1 \lor h_2)}$$

The probability of one thing or another thing happening, provided that the two things in question are independent of each other, is the same as the probability of the first plus the probability of the second. For example, since the result of any flip of a coin doesn't depend in any way on the prior results of previous flips of the same coin, each flip of a coin is independent of every other, and so, the probability of my getting heads or tails is the probability of my getting heads plus the probability of my getting tails. Applied to our billiard balls we get:

3. $\dfrac{P[(r \bullet h_1) \lor (r \bullet h_2)]}{P(h_1 \lor h_2)} = \dfrac{P(r \bullet h_1)}{P(h_1 \lor h_2)} + \dfrac{P(r \bullet h_2)}{P(h_1 \lor h_2)}$

Now, given that there is no reason for the ball to favor either hole over the other, we have that

4. $P(h_1 \lor h_2) = 2\,P(h_1) = 2\,P(h_2)$

Therefore, (3) becomes (5) and (6)

5. $\dfrac{P(r \bullet h_1)}{P(h_1 \lor h_2)} = \dfrac{P(r \bullet h_1)}{2P(h_1)} = \dfrac{P(r|h_1)}{2}$

6. $\dfrac{P(r \bullet h_2)}{P(h_1 \lor h_2)} = \dfrac{P(r \bullet h_2)}{2P(h_2)} = \dfrac{P(r|h_2)}{2}$

This, finally, allows us to infer

7. $P(r \mid h_1 \lor h_2) = 1/2\,[\,P(r \mid h_1) + P(r \mid h_2)\,]$ [3]

No doubt, you had no idea that all that was involved in the informal rendering of the of the argument that I first gave, but when we formalize probabilistic thinking to make clear why that informal argument is correct, this is what we arrive at.

Returning to the two-hole experiment in quantum mechanics, a similar sort of reasoning leads us to think that the probability of an electron hitting some region, r, on the screen when both holes are open should be one half of the probability of its hitting that region when each of the holes is open one at a time. But this, of course, is not what we find. Since the pattern on the detector screen is an interference pattern when both holes are open, the probability of an electron's hitting that region, r, is less than 1/2.

---

[3] "Is Logic Empirical?", Putnam, Hilary (1968) *Boston Studies in the Philosophy of Science,* eds., R. Cohen and M. Wartofsky, Dordrecht, Holland: D. Reidel.
Reprinted under the new title "The Logic of Quantum Mechanics" in *Mathematics Matter and Method,* Putnam, Hilary (1979), New York, Cambridge, Melbourne: Cambridge University Press.

According to Putnam, however if D1 is no longer valid, then we should not ever form the belief that turns out false. Without D1, in other words, we will never come to form the belief that the probability of a particle hitting r when both holes are open is 1/2 the probability of its hitting r when only one is open at a time. And if we are barred from forming the belief, then we won't make the prediction either, and so our experimental evidence will not go against our expectations.

The rationale behind Putnam's argument is quite simple. If a rule of inference is not valid in some domain, then the conclusions licensed by that rule in that domain will no longer follow. After all, in general, if a sentence is a consequence of an invalid rule of inference, the sentence in question is not licensed logically. For example, returning to the argument from Chapter 1, suppose that Hannah uses my funny Dysfunctional Syllogism rule to go from the sentences

Either my husband is at home or he's at the store.

He's not at home.

to the sentence

My husband is not at the store either.

In this case, presumably, we don't think Hannah is entitled to believe the concluding sentence because the rule that underwrites it is not a good one. In the same way, if some distributive rule is not a valid rule of inference, then using it to arrive at a sentence that predicts things that are contrary to our experimental evidence would be illegitimate as well.

Note that the distributive rules clearly do preserve truth in many, perhaps even most contexts. If it is true that Jill is going to the store and then either going to the movies or to dinner, then its true that she is either going to the store and the movies or to the store and dinner. With this in mind, Putnam argued that the distributive rules are perfectly valid in most contexts, and they should only be restricted when we're dealing with quantum phenomena. In other words, Putnam's revision of logic was meant to be local (restricted to one domain) and not global (applying to every possible domain we could think about).

## III—PROBLEMS WITH QUANTUM LOGIC

Criticisms of Putnam's arguments were many and various. One difficulty pertained to the actual adequacy of Putnam's proposed solution. Many commentators were skeptical that every anomaly of quantum mechanics actually did depend in some way or another on one of (D1) through (D4) above. If this skepticism were warranted, then Putnam's solution would obviously fail. However, I propose that we skip over this detail and just grant Putnam his claim. This will allow us to pursue some of the more philosophically interesting criticisms of Putnam's arguments.

The first that we will look at concerns the explanatory adequacy of Putnam's solution. Putnam claimed that his solution explained better than other interpretive solutions the anomalies of quantum mechanics, but its not at all clear how adopting quantum logic will do anything to solve the interpretive difficulties that I briefly outlined in the first section of this chapter. After all, as a solution, quantum logic simply doesn't allow us to infer various false sentences. But even assuming that every anomalous conclusion is forestalled, this doesn't really tell us how to interpret particle-wave duality, or how to make sense of the littlest bits of matter that confound our common-sense understanding of the world. In the case that we have been focusing on, we are simply prevented from ever concluding that the probability of an electron hitting the region r when both holes are open should be ½ the probability of its hitting r when one hole at a time is open. Nevertheless, the fact that electrons sometimes behave like particles and sometimes behave like waves, as manifested by the different patterns that emerge on the detector screens, is still extremely puzzling.

By analogy, suppose that Hannah's husband really is going to be either at home or at the store, and suppose further that he is in neither place. Of course this is completely crazy, but play along for the sake of the argument. The analogy to Putnam's argument in this situation would be to limit the validity of Disjunctive Syllogism. So, suppose that we did this, thereby disallowing Hannah from concluding "My husband is at home." In this case, there would be no clash between the belief that Hannah forms and reality. But isn't it obvious that we haven't really explained what is going on with Hannah's husband? How can he both be in either place, and also not be in either place? Clearly, simply blocking Hannah from forming a conclusion does nothing to tell us about why her husband is able to simultaneously do both.

Quantum mechanics reveals a strange world in which things behave in ways that are radically different than ordinary medium-sized objects. Making sense of all of this strangeness requires more than simply barring us from forming certain conclusions. It requires actually explaining how assumption 1 and assumption 2 from the first section could be false. In addition, a good solution should explain particle-wave duality in a way that makes it somehow make sense. Since Putnam's solution does none of these things, it is at best a stop-gap measure. Put simply, Putnam's solution might save us from making false conclusions, but it won't really tell us why those strange conclusions aren't warranted in the case at hand.

A second difficulty with Putnam's argument doesn't concern its adequacy as a solution so much as the repercussions of taking it seriously. As I noted above, Putnam's recommended revision of logic is meant to be local, not global. This raises the question of how much local revision of logic is going to be acceptable. Supposing that more and more parts of the universe could be made sense of by appealing to non-standard logics, what's to stop us from revising logic again and again, as we see fit? For example, in Chapter 4 we encountered the following argument involving color terms:

> This sweater is green.
> So, this sweater is not red.

There, I noted that the only reason why the truth of the conclusion seems guaranteed by the truth of the premise is that meaning of the word 'green' guarantees that if some patch is green that very same patch can't be other colors. Now, suppose that someone developed a logic of colors that could guarantee that whenever the premise of this argument is true, the conclusion would also be true. Should we thereby adopt this color logic, and stipulate that the new logic applies only to the domain of colors?

There are many reasons to think that the answer to this last question should be no. As we have seen, the supposed topic-neutrality of logic means that logic is supposed to work regardless of the topic under discussion. If we start to think in terms of local revisions of logic, we are going to have to start considering more issues of content, and so the seeming topic-neutrality of logic would be lost. To put it in Fregean terms, logic would no longer be the most general of disciplines, and so it would be harder (if not impossible) to see what made logical functions differ from other seemingly non-logical functions.

Of course, we have seen many logics in the course of this book that seem to similarly put pressure on the clarity of the line that distinguishes the logical from the non-logical, so considerations like these are probably not decisive. But topic-neutrality to the side, what's to stop us from revising logic again and again? If Putnam's argument is right, the answer to this question might be "Nothing."

Thus, Putnam's argument raises the possibility that a plurality of logics might be true, each in its own domain. Though there are some philosophers who would not be bothered by this possibility, it's fair to say that most would not be happy with it. Just as ethicists hope to find principles of right and wrong that apply always and everywhere, many philosophers of logic would like to find logical principles that apply always and everywhere.

The final difficulty I will discuss is perhaps the most fundamental. Putnam's suggestion depends on a fairly radical assumption, namely that empirical evidence might be relevant to the question of which logic we ought to use. In philosophy, there is a tradition of dividing kinds of knowledge into what can be known rationally (by reason) and what can be known empirically (by experience). Rational knowledge concerns concept understanding and the relating of ideas, whereas empirical knowledge is knowledge that depends on one's experiences. The paradigms of the former kind of knowledge have been mathematics and logic. Suggestions that logic should be revised because of things that are true and false at the worlds that we think about have seemed just as outrageous as saying that we should revise arithmetic in worlds where it seems as though two objects added to two objects makes five objects. The problem for Putnam, therefore, is that his argument flies squarely in the face of a tradition that has not regarded evidence as relevant to the truth of logic at all.

One point in Putnam's favor and against the traditional view is the fact that geometry, once touted by philosophers as the paradigm of reason based knowledge, has turned out to be a lot more empirical than anyone had previously thought. For the vast majority of recorded intellectual time, the principles of Euclidean geometry have been identified as truths of reason, knowable using pure thought alone without any reference to experience. During the $18^{th}$ and $19^{th}$ Centuries, however, non-Euclidean geometries were developed. At the time of their development, they were largely regarded as intellectually puzzling but physically insignificant. However, in 1919 Arthur Stanley Eddington observed during a solar eclipse that light rays bend when they are passing near the sun. This observation confirmed Einstein's theory of relativity and established that space, itself, is non-Euclidean, as Einstein had predicted. Thus, one standard truth of reason turned out to be empirical. Those, like Putnam, who think that logic should be seen as more empirically determinable, argue that the case of geometry is a good model for how it is with logic. That is, though many do regard logical truths as truths of reason, they might be wrong, just as many were wrong about the status of geometry.

Against this, some philosophers don't even agree that geometry is a good example of a field of study that we thought was purely conceptual but which turned out to be empirical. According to these philosophers, geometry is still a field where justification is given by reason. It's just that there are a lot of different systems that can be defined by reason (e.g., both the Euclidean and the non-Euclidean geometries). What Eddington showed was that the space that we live in is non-Euclidean. But the question of which space we live in is (and has always been) an empirical question, even if previous thinkers have failed to recognize that this is so. Geometry is still a model of pure reasoning. If this is right, the existence of alternative logics does nothing to suggest that logic might be empirical, either.

The suggestion that we adopt a quantum logic as a solution to the anomalies of quantum mechanics raises interesting issues about the status of logic, and these issues are relevant and important to think about whatever the ultimate status of Putnam's arguments. Even if arguments for quantum logic weren't all that plausible, this doesn't mean that there never will be a good empirical reason to change our logic. There might well be, and we should think about this possibility whether or not it ever becomes an actuality.

# 11

# Which Logic is Right?

## I—NOT TONK

We've looked at a number of different logics, and a number of the considerations both for and against each logic. In the face of such choices, it is kind of hard not to wonder which logic is right. Now, if I were going to write a chapter actually addressing this question, this would be a mighty short chapter:

I don't know.

So, instead of answering the question, I'm going to consider some of the broader issues that come up in trying to answer it.

The first thing to do is canvas some of the sorts of considerations one might have in answering the question that is the title of this chapter. A good way to begin doing this is to consider a very famous logical connective that is most definitely not right. The connective is due to the work of Prior, who we met in connection with the logicality of modal terms. Prior's point in introducing this connective is not the same as mine. I just want to consider more carefully why one would be ill-advised to use a logical connective like this one, whereas Prior was trying to criticize a particular theory about the meaning of the logical connectives.[1] Nevertheless, I think it can profitably be put to my use as well as his original one.

---

[1] In particular, according to one popular theory of the meaning of the logical connectives, logical terms are just defined by the rules that govern their operations. What Prior's tonk example makes clear is that merely giving the rules for a logical connective is not the same as defining a legitimate logical term.

The connective, called *tonk*, is defined by the following two rules of inference:

p

So, p tonk q

p tonk q

So, q[2]

A sentence that contains tonk is called a *contonktion*. Here's an example of a valid inference involving a contonktion:

Julie is at the store.

So, Julies at the store, tonk Bill is at the beach.

This inference uses the first inference rule. Now, using the second, we can infer as follows:

Julie is at the store, tonk Bill is at the beach.

So, Bill is at the beach.

The problem with this connective, as you may have already guessed, is that it allows us to go from a sentence, p, to any other sentence, q, whatsoever. That is, I could have inferred from my belief, "Julie is at the store," that the moon is made of green cheese, that $2 + 2 = 5$, or that I am Bigfoot. Thus, tonk allows us to go from sentences that we believe to be true to sentences that we know to be false. One thing that we can say about tonk, then, is that the rules that define it are not valid.

We discussed very early on in this book why valid arguments are important. Only valid arguments provide the guarantee that one will not go from true beliefs to false ones. Licensing invalid inferences, of course, is a significant mark against tonk, but the problem with tonk is not simply that the rules that define it are invalid. Rather, it is that it doesn't allow us to distinguish *in any way* good sentences to believe from bad ones. Since one can infer any sentence, q, from any sentence, p, using both rules of contonktion, a belief set that was governed by the rules of tonk would not be a very useful belief set since it would license belief in anything and everything. The account

[2] "The Runabout Inference Ticket," Prior, Arthur (1960) *Analysis*, vol. 21.
Reprinted in (1976), in *Papers in Logic and Ethics*, eds. P.T. Geach and A.J.P.Kenny, Amherst: University of Massachusetts Press.

of logical consequence defined by the tonk rules does no work at all by way of guiding us as to what we ought and ought not to believe. This defect with tonk suggests that one of the things that it would be good for an account of logical consequence to do would be to distinguish the sentences that are good for us to believe, given our starting beliefs, from the ones that are bad. The trick, of course, is to say just what should count as a good sentence to believe. Most of the non-classical logics that we've examined can be seen as pressing classical logic on just this issue. Take intuitionism, for example. According to intuitionists, classical logic just gets it wrong on LEM. Dummett in particular has argued that it is just not true that every sentence is such that either it or its negation holds, because at least some things are not the sorts of things about which realism is the correct philosophical viewpoint. Thus, the classical logician and the intuitionist logician just disagree about whether or not a particular sentence (for example, "Either Jones is brave or its not the case that Jones is brave") is a good one to believe.

What this shows is that when rival logicians disagree, their disagreement is not only about which rules of logic are right. It's also a disagreement about which sentences are good ones to believe. This is one reason why adjudicating between the many logics out there can be so difficult. Disagreements about logical consequence are only partly about logic. They are also, perhaps even mostly, about quite fundamental issues like whether or not a belief is a good one to have given one's other beliefs. And, as we have seen, one's views on which sentences are good to believe will frequently depend on one's views in other fundamental philosophical areas. At any rate, however difficult it may be to decide which of the many logics we've examined is correct, one thing is clear. Any language with tonk as one of its connectives will not be very desirable, since according to a language like this every possible sentence is equally good to believe.

Having said what the right account of logical consequence ought not to do (license belief in everything), is there anything in particular it ought to do? I'll mention three. The first two are soundness and completeness. A system in which everything that is provable is also true is *sound*, and it is *complete* if everything that is true can also be proven. Classical logic is both sound and complete, and so too are the other logics that we've looked at. The soundness and completeness of logic amounts to this: any sentence that gets formed using the rules of the logic in question is guaranteed to also be true, and every sentence that is true is going to be provable using its rules. Thus, anything that's true as a matter of logic will be provable, and everything that is provable will be true. Put somewhat flippantly, the truth shall be revealed, provided the rules are applied correctly.

Another quality frequently mentioned is *strength*. By strength, I mean the number of theorems that can be proven using the rules of the logic in question. For example, one factor frequently cited in favor of classical logic over intuitionistic logic is that classical logic is stronger in the sense that more theorems can be proven using classical inference rules than can be proven intuitionistically. Of course, intuitionists think that the more that can be proven is ill-gotten gain since it wasn't proven constructively, and so citing strength does nothing to convince the devoted intuitionist. I suspect that this will be true in a lot of cases of rival logics, i.e., the sentences that can be proven in one but not the other will be the very sentences under dispute as good to believe.

Soundness, completeness, and strength, then, are some of the qualities that reflect favorably on an account of logical consequence. Nevertheless, none of them proves terribly useful in adjudicating among rival logics. As to the first two, many if not most rival accounts of logical consequence are sound and complete, and so the logics are not distinguished by their possession of these qualities. Strength, on the other hand, does distinguish each rival logic from its competitors, but not in a way that would allow a definitive assessment. Even if we want a strong logic, we don't want one that's so strong that it licenses us to believe things that we aren't really entitled to believe, and the disagreement among advocates of rival logics is frequently a disagreement over the proper bounds of this entitlement. Thus, even knowing some of the things that make an account of logical consequence desirable or not doesn't help us to know which logic is the right logic.

## II—MAKING SENSE OF THE TITLE
## QUESTION OF THIS CHAPTER

It might seem like the title question of this chapter makes perfect sense. Haven't I spent the last six chapters essentially listing some of the considerations that go into answering it? As obvious as this may seem, a number of philosophers have argued that there is a problem with even making sense of the question of which logic is correct and which one isn't. That's because these philosophers don't think that there can be a genuine rivalry between logics.

To see why, let us begin with a silly story. Suppose that you have one theory of cats, and I have another. Let us say that both of our theories of cats agree on the following:

1. Cats purr.
2. Cats meow.

The disagreement in our theories centers around the eating habits of cats. According to your theory, which makes cats carnivores,

3. Cats eat meat.

But according to my theory, which makes cats omnivores,

4. Cats eat meat and vegetables.

It seems reasonable to suppose, given my theory of cats, that rules 1, 2 and 4 define 'cat' for me, and given your theory of cats, that rules 1, 2, and 3 define 'cat' for you. Indeed, to the extent that concepts are understood by how we define them, we can even say that we each have a different concept of cats. We can indicate this by giving each of our terms its own little subscript (yours can be $cat_3$ and mine can be $cat_4$). Now, let us suppose that we have the following scintillating discussion:

Me: $Cats_4$ eat meat and vegetables.

You: $Cats_3$ eat meat only.

Are we disagreeing with one another when we have this conversation? In one sense no. What we both said is true because the concepts under discussion are actually different. But in another sense we clearly are. We disagree about what the correct thing to say about cats is.

In this latter case, the thing that we disagree about is clear. We disagree about the nature of cats. And our dispute can be adjudicated by appealing to the behavior of actual cats, those furry meowing creatures that live among us. That is, our disagreement is over something whose nature is independent of the beliefs that we each have about cats. This is because, for both of us, the bottom line is that 'cat' is supposed to refer to cats in the world, so one of our definitions will turn out to be correct and the other will be incorrect.

Now, suppose that we disagree about which logic is correct to use. Since different logics are defined by their different rules and theorems, our disagreement must be over the rules and theorems.[3] Let's say that I think that classical logic is correct, and you think that $L_3$ is correct. For ease of discussion, lets just focus on LEM which is a theorem in classical logic but not in $L_3$, and the meaning of the English logical term 'or'. Like 'cat' above, it seems reasonable to say that you and I have different concepts of 'or'. Mine is $or_{CL}$ and yours is $or_{L3}$. Now, just like above, suppose that we have the following discussion:

> Me:   It is certainly the case that either every sentence $or_{CL}$ its negation is true.

> You:   It is definitely not the case that every sentence $or_{L3}$ its negation is true.

Once again, we can ask whether we disagree, and once again, the answer is both yes and no. In one sense, no, since what we both said is, strictly speaking, true. What I said is true of $or_{CL}$ and what you said is true of $or_{L3}$. But in another sense, yes, since we disagree about which logic is correct.

But herein lies the rub. When we disagreed about the correct definition of 'cat', we could adjudicate our disagreement by studying cats. But there is no corresponding way to adjudicate our logical disagreement. There are no ors in the world for us to study and discover their true nature. Since all that there is to a logic are the rules and theorems that define it, any disagreement about those rules and theorems is necessarily a disagreement concerning the very subject under discussion.

If all this is correct, then the problem with the title question of this chapter is clear. You can only ask which theory is correct where there is a genuine disagreement between theories. If we cannot have a genuine disagreement, then it's hard to see how one logic could be a rival to another logic. In a sense, it's as though every time we go from talking about one logic to talking about a different logic, we've just changed the subject (in our example, from a discussion of $or_{CL}$ to a discussion of $or_{L3}$). Indeed, proponents of the view that there can be no genuine rivalry between alternative logics sum up their view with the slogan, "Change of logic, change of subject".

---

[3] This is a simplification, since the difference between rival logics is not limited to a difference between rules and theorems. For example, as we have seen, intuitionists understand the logical connectives completely differently than classical logicians. For current purposes, though, we can focus on just the rules and theorems since the point I'm making would go through just the same no matter what accounts for the differences between rival logics in particular cases.

The question is, is this argument correct? I think it is not, and the best way to see why is to consider one more example of rival theories, this time from ethics. Suppose that you and I agree on the following:

5. Murder is wrong.

6. Lying is wrong.

But we disagree about whether or not something else, say abortion, is wrong. In particular, I think

7. Abortion is wrong.

But you think

8. It is not the case that abortion is wrong.

Just as with 'cat' and 'or', we might say that you and I have two different concepts of wrongness. Let us call mine 'wrong$_7$' and yours 'wrong$_8$'. Since wrongs are a lot more like ors than they are like cats (they are not physical objects existing independently of us and our conceptual schemes), it seems we should have to conclude that you and I don't really disagree, since there can be no genuine rivalry between our theories of wrongness. When you try to convince me that abortion is not wrong, from my perspective, you've just changed the subject from wrong$_7$ to wrong$_8$. In addition, it's hard to see how we can ask whose theory is correct, since when we consider each of our differing theories, we seem to be going from one subject to another.

I'm hoping this version of the change of meaning change of subject argument is clearly wrong to you. We obviously do have genuine moral disagreements, and these disagreements are usually engaged in with an eye toward figuring out who is right. Two questions, therefore, confront us. What are we disagreeing about? And what is there to be right about? It seems to me that the answer to both of these questions is not hard to find. What we disagree about, and the thing that there is to be right about, is how we ought to behave. In other words, the thing that we disagree about is a normative issue, not a descriptive one.

In all three of the examples that we've looked at (those involving cats, ors, and wrongs), it is certainly possible to conceive of our disagreement as a disagreement over the best definition of a term. What distinguishes the cat case from the others (so far), is that cats exist independently of us, and we want our theories to correctly reflect the actual behavior of cats. Cats, themselves, make disagreement possible because, whatever the differences between our concepts at the outset, we want our concepts to be true of these.

Now, in the case of wrongs, the thing that we want to be correct about is not an object that we can describe physically, like a cat. Rather it is a question of what the right way to behave is, and to answer this question we must prescribe norms. But this difference shouldn't stop us from saying that there is still something we can disagree about. Determining the correctness and/or incorrectness of norms may be trickier than determining the correctness and/or incorrectness of descriptions, but it is not, for all that, impossible.

And so too, with logic. If the working assumption of this book is correct, rival logicians who disagree about logical consequence are disagreeing about how we ought to reason. True, oughts are not things in the world like cats. There is no physical thing independent of us that we can look to in order to adjudicate our disagreement. We'll have a full discussion of the metaphysics of these oughts in Chapter 12, and as we'll see there, dealing with these is not any easy or straightforward matter. Right now the point is that advocates of different logics can certainly be rivals in their claims that their favored logic is the right one to use. Correspondingly, there is definitely something that these rival theories disagree about.

Let me end this interlude by reiterating a point that was made in the first section. Tonk is definitely not right. And what makes it not right is that it fails to distinguish in any way good sentences to believe from bad ones. I wanted to reiterate this for two reasons. The first concerns the point just being made. In some sense, one could just define a language with the tonk connectives and say that in that language, it is true that "Julie is at the store" implies "Bill's at the beach" (and "The moon is made of green cheese," and "I am Bigfoot," etc . . . ). But even if that's true, we can object to this language on many grounds, such as that it's not a very useful language or that it would be an irrational language to use. That is, we do clearly judge the goodness of other logics, even if those logics can, in some sense, be well-defined. That we do judge in this way is indisputable. That our so judging is conceptually possible has been disputed, though. I have tried to show that those who dispute it are mistaken as to the object of the disagreement.

The second reason I wanted to remind the reader of the clear wrongness of tonk is that it is all too easy, I think, to feel that adjudicating between rival logics is going to be a near-impossible task. Oughts really are a lot more slippery than cats. But even if this is true, that doesn't mean that the task is hopeless. Just as in ethics, where there is near universal agreement on certain things (you shouldn't punch babies in the face, genocide is wrong), in logic there is universal agreement that tonk is not really a good logical connective to include in one's logic. So, even if determining which logic is right and which logic is wrong in many cases is difficult, we all do agree on one thing. It may not be much, but it's something.

# 12

# The Metaphysics of Logic

## I—MAKING SENSE OF LOGICAL FACTS

In the final three chapters of this book, we will look at three traditional areas of philosophy, and consider some of the special sorts of questions that logic raises for them. The first issue is the metaphysics of logic. Metaphysics, you'll recall, is the study of the fundamental nature of reality. While physics describes the world of the five senses, metaphysics explores the fundamental underpinnings of our conceptual structures or world views.

To see what the metaphysical issues with logic are, consider first an ordinary descriptive sentence like "Cats have four legs." What makes sentences like this true is something about the world, in this case, the fact that cats, typically, have four legs. Now, let's just suppose that classical logic is the logic that we ought to use in our own reasoning. For simplicity, let us say that this amounts to the truth of the following four sentences, the set of which I will refer to as CL:

CL    Either p or not-p.
      Its not the case that both p and not-p.
      From p and not-p, infer q.
      From p or q and not-p, infer q.

What makes the sentences of CL true? Are there any logical facts in the world? If so, what kind of facts are they? And if not, can we still talk about the truth and falsity of sentences like these? These are the sorts of questions that we will consider in this chapter.

Theories concerning the metaphysics of normative sentences can profitably be divided into two main camps. In the first camp are those theories that hold that some fact makes these sentences true. In the second, there are theories that hold that there are no such facts. Let us begin with the former kind of theory, of which there are many variants.

## A. Psychologism

The first variant, psychologism, is one that was very briefly mentioned in Chapter 1. I include it here not because any philosopher today takes it seriously, but because it will clarify the general idea of how a fact could make sentences like those in CL true. *Psychologism* is the view that the truth of the sentences in CL, and others like them, is determined by the logic we use. Let us suppose that we discover that people are born with the ability and the inclination to reason classically. Never mind how we come to discover this fact, just play along for the sake of explaining the view. According to psychologism, what would make the sentences of CL true is the fact that this is how people actually reason. If we had discovered that people were hard-wired to reason intuitionistically then the sentence "Either p or not-p" would be false. And if we discovered that people were hard-wired to reason paraconsistently, then the sentences "Not both p and not-p" and "From p or q and not p infer q" would be false. In both cases, what would make those sentences false is some fact about us and our cognitive architecture. In the same way that facts about cats make sentences about cats either true or false, facts about us and our hard-wiring would make sentences like those in CL either true or false.

There are many reasons to reject a theory like this. One practical problem is who to include in the "we" indicated in the initial characterization of the view above, i.e, that "..the truth of the sentences in CL, and others like them, is determined by the logic *we* use." Though people might agree on many cases, this book is testament to the fact that there are a range of principles and/or inferences about which people disagree. Clearly, if an advocate of psychologism tried to include everyone in the "we," then the truth of any one of those sentences might well vary from person to person, or from group to group. The idea, however, that what is true in logic for one person might not be true for another person has some pretty major drawbacks. Most importantly, "From p or q and not-p, infer not-q," would have to be true for someone who was hard-wired that way.

Therefore, an advocate of psychologism would want to include some people and exclude others in their account of how "we" reason. But this is impossible to do unless she already knows which logic is right. To see this, suppose that Joe thinks that the sentence "From p or q and not-p, infer not-q," is true, and Phil thinks it is false. The only way that our advocate of psychologism could exclude Joe from her calculations is if she already knew that Dysfunctional Syllogism is not a good argument form, i.e., if she already knows that "From p or q and not p infer not q" is false. But this, of course, is precisely the issue that she is supposed to be trying to determine by discovering the facts of how people do reason.

In fact, even if the practical problem of figuring out who "we" are got resolved, psychologism would still not be a very good theory. The heart of the problem for psychologism as a theory about the truth or falsity of logic is that it seeks to describe, not prescribe. That is, it's hard to see how psychologism could ever be a good theory concerning the truth or falsity of logical rules and principles because determining this truth or falsity is inextricably connected to normative questions like how people ought to reason. In asking which logical rules and principles are true we are asking how people should reason, and to do this we have to look beyond how people do reason, because people often reason poorly. Indeed, even if we could determine that people all do reason in some particular way, the fact that they do is hardly a justification for saying that they should reason that way. This is the primary reason no philosopher really takes psychologism seriously as a theory of logic.

## B. Conventionalism

The next view we'll look at is called *conventionalism*. According to conventionalists, what makes sentences like those in CL either true or false are the conventions that govern the language that the sentences are in, in this case English. To get an idea of the motivation for a view like this, consider what we should say about someone who thinks the following sentence is true: "Two added to two makes six". First and most obviously, the person in question has uttered a false sentence. Two and two do not make six. The question is what account to give of why this person has uttered this particular false sentence.

Suppose that on querying this person, it becomes clear that their understanding of arithmetic is otherwise without problems, it's just that they use the word 'two' where every other speaker of English uses the word 'three' and vice versa. For example, when you hold up three fingers they say that you are holding up two fingers. And they say that three and three makes four, and that people have three eyes. Given this, it would seem wrong to say that this person misunderstands arithmetic, or that they're under some sort of conceptual confusion about the nature of the numbers two and three. Rather, it seems more plausible to say that this person just hasn't quite learned English correctly. They speak a language a lot like English, it's just that for some reason they have mis-learned these two particular words.

In saying that this person hasn't quite learned to speak English correctly, we are appealing to the fact that there are certain rules that govern how English speakers are supposed to use English words. We might well have spoken a language in which 'three' meant two and 'two' meant three. But that's not the way it is in the English language that is currently spoken. The conventions of the English language are such that 'two' refers to two and 'three' refers to three.

That there are conventions (either implicit or explicit) that govern the correct usage of linguistic terms seems beyond question. From this truism arises the motivation for conventionalist accounts of logic. According to conventionalists, what makes sentences like those in CL true are the conventions of the English language. Conventions here can be thought of as something like rules for the correct usage of a language. So, those sentences will be true just in case the conventions that govern the logical connectives are the rules of classical logic. And they will be false if the rules that govern the conventions are non-classical. For example, if they are intuitionistic, then "Either p or not-p" will be false.

There are three major problems with this theory. The first concerns how to make sense of the conventions themselves. The conventions are supposed to define how English speakers are supposed to use terms of English. So, for example, the convention for a term like 'cat' might include things like, "Cats are furry feline animals," and this convention is something like a rule that one should only use 'cat' to refer to furry feline animals. This rule can be used whether one knows what cats are or not. As long as one knows what a furry feline animal is, one can use this rule to appropriately apply the word 'cat'.

In the same way that the convention for 'cat' is supposed to be a rule for helping English speakers use the term, so too a convention for 'or' will be some kind of a rule for helping English speakers use that term. For example, among the rules that define 'or' one is likely to find rules similar to the ones containing 'or' in CL above. But in order to correctly use 'or' in English, one needs to know more than what can be inferred from disjunctions and when. English speakers need to know how and when it is appropriate to form a disjunction. In addition to things like rules defining correct inferences with disjunction, therefore, there will have to be at least one convention that guides English speakers about when they are entitled to form an 'or' sentence. And it is here that conventionalism starts to run into difficulties.

To see the problem, consider the following suggestion:

'p or q' will be true just in case either p is true or q is true.

Unlike the convention that defined 'cat' above, to understand this convention a speaker must already know what 'or' means, since the term appears in the conventional instructions for its basic use. Of course, one could fiddle with the details here. But just try to come up with a rule that would make clear to speakers when it was appropriate to utter a sentence with the word 'or' that didn't, in some way, already use or. As you will quickly discover if you really try to come up with a rule, there is no way to explain the nature of disjunction without appealing, either implicitly or explicitly, to some prior understanding of the term 'or'.

The second problem is that, unlike 'two' and 'three', it is just not as plausible that there is one clear convention which governs our use of 'or', or, even worse, 'if...then'. Though it is very clear that Dysfunctional Syllogism is not a rule which governs our conventions for 'or', there are many cases where excellent English speakers either don't have intuitions or where intuitions vary from person to person. As we have seen, Disjunctive Syllogism is generally a good rule of inference, but when it licenses us to believe that any q follows from a contradiction, it is not so clearly a part of what should define the term for us.

Third and finally, there are many different sets of conventions that could, in principle, define many different languages. There is English$_{CL}$ (which is English where the conventions for the logical terms are defined by the rules and principles of classical logic), there is English$_{IL}$ (which is English where the conventions for the logical terms are defined by the rules and principles of intuitionistic logic), there is English$_{L3}$ (which is English where the conventions for the logical terms are defined by the rules and principles of L$_3$), and on and on. It is certainly something to make sense of the truth conditions for sentences containing logical terms in each one of these variants of

English (though as we have also seen, conventionalists didn't make as much sense of this as they had hoped). But pressing, and to many people's minds, more interesting questions are left unanswered, even after we have made sense of these truth conditions. In particular, we want to know whether we should speak English$_{CL}$ or English$_{IL}$ or English$_{L3}$, because what we want to know is how we should reason.

The problem, of course, is that we don't really want to know what the conventions are, we want to know what they should be. And conventionalism about logical truth doesn't really tell us a whole lot about that. Now, to be fair, most conventionalists were certainly aware of this problem, and they did offer a response to the normative issues that concern us. I'll consider the kind of response they gave in the second section of this chapter. But in and of itself, the conventionalist account of logical truth can't really tell us why the sentences of CL are true, as opposed to some other set of sentences.

## C. Rationalism

Thus far, we have looked at psychologism and conventionalism as examples of theories that posit the existence of logical facts to explain the truth of sentences like those in CL. The last theory that I will discuss in this vein can tend to be a little less intuitive to the philosophically uninitiated. This view, which I will call *rationalism* (it goes by many names) states that there are abstract facts accessible to reason that make sentences like those in CL true. Let us begin our discussion of rationalism by briefly exploring an analogous position in ethics.

Perhaps the most well-known and popular theory that grounds ethical facts in reason comes from the philosopher Immanuel Kant. Kant thought that there were objective facts of reason that make ethical laws either true or false. For instance, Kant argued that lying was never permissible, so that the sentence, "It is wrong to lie" is always true. The reason, according to Kant, is that lying demonstrates a practical inconsistency in the will. Kant thought that in order for some act to be considered moral, it would have to be something that would be okay for everyone to do, or in his terminology, that it would have to be universalizable. Now, in order for a lie to succeed, there has to be a general practice of truth telling. After all, if there weren't this general practice then no one would believe anyone, and so a lie would not be believed. But this makes clear that if a willing subject universalized her lie, i.e, asked herself what if everyone lied when they wanted to, she would see that her very lie undermines the practice that she exploits in her lying. Liars, in others words, make use of a practice which their lie undermines. This is why the problem is a practical inconsistency. It is not strictly inconsistent to believe "It is wrong to lie" and then to tell a lie, because it is not an instance of p and not-p, but there is certainly something like an inconsistency on the part of the willing subject.

The important point for current purposes is that the fact that makes lying wrong according to a view like this is not to be found in nature or the concrete world. Rather, it is to be found in pure reason. Kant thought that truths about ethics were like truths about mathematics. In the same way that anyone who understands the concepts of two and addition understands the truth of the sentence "Two plus two is equal to four," so too anyone who understands the concept of lying understands that the sentence "Lying is wrong" must be true. In particular, it is clear that anyone who understands the concept of lying can see how a lie involves one in behavior that can't be universalized without being practically inconsistent. We don't need to see how things turn out in the real world, or to do any investigation into the nature of people's psychological propensities. Reason alone is sufficient to tell us that lying is not good.

In the same way that abstract facts of reason make lying wrong, some philosophers have argued that there are abstract facts of reason that determine the truth or falsity of sentences like those in CL. Frege, for example, argued that logic has the job of tracking truth, as we saw in Chapter 1. To see why we can assess truth-tracking by reason alone, let's go back to tonk, and see what a view like this would have to say about the truth or falsity of the sentences, "From p infer p tonk q" and "From p tonk q, infer q." Let's call these two sentences the tonk sentences. As long as we understand the tonk sentences, it is clear that tonk can not guarantee that we will only go from true sentences to other true sentences. As we saw, tonk doesn't distinguish in any way good from bad sentences to believe, since any sentence, p, is inferable from any other sentence, q. Given this, it is clearly false that the tonk sentences will track truth. Consequently, the tonk sentences must be false. This fact about tonk is something that we can see simply by considering the tonk sentences in the abstract. That is why this would count as a truth of reason. For rationalists, therefore, the facts that make logical rules and principles true or false are accessible to reason alone.

The biggest problem with rationalism about logic is that it is not clearly capable of doing the kind of work that we want done. It is one thing, after all, to be able to say why the tonk sentences are false, but quite another to say why the CL sentences are true. The problem, of course, is that the controversial aspects of classical logic tend to arise in precisely the places where we're just not sure whether or not a rule tracks truth. For example, though the truth of disjunctive syllogism certainly seems, in the abstract, to be a kind of fact of reason, when the rule is used in such a way that we can infer anything from a contradiction, the facts are a lot less clear. In short, rationalism might be a plausible story to explain the falsity of a sentence like "From p infer p tonk q," but it loses its plausibility when it comes to the more difficult cases.

Another way to see the difficulty I have in mind is this. Arguably, every logic we've looked at tracks truth in the sense that, using its rules, one cannot go from true sentences to false ones. The only apparent exception would be paraconsistent logics, but even here, one could question how much of an exception these are, since para-consistent logics will never take one from designated values to non-designated values. So, one can go from true and true only beliefs to beliefs that are both true and false, but paraconsistently one cannot go from true and true only beliefs to false and false only beliefs.

In light of these considerations, the rationalist faces a choice. One thing he can say is that many different, mutually incompatible logical sentences can be true, depending on the logic that is under discussion. So, even though the sentences of CL might be true, the last two

From p and not-p, infer q.

From p or q and not-p, infer q.

would be false in a relevance logic. In other words, the rationalist can admit that by the truth-tracking criterion, many different logics pass the test, and so though it might sound a bit strange, one and the same logical sentence might be either true or false depending on the logical system that one is doing the evaluating in.

While certainly possible, this alternative is not terribly attractive to many rationalists. Mainly, it means that reason alone leaves open many different possibilities, and in general, rationalists have wanted reason to function in exactly the opposite direction. Indeed, at least some rationalists appeal to reason precisely to preclude this kind of a situation. The analogous situation in ethics would have it that according to pure reason, lying is never permissible, but also that lying is sometimes permissible. In other words, it would leave open the possibility that both ethical judgments might be true. It is just a fact of the history of philosophy that many rationalists would not find this move acceptable.

Another thing a rationalist might say to escape the difficulties I've raised is that reason can appeal to many other qualities in addition to a logic's ability to track truth. For example, perhaps they might say that it is always rational to prefer the stronger over the weaker logic (or something like that), and then explain this rational preference in terms of some other truths of reason. There certainly are theories of rationality that claim to ground their fundamental principles in reason. *Decision theory*, for instance, which is a formalization of the rules and principles for correct decision making, claims as a sort of fundamental principle that if one prefers some outcome, say, A, over a different outcome, B, and one prefers B over a third outcome, C, then one should always prefer A over C as well. This principle, that one's preferences should be transitive, seems right by the light of reason. Actually giving an account like this would not be easy, but it is certainly a possible move the rationalist could make in light of the difficulties I've raised here.

In sum, there are ways that a rationalist could clarify why the sentences in CL, for example, are true, which also makes clear why no conflicting sentences of any other logic are true. But at the very least, rationalists are going to have say a lot more about what it is that reason can discern, and why we can be sure that reason can single it out, since simply appealing to a logical rule's ability to track truth will make many incompatible rules true.

## II—GIVING UP TRYING TO MAKE SENSE
## OF LOGICAL FACTS

Given the difficulties that surround the possibility of clearly explaining logical facts, some philosophers have abandoned the quest. There are many different ways of denying that there are normative facts, but I will focus on only one of them in what follows. Though it goes by many names in the literature, I will call the view that I spell out in the remainder of this chapter *non-cognitivism*. Non-cognitivism about a particular subject matter is the denial that the sentences of that subject represent facts. In addition, according to the non-cognitivism that I will focus on, the sentences pertaining to that subject matter are neither true nor false. In other words, non-cognitivists about logical truth would both deny that there are facts like any of those discussed in the last section, and also deny that the sentences of CL can be either true or false.

Let us first explore this view in terms of ethics. Non-cognitivists about ethics don't believe that the sentence "It is wrong to lie," is either true or false. They think that it expresses an emotional reaction, something like abhorrence at lies. Non-cognitivists still think that such a sentence might be a good one or a bad one to believe, but they don't think that there are any facts that justify one in either believing it or not. Rather, what compels a person's belief about lying is her feelings about lying.

The view might sound crazy at first. What if someone feels really happy at the thought of lying? Would that make it okay? The non-cognitivist wants to answer no to this last question, because if she said yes then her view would be objectionably relativistic. Relativism is the view that the rightness or wrongness of an action can only be determined relative to a person's ethical beliefs. To see what's wrong with this view, one need consider no more than the fact that according to some ethical systems (e.g., Hitlter's), genocide is okay. Since, intuitively, that doesn't make genocide okay, it can't be the case that what is right and wrong is determined by one's ethical system. For this reason, non-cognitivists are right to want to avoid being relativists.

How, then, do they avoid it? To see the answer to this, consider humor for a second. In many cases, humor is a matter of taste. Most five year olds find bathroom humor hilarious, but many people don't find much humor in it at all. Our humor reactions to situations are non-cognitive in the sense that it doesn't seem right to say that "Fart jokes are funny" is either true or false. In addition, it doesn't seem like people's reactions are justified by some clearly determinable fact in the world. Most children (and some adults) just happen to find gross humor funny, but if you don't, very few would argue that you're wrong.

That said, most people do think that there are certain things that no one should find funny. It is not funny to watch someone painfully suffer and then die, and anyone who has that emotional reaction to watching someone do this would be wrong to do so. A non-cognitivist about funnyness would want to say that sentences like "Watching people painfully suffer and die is funny" are neither true nor false, because there are no facts about funnyness in the world. Nevertheless, the non-cognitivist can certainly disapprove of someone's finding suffering funny. Thus, even emotional reactions like funnyness can be subject to the approval or disapproval of our fellows.

Returning, then, to the ethics case, if someone gets really happy at the thought of lying, a non-cognitivist does not have to merely accept this as okay. She can try to convince this person that his emotional reaction is inappropriate in some way, and if that doesn't work, the non-cognitivist can even try to apply some kind of social pressure. For example, she might say, "If you find lying to be a good thing, I don't want to be friends with you." The bottom line for the non-cognitivist, however, is that there are no facts about lying in the world. Where there are facts, one can adjudicate disagreements (if you say cats typically have three legs and I say they have four, one of us is right and the other is wrong because there are facts about the number of legs that cats have). In the absence of ethical facts, non-cognitivists must appeal to persuasion, brute social pressures, and other mechanisms to try to solve disputes.

Now to finally turn to non-cognitivism about logic. According to this view, the sentences of CL are neither true nor false, since there are no logical facts either of reason or nature or language. So, what is it a matter of? For starters, it is a matter of our intuitions about what follows from what. Where these intuitions come from is an interesting question,[1] but that we have them is undeniable. Recall Hannah's and Jake's arguments from Chapter 1. Everyone has intuitions about the goodness of each of them. Brute intuitions, however, are not enough (unless we want this view to collapse into a variant of psychologism), since some of our intuitions are not as refined as we might like. So the second component central to determining what follows from what is that we consider our intuitions in some rigorous and critical way, and try to arrive at a theory of what should follow from what which meets as many standards as possible. The details of this process will be presented in the next chapter, but for now, the important point according to the non-cognitivist is that however we arrive at our conclusions concerning which logic is correct, there are no logical facts that make these conclusions either true or false, and the sentences that represent these conclusions should be regarded as neither true nor false.

I noted in my discussion of conventionalism that conventionalists were certainly aware that their account of logical truth did not have any real normative clout. In fact, when it came to the normative issues in logic, conventionalists denied that there were any facts at all.

---

[1] Psychologists have studied how people reason and have proposed a number of theories to account for where our logical intuitions come from. The two most prominent are that they are innate (selected for in the same way that language ability has been selected for: because it helps with our survival), or that they come from "mental models" that we construct by considering the objects around us. See Further Readings for references to these two theories.

So though conventionalists hoped that conventions made sense of how sentences like those in CL could be true or false, they didn't think that there were any facts which determined which logic was the correct one to use. Or, put slightly differently, conventionalists believe that there are facts that make sentences like "Either p or not-p" true or false, but they don't think there are any facts about sentences like, "Classical logic is the best logic."

So how, according to non-cognitivists, should we decide whether we should speak English$_{CL}$ or English$_{IL}$ or English$_{L3}$? One famous answer came from the philosopher Rudolph Carnap. According to him, we should decide which language to speak by considering pragmatic factors like which language best furthers our interests and goals. By way of illustration, suppose that in order to further our interests and goals it turns out that we need all of classical arithmetic. In this case, according to Carnap we should speak English$_{CL}$, or some other English that gives us classical arithmetic. The point is that in a case like this, we should definitely not speak English$_{IL}$.

Unlike most philosophers, Carnap explicitly embraces pluralism. *Pluralism* is the view that many different logics might be true. Carnap argued for what he called a principle of tolerance, whereby it is not the philosopher's business to set up prohibitions, but merely to establish possible ways of conventionally defining a language. According to this view, we should let a thousand flowers bloom, and fully explore the many different logical systems that have been proposed. Only by keeping an open mind can we come to fully appreciate the advantages and disadvantages of each. Presumably, we should keep exploring all of these systems until one emerges as clearly preferable to the others.

Carnap's view has one serious drawback.[2] I noted earlier that ethical non-cogntivists want to avoid relativism, but this kind of non-cognitivism seems unavoidably relativistic. Whether or not we ought to use a logic depends on (is relative to) what our interests and goals are. This seems to leave open the possibility, for example, that a logic with the tonk rules could be right for a person who didn't value distinguishing good from bad beliefs, while it could be wrong for a person who did value that.

In one sense, this criticism of non-cognitivism is correct. If a person really didn't value distinguishing good from bad beliefs, then for that

---

[2] Actually, non-cognitivism has several major and well recognized difficulties, but I'll only discuss one here.

person, the tonk rules might be fine. The question is how much this ought to bother the logical non-cognitivist. In the first place, one has to wonder about this imaginary person, and ask whether or not he could really ever exist? After all, if he really didn't care about distinguishing good from bad beliefs, then what's to stop him from believing that drinking arsenic is good for his health? It doesn't seem likely, in other words, that a fictional person like this would live for very long, and even if he did, it certainly seems unlikely his genes would prove beneficial to his offspring. Unlike the case in ethics, in other words, where we know that there are sadists, it is just not clear how we can make sense of people who really truly do not care at all about distinguishing beliefs that are good ones to have from those that aren't good ones to have. If this first thought is correct, then it is not clear that the logical non-cognitivist really needs to worry much about someone embracing the tonk rules, since no real person who ever existed really doesn't care about distinguishing good from bad beliefs.

The second response to the charge of relativism takes off where the first one ended. Given that we can rule out truly terrible logics like those containing the tonk rules, who cares if it turns out that different logics might be better or worse depending on one's goals and interests? Whereas in ethics it is clearly intolerable that it should be right for one person to harm others against their will, it is not at all clear what the harm would be in two different people using two of the different logics we have looked at. Perhaps we might have to be a bit more careful about simply believing any and every sentence that someone else believes, since for all we know, a person might have to come to their conclusions using a logic that we disapprove of. But this kind of skepticism may be warranted whether or not we all use the same logic.

A third response is perhaps the most important defense against the charges of relativism. Suppose that we do, in fact, agree on our basic goals and interests. This might be the case in a limited way, for example, for scientists working in one field, or maybe for mathematicians. More generally, it is clear that most people do have very similar goals and interests, broadly defined. Everyone needs food, water, shelter, and basic medical care, and most people also desire things like a mate, close friends and family. Two things might occur in these scenarios where goals and interests are agreed upon. Either no one logic would emerge as clearly the best logic for us to use, or one logic would clearly be the best given our shared goals and interests. If the latter, then we could all agree to use it. If the former, then any of the logics that might be efficacious would be acceptable. It is worth noting here that when there are disagreements among scientists as to which theory is correct, different scientists generally work with their different pet theories unless and until one emerges as the clearly better theory. As I noted above, Carnap thought that we should let a thousand flowers bloom. In other words, in practice, it might turn out either that there is a lot more agreement than we think, or, where there isn't, that disagreement is appropriate and healthy.

# 13

# The Epistemology of Logic

## I—A TRADITIONAL DISTINCTION

The second general philosophical area we will examine is epistemology, which you will recall, is the theory of knowledge. Epistemology is concerned with questions like how we know the things we do, and what can (or can't) be known. These traditional questions turn out to be especially tricky when the subject is logic.

At the end of Chapter 10, I briefly discussed the radical claim that logic might be revisable in light of quantum mechanics. There, I introduced a traditional philosophical distinction between rational and empirical knowledge. To begin our discussion of the epistemology of logic, it would be useful to first say a little bit more about this distinction.

Some new terminology at the outset. What I have been calling rational knowledge is traditionally known as *a priori knowledge* (which in Latin, means literally, from what comes before), and what I have been calling empirical knowledge is traditionally known as *a posteriori knowledge* (which means from what comes after). A priori knowledge is supposed to be knowledge that is justifiable independently of any experiences we might have. That is, the justification for a priori knowledge is theoretically independent of our experiences of the world. A posteriori knowledge, on the other hand, is knowledge that requires experience for its justification. Or, in other words, the justification for a posteriori knowledge must come after experience.

As we saw in that discussion in Chapter 10, the paradigm of a priori knowledge is mathematics. The truth of $2 + 2 = 4$ has nothing to do with the fact that if I add two stones to two stones, I will have four stones. Of course, humans need to count objects like stones to have an understanding of the concepts 'two' and 'four.' But even if we need experience to possess these concepts, the experience itself is not supposed to be what justifies us in thinking that $2 + 2 = 4$. That knowledge is something that follows simply from our understanding of the concepts in question.

To see this, consider two quick points. First, we can imagine beings, unlike humans, that don't require experiences in order to acquire concepts. Let's suppose that God is just such a being. Clearly, God could have a purely rational understanding of the concepts of 'two' and 'four', and be certain that $2 + 2 = 4$, even if God never actually needs to count any objects. Second, even if $2 + 2 = 4$ seems like it could be something we learn through experience of objects, we know just as certainly the truth of

$$\begin{array}{r} 123{,}456{,}789 \\ + \, 987{,}654{,}321 \\ \hline 1{,}111{,}111{,}110 \end{array}$$

and it is not because we've counted this many objects.

A posteriori knowledge, on the other hand, constitutes the vast majority of things we know. I know that the sky is blue, that unsupported objects fall to earth, and that tigers have stripes, and all of these bits of knowledge depend on my experiencing the world as being one way rather than another.

A traditional way of explaining the a priori/a posteriori distinction is in terms of what we can and can't conceive. One is not supposed to be able imagine the opposite of anything known a priori, whereas one can always imagine the opposite of anything known a posteriori. In terms of our examples, we can't imagine two and two not equaling four, but we can imagine the sky not being blue, objects floating when unsupported, and tigers being spotted or solid colored.

As I noted in Chapter 10, logic has traditionally been grouped with mathematics as being a subject that is knowable by reason alone. Thus, knowledge of logic has long been thought to be just as a priori as knowledge of arithmetic. But we've seen over the course of this book that there is more than one logic, and even assuming that classical logic is correct, it is certainly conceivable that various rules or theorems might not hold. We have conceived of just such possibilities in all the previous chapters exploring non-classical logics. At the very least, therefore, the a priority of logic is not quite as straightforward as the a priority of arithmetic. So is logic knowable a priori or not? Let's begin by seeing whether or not logic is justifiable independently of experience.

## II—JUSTIFYING LOGIC

Suppose I wanted to justify some belief to you, say my belief that pigs can't fly. Presumably, I would point out that things that can fly either have wings or some other device for leaving the ground. I would also note that things than can fly tend to be light for their size, and aerodynamic. Finally I would conclude by making clear that pigs have neither wings nor any other device for leaving the ground, and that pigs are very dense and not terribly aerodynamic. I would, in other words, give you an argument that claimed to establish that pigs can't fly. But, what is an argument? We are assuming (at least until the next chapter) that an argument is just a piece of reasoning, and that reasoning is something that involves logical inference. In other words, in order to justify my belief that pigs can't fly, I would use logic.

How then could I justify my belief that classical logic, for example, is correct? Clearly, I would have to give an argument, since it's hard to see how to justify any belief without giving some kind of argument for it. But this seems to put me in a bit of a bind. Any argument to justify classical logic will either be valid according to classical rules, or not. If the latter, then the argument that I give will be incorrect by my own standards. Since I think classical logic is correct, any classically invalid argument has to be a bad argument for me to use, and presumably, so, I would not use rules that I regarded as incorrect to justify my beliefs. Thus, I would have to use the very rules whose justification I was trying to establish. But in this case my argument would seem to presuppose what it is supposed to explain. I want to justify classical logic as the correct way to reason, but in using classical logic for my argument, I must assume that reasoning according to classical rules is justified.

Arguments like this assume the legitimacy of the rules that they are trying to establish, and as such, involve a kind *circular reasoning*. Circular reasoning is just what it sounds like, reasoning that goes in a circle, either by assuming the truth of the conclusion in one or more of the premises or, as in our case, by assuming the legitimacy of some rule in a derivation meant to establish the justification for that same rule. In general, circular reasoning is not very highly regarded, and it's not hard to see why. One could prove anything at all if one just assumed (either implicitly or explicitly) the truth of what one was trying to prove. I could prove that there are green fairies living on my lawn, for example, by citing the fact that the green fairies wrote a book about themselves and left it on my doorstep. Clearly, in order for them to have written and left a book on my doorstep, green fairies must exist.

The difficulty with justifying logic, then, is that there doesn't seem to be a way to avoid circular reasoning. This is problematic for two main reasons. The first relates to the point that I just made. It seems that I could justify the legitimacy of just about any rule of inference using a circular argument. This is a point that the philosopher Susan Haack made rather humorously with a rule of inference that she called Modus Morons (MM):

MM      q

         $\underline{p \supset q}$

         So, p

Haack gave the following as a justification for this rule:

If A $\supset$ B is true, then B is true.

If A is true, then if A $\supset$ B is true, then B is true.

So, A is true.[1]

This argument uses MM to justify itself. In this argument, q is the sentence "If A $\supset$ B is true, then B is true," and p is the sentence "A is true." (Remember, those p's and q's can stand for any complete declarative sentence whatsoever, and a conditional, though complex, is a complete declarative sentence.)

In fact, even tonk, the rule of inference that everyone can agree is not a good rule to use, can be used to justify itself.

A is true.

A is true tonk A tonk B is true. (by the first rule of Tonk)

So, A tonk B is true (by the second rule of Tonk)

---

[1] "The Justification of Deduction", Susan Haack, first appeared *Mind* 85 (1976), pp. 112–119. Reprinted in *Deviant Logic Fuzzy Logic*, Susan Haack (1996) Chicago, London: The University of Chicago Press

In this argument, p is "A is true" and q is "A tonk B is true". The first premise is an assumption, though a pretty reasonable one. Surely some sentence A is true. Essentially, by applying the two rules of tonk to that assumption, we are able to show that the rules for tonk are justified.

A second problem with the circular nature of justifying logic concerns how we go about adjudicating disputes between advocates of rival logics. How can I possibly convince you that my logic is correct, using my logic, if you disagree that my logic is correct? And how can you possibly convince me, using your logic, that your logic is correct, if I don't already agree with you that your logic is correct? It seems, given the problem of justifying logic, that there is no neutral ground from which we can present our arguments, since our arguments all depend on the very issues about which we disagree.

Of course, there can be overlap and agreement among competing logics, as we have seen. This means that neutral ground can sometimes be found even among advocates of competing logics who differ greatly on certain issues. For example, though $L_3$ differs from classical logic in countenancing three possible truth values rather than two, when the truth value of a sentence is classical, $L_3$ and classical logic are indistinguishable. And though intuitionists reject LEM, they endorse LNC, and the intuitionist conditional is subject to the same paradoxes of material implication as is the conditional in classical logic. So though intuitionism is clearly distinct from classical logic, an intuitionist and classical logician can agree on a great deal. Another kind of overlap might be found in the paraconsistent logicians assertion that disjunctive syllogism is fine to use when the subject under consideration is known to be consistent. Though paraconsistent and classical logicians clearly disagree on the validity of disjunctive syllogism, the fact remains that on many subjects, they can agree in practice.

Even if this is true, however, there is no guarantee that one can always find some sort of neutral territory. So the problem might still occasionally haunt us. At the very least, then, the problem of justifying a logic to someone who doesn't already endorse it remains a potential wrench in the works.

Where does all of this leave us, vis-à-vis the a priority of logic? The fact that one can't justify logic without using some form of logical reasoning suggests that logic must be justifiable independently of experience in at least a pragmatic sense. To see what I mean by this, suppose that humans decided that they should never use any rule unless they had a justification that that rule was correct to use. In all sorts of cases (rules of ethics, rules of driving, rules of cooking, rules of war, and so on), this requirement would pose little problem. One can clearly justify the rule, for example, that everyone should drive on the right (or the left, depending on which country you're in) by citing the fact that when everyone drives on the same side of the road when they are going in the same direction, there are fewer accidents. And though the justifications for things like ethics and war are a little more controversial, there is no principled reason why justifications couldn't be found. But in the case of rules of inference, this requirement would prohibit us from ever using a logical rule. For one can't justify a logical rule without using a logical rule. In practice, therefore, the requirement that we have a justification prior to using a rule would mean that we couldn't use logic. But this is clearly an unacceptable result. If we didn't use logic, we would never be able to engage in structured thinking about any subject at all. So what justifies us in using a rule of logic, independently of experience or not, is that if we didn't, we would not be able to reason.

That might seem like some kind of trick. I started this section trying to justify logic by structured argument, but I concluded that logic is justified as a matter of practical necessity. In the interest of clarity, therefore, let us disambiguate the term 'justification' by distinguishing logical justification from practical justification. In that case, the conclusion of this section should be that logic can not be logically justified by logic (at least not in a non-circular way), though it can be practically justified. Though it is certainly true that the sense of 'justification' morphed from the beginning of this section to the end, there was no trickery behind it. Having seen that logic couldn't be justified by logical arguments, I settled for the next best thing. Both senses of 'justification' are clearly legitimate definitions of the English term. Since a priori justification could mean logical justification independently of experience or practical justification independent of experience, we can conclude that logical rules are a priori justified. Practically, we must use logical rules whatever our experiences may be.

## III—REVISING LOGIC

In the discussion of quantum logic, I noted that quantum logic challenged the traditional conception that logical truths are, like mathematical truths, knowable a priori. We have just seen that logic seems to be a priori justified in at least a practical sense. We must be justified in using some rules of logic independently of experience because if we weren't, we would never be justified in using any rules of logic at all. But it is hard to see why the a priority of logic in this sense is challenged, in any way, by the possibility that we might change our logic for empirical reasons. After all, the practical conclusion is that we've got to use some logic, but this leaves open which logic is the one that we've got to use. Intuitionist logic is presumably just as practically justifiable independently of experience as is classical logic.

So why all the fuss about quantum logic? The short answer is that many philosophers have thought that if something can be known a priori, then that knowledge would not be revisable for empirical reasons. Let me briefly explain this last phrase. Philosophers prefer the term *revision* for talking about what happens when we change our beliefs. The idea here is to think of our beliefs as a set of sentences. Whenever we have a reason to change those sentences, say, to delete a sentence because we no longer believe it, or to replace one sentence with a new one that we think is better justified, we are revising our beliefs. Philosophers who have thought that a priori knowledge is not revisable for empirical reasons, then, have thought that the reasons for revision can't, themselves, be a posteriori.

To see why philosophers have thought that a priori knowledge should not be revisable for empirical reasons, let's return to the domain of arithmetic again. Just ask yourself whether it would ever be reasonable to conclude that $2 + 2 = 5$? Suppose, for example, that on some far distant planet, astronomers discover a new class of objects which seem to have the unusual property that two of these objects added to two other of these objects makes five of these object. If you think that there must be some counting mistake or illusion in any world in which it seems that $2 + 2 = 5$, then you can see why mathematical knowledge is thought to be a priori in the sense that it is not revisable for empirical reasons. Even experiences that seem to contravene mathematical knowledge can't undermine it. Or, put slightly differently, $2 + 2 = 4$ seems like something that's true no matter what our experiences in the world.

If logical knowledge is a priori in this sense in addition to being a priori in the practical sense argued at the end of the last section, then the fuss caused by quantum logic is clear. We should no more revise logic in light of our experiences than we should revise math in light of our experiences. This is the locus of the disagreement among philosophers concerning logic's a priority, and this is why quantum logic was such a radical suggestion.

In this section, then, I wish to focus on the question of revising logic. Just as with the justification of logic, there are problems that arise in figuring out whether, and how, logic is revisable. As we will see, they stem from the same source as the problems of justifying logic.

The first difficulty that I will discuss attacks the very possibility that we might revise logic for empirical reasons. To see what the problem is, let's focus on quantum logic. In the quantum logic case, Putnam argued that the evidence of the two hole experiments, among others, should cause us to revise our logic. But how do we go about gathering and assessing evidence? Here's one extremely simplistic answer: we make a bunch of observations, and then generalize from those observations. So, for example, after observing ravens all over the world in many different seasons and finding them all to be black, I might conclude that all ravens are black. This kind of argument is what is called an *inductive generalization*.[2] Arguments like this are common and important, but they will only get one so far. In particular, inductive generalizations are not going to yield highly abstract physical theories like quantum mechanics. It's not as though the model of the atom came about in virtue of our observing atoms. So, a more complex and realistic answer to the question of how we go about gathering and assessing evidence is something like the following. Scientists come up with a theory about what atoms might be like, and determine what observable consequences would follow if their theory about atoms is true. They then construct an experiment to see whether or not the predicted consequence occurs, and if it does, they consider their theory tentatively confirmed and if not, they consider their theory tentatively disconfirmed.[3]

The problem with revising logic for empirical reasons, then, is that this whole process itself makes healthy use of logical rules and principles. For example, some logical rules are essential to the whole

---

[2] The form of inductive generalizations is:

n% of observed A's are B's.

So, it is likely that n% of all A's are B's.

[3] I say tentatively because it involves a lot more complexity than I have indicated. In particular, any predicted observable consequence only comes about given many background assumptions. Sometimes, if an observable consequence doesn't occur, it is because one of the background assumptions is incorrect, not because the theory in question is incorrect.

structure of confirmation and disconfirmation (*if* the predicted consequence occurs, *then* the theory is tentatively confirmed). In addition, figuring out the consequences of our theories will surely involve at least some logic as well. Really this should come as no surprise. Evaluation of any sort generally involves some kind of logic. If it didn't, then it would seem to be purely random and unstructured. Given the indispensable role of logical rules and principles in scientific evidence gathering and assessing, it is hard to see how one could gather and assess evidence against the logical rules and principles in question. How can one assess evidence against a rule of logic when the rule of logic plays an essential role in the evidence assessing itself?

Such considerations cast serious doubt on the possibility of revising logic for empirical reasons, and so they lend credence to the claim that logic must not be revisable for empirical reasons. Of course, many philosophers will still want to claim that logic might be revisable for more conceptual reasons. With the exception of the quantum logic discussion, all of the motivations for non-classical logics that we've looked at could arguably be classified as conceptual arguments against classical logic. For example, intuitionist arguments concern issues about meaning and realism, and these clearly involve abstract theoretical considerations as opposed to empirical and evidential considerations. Likewise, relevance logicians urge us to reconsider the material conditional because they claim that it grossly misrepresents the conceptual role that a conditional ought to and/or does have.

But revising logic for conceptual reasons seems no more possible than revising it for empirical ones. Suppose that I currently believe that some logic, call it L, is the correct one to use. Could I ever come to believe for conceptual reasons that a different logic, call it L$\star$, might be better? On the face of it, it seems not. After all, if my reasons for thinking that L$\star$ is better are founded on arguments, then I seem to be in a bind similar to the one that surrounded the justification of logic. My reasons could be based on the rules of inference of L or on the rules of inference L$\star$. If the former, then it seems that I think that the inferences of L do provide good reasons, and so the question arises as to why I think I ought to use L$\star$. Put slightly differently, if an inference in L has a conclusion which says to use a different logic, L$\star$, then this seems a little self-defeating. But if my decision to revise is based on some rule of inference in L$\star$, then it is not clear that this should really count as a reason to revise. After all, we're supposing that I currently believe that some logic L is the right one to use. If my reason for thinking L★ is a better logic comes from L★ and not L, then by my current allegiances to L, my reasoning shouldn't be legitimate. So, it seems that a problem arises no matter what logic my decision to revise is based on.

Now we really seem to be in trouble, however. If we cannot revise logic for either empirical or conceptual reasons, then it would seem that the logic that we use is the logic that we're stuck with. Furthermore, in light of the problems of justifying logic it would seem that whatever logic we use (and get stuck with) cannot be preferred for any particular reasons, other than that we actually use it. All of these considerations make it seem like the logic we use is a matter of chance rather than a matter of reasoned deliberation. Can this really be right?

## IV—A MORE POSITIVE NOTE

Let me try to end this chapter on a more positive note by saying why I think the answer to that question is no, in spite of the epistemological difficulties with justifying and revising logic that we've encountered. In the first place, there is the fact that we actually have revised the logic that we think we ought to use. As I noted in Chapter 1, for many centuries, Aristotelian logic reigned supreme, and it was replaced by classical logic only fairly recently.[4] And make no mistake about it, though there certainly is a lot of overlap and agreement between Aristotelian logic and classical logic, some syllogisms that were valid in Aristotelian logic are not classically valid.[5] Classical logic was deemed better than Aristotelian logic for many reasons. For example, it is a stronger logic, and it provides a systematic treatment of logical notions that Aristotelian logic either couldn't account for or

---

[4] Of course, we have seen a lot of reasons to think that the classical logic isn't the right replacement, but it is undeniable that for many philosophers of the last century, classical logic was regarded as the proper tool for philosophical and other reasoning.

[5] For example, the syllogism

All M are P
All M are S
So, some S are P.

is valid in Aristotelian logic but (on the canonical understanding of how to best translate these categorical sentences into the notation of classical logic which I used in Chapter 1) classically invalid.

CHAPTER 13

accounted for in myriad different ways. In other words, the switch from Aristotelian logic to classical logic seems to be both a reasonable and a thoughtful one.

Secondly, there are ways of making philosophical sense of the revision that I've just described. I'll discuss two of these ways. The first has generally been advocated by philosophers who believe that logic is a priori and knowable through reason alone. According to these philosophers, reason, in some broad sense, tells us that classical logic is preferable to Aristotelian logic, because classical logic is stronger and more systematic, and these qualities can be both valued and known by pure reason. Of course, these philosophers have to acknowledge the limits on justification that we have canvassed (i.e., that this justification probably wouldn't be convincing to advocates of non-classical logics). And they also must be prepared to admit, in light of the problems with revising logic, that the revision from Aristotelian to classical logic was, in some sense, like a gestalt switch, not done using the principles of either logic, but just seen (by the light of reason) to be better.

The general picture here is similar to the view about the nature of geometry that I briefly discussed in Chapter 10, according to which one must distinguish pure from applied geometry. Pure geometry (as given by the axioms of each geometrical system) is a priori and knowable using reason alone, while applied geometry is a posteriori and so, consequently, must make use of empirical evidence. According to these philosophers, geometry is and always has been a priori, even if the question of what kind of space we live in is empirical.

Likewise, in logic we can distinguish pure from applied logic. According to this theory of how we go about justifying and revising logic, each pure logic is an account of a possible way that people could reason. In addition, the account of logical consequence defined for each pure logic is knowable a priori through an act of reason alone. Applied logic, on the other hand, concerns the question of which logic we ought, actually, to use. Unlike the question of what kind of space we live in, however, discovering what kind of logic we ought to use is not something that requires empirical evidence. On this view, there are many conceptual and purely philosophical issues that go into deciding which logic is correct, and so even applied logic should be regarded as essentially a priori.

The downside to a view like this is its fundamental mysteriousness. What is this light of reason and how does it work? How can we be sure that it is trustworthy, especially given the dismal history of ideas which seemed true by the light of reason but which later came to be regarded as false? Worse still, why should we trust a faculty (pure reason) that seems to yield such different answers to different people?

Defenders of the rationalist picture claim that, mysterious or not, we clearly do have these kind of insights, and to deny them simply in virtue of their mysteriousness would be as silly as denying that we have consciousness simply because the nature of consciousness is rather mysterious as well. In addition, though many rationalists in history have thought that rational insight was infallible, there is no reason for contemporary rationalists to do so. They rightfully argue that just because some mode of attaining knowledge can sometimes be wrong doesn't mean we should never rely on it. After all, sometimes our visual systems lead to judgments that are later found to be wrong, but that doesn't mean that we should eschew vision as a legitimate mode of coming to know the world.

The other way of making philosophical sense of the justification and revision of logic is generally advocated by those who think logic is not a priori, and so not determinable using reason alone. On this view, deciding which logic is correct is best achieved through a process known as *reflective equilibrium*. This phrase is most famously associated with the political philosopher John Rawls, who uses it to describe the process for determining what the principles of justice ought to be. The idea behind reflective equilibrium is quite simple. We begin with our intuitions about what is just (e.g., that punishing someone who hasn't done anything wrong is not just), and we try to formulate a theory that captures all our intuitions. We then see what consequences flow from the theory that we've constructed. Frequently, the more abstract theory will have consequences that we didn't anticipate, and which go against our intuitions about justice. In this case, we can either decide that the intuitions were wrong or we can adjust the theory. This process goes on until we have arrived at a state of reflective equilibrium, which is state that we are in when our theory and our intuitions become completely aligned. Every intuition is accounted for by theory, and no theoretical consequences go against our intuitions. In this way, our intuitions and our theories kind of grow and develop together into one harmonious whole.

The philosopher Nelson Goodman was the first to argue that the process with logic is similar. We begin with our logical intuitions regarding things like which arguments seem right, what sets of sentences seem inconsistent, and the like, and then we try to construct a theory which captures those intuitions. The theory that we construct will usually have some fairly unintuitive consequences that we didn't anticipate, like the paradoxes of material implication, and so we must decide whether our intuitions or our theory is wrong. The process goes on until we reach a state of reflective equilibrium, whereby our intuitions about good inference are fully captured by our logical theory and our theory no longer has any counter-intuitive consequences.

The reflective equilibrium approach avoids the problems with revising and justifying logic by incorporating many non-logical considerations in the process. That is, what would make a logic justified is the fact that it accords well with our overall theories about the world, and what would make a logic ripe for revision is that it didn't. Of course, making clear just what it means to 'accord well' is no small task, but at the very least, some loose sense of fit which goes beyond the merely logical will be important. Advocates of this view need to say a lot more about how we judge fit and overall equilibrium, and though clarifying these notions will certainly not be easy, there is no reason to think that they couldn't be explained well enough to make the view plausible.

The downside of the reflective equilibrium approach to justifying and revising logic is that if we begin with intuitions that are wildly off base, our final, reflectively equilibrated logic will be similarly wildly off base. For example, someone who begins with the intuition that the rules for tonk are good will not arrive at a final judgment on logic that is much better. In addition, many philosophers are greatly bothered by the unsystematic nature of this approach. When there is a clash between intuitions and theories, different philosophers can justifiably go different ways (one might lose the intuition, another might change the theory), and this is perfectly acceptable.

In response to these difficulties, advocates of the reflective equilibrium approach reply that a survey of the history of philosophy reveals a long line of theories and beliefs which were claimed, at the time, to be knowable using pure reason alone, but which were later deemed fairly loony. In practice, therefore, the other approach to justifying logic may not fare much better. As to the unsystematic nature of this approach, one possible response is that sometimes people can reasonably disagree. For example, reasonable people might well take very different paths in light of the paradoxes of material implication. Classical logic has many advantages over its non-classical rivals, and so biting the bullet and explaining the paradoxes away à la Grice is not crazy. Then again, it is also far from crazy to think that these paradoxes are just too counter-intuitive to be maintained. In light of the tremendous difficulty of coming up with definitive arguments in favor of either response, maybe we really should think that people can reasonably disagree about which logic we ought to use.

The important point about both of the methods for justifying and revising logic is that they get around the problems of justifying and revising logic by making these matters depend, in essence, on something other than logic. The first approach posits that we can see by the light of reason, broadly conceived, that some logic is better than another. And the reflective equilibrium approach depends on a loosely defined notion of fit that tends to include such considerations as overall coherence, explanatory strength and simplicity. In other words, given the problems with using logic to either justify or revise logic, philosophers have turned to non-logical means to do both.

This is important because it raises an extremely interesting possibility. Maybe logic isn't the fundamental and foundational basis of thought that we have been taking it to be. Clearly logic is fundamental to reasoning in some sense, but there's more to what we should believe and how we should come to believe it than can be found in logic, alone. In the final chapter of this book, we will consider just this possibility.

# 14

# Rationality and Logic

## I—THE WASON SELECTION TASK (AGAIN)

Ancient Greek philosophers like Plato and Aristotle thought that rationality distinguished humans from other animals. But what is rationality? At the very least, we are rational when we make decisions as to what we are going to believe or how we are going to act based on good reasons. It seems obvious that such behavior will certainly include thinking and acting according to the rules of logic. So it is no surprise that many philosophers have argued that at least a part of our rationality consists in our logicality. In spite of this intuitive connectedness, however, there are questions about how much one can be defined in terms of the other, and what their overall relationship really is.

At the outset of the book, I gave the following version of the Wason selection task. I asked the reader to imagine four cards from a set of cards, each with a number on one side and a letter on the other, laid out on a table as follows:

I then posed the question, which cards are relevant to the truth or falsity of the rule "If there is a vowel on one side, there is an even number on the other."? As I noted at the time, 80–90% of test subjects do very poorly on this version of the selection task, meaning they don't pick out just the E and the 7.

There are many conclusions that one could draw from this poor performance. At the very least, tests like these seem to show that people have a less than stellar understanding of the conditional. Given what we've seen about the difficulty of giving a correct account of the conditional, this really should come as no surprise. But some philosophers and psychologists have argued that these results suggest a stronger conclusion, namely that people can't reason well, or even that they are systematically irrational in many respects. These latter, stronger conclusions, however, have not gone unchallenged, and both the tests and how the results get interpreted have been contested on several counts.

To begin, let's first clarify the overall structure of the test. The test involves a conditional rule, if p then q, and a series of 4 cards in the following order:

We are asked which of the cards are necessary to turn over to show that the rule is or isn't true. We now know that the only time a conditional can be false is if the antecedent is true and the consequent is false (p and not-q, respectively), and this is why those are the only cases we logically need to check. The others just aren't relevant to the truth of the conditional.

One kind of challenge to the stronger conclusions that people can't reason or are highly irrational is aimed at the experimental set-up. For example, some psychologists have argued that the poor performance of test-subjects can be explained by the subject matter of the test itself (i.e., the numbers and letters on the cards). The gist of this challenge is simple. Even if the selection task shows that people are not very logical when confronted with rules that have no real connection to their daily lives or decisions, the test shows nothing about people's reasoning abilities when it comes to thinking about things that they are familiar with, or that matter in some practical way to them. Since very few people really need to think about cards with letters on one side and numbers on the other, subjects' poor performance on the number/letter cards needn't be an indication of much of anything at all regarding peoples' overall reasoning abilities.

This challenge has been empirically supported by variants on the original selection task. For example, consider the following cards and the rule, "If you borrow my car, you must fill up the gas tank."

Notice that this test has exactly the same form as the original one. The rule is a conditional, if p then q, and the four choices on the cards are p, not-p, q, and not q. The only difference is that the subject matter is something that people understand in a concrete and practical way. It turns out that subjects perform much better on experiments like these, a fact which some take to support this criticism of the original selection task. Though subjects do poorly when they have to engage in abstract logical reasoning, they do much better at being logical when they are thinking about things that they might have deal with on an everyday basis.

Against these critics of the original Wason selection task, defenders of the conclusion that people are poor reasoners or less than fully rational acknowledge that content does seem to affect people's reasoning abilities, but still claim that, for all that, people reason poorly. According to this defense, people should be able to reason abstractly, because good reasoning necessarily involves an ability to abstract from the concrete.[1] As I noted at the outset of this chapter, philosophers have long thought that rationality is what makes us distinctly human, but arguably non-human animals can seem to reason about content specific domains. The cat thinks to itself, as it were, "If I hide behind this tall bush, the mouse won't see me," but it knows nothing at all about conditionals or logic. What separates us from the cat is that we can extrapolate from particular situations and apply what we've learned to new ones. Thus, even if it's true that people do better at reasoning when they are thinking about familiar subject matters, the less able people are to formulate the abstract and general principles that underlie their reasoning, the less rational they are as well.

---

[1] By analogy, people rarely encounter a need to count and add things that number in the millions. But no one would say that a person is perfectly good at addition because he can add smaller numbers (i.e., numbers that he might encounter in his daily life), but not large ones.

Another, deeper challenge to those who take a dim view of human rationality in light of these tests attacks the very idea that people are or could be systematically irrational. According to a number of evolutionary psychologists, we simply can't reason in ways that are systematically irrational because if our patterns of reasoning were really so bad we would not have evolved to reason the way we do. After all, inference strategies must have been subject to selection pressures every bit as much as body type and coloring are. Since it just doesn't make evolutionary sense for us to have evolved into creatures with seriously maladaptive body types and coloring, the idea that we could be creatures who have evolved multiple systematically irrational strategies shouldn't make sense either. Given this, the argument goes, it is just not possible that we are systematically prone to reason poorly. Our ancestors evolved reasoning strategies that must have been by and large successful, or else these ancestors wouldn't have had breeding success and been able to pass on their genes.

In fact, some researchers have even argued that slavishly following the rules of logic would sometimes be irrational. To see why, think about what kinds of reasoning might have been helpful to our early ancestors. One very important aspect of human life is the fact that we live together in groups. Like ants and bees, we are social creatures that flourish when we live together and are less successful when we are isolated. This has made us very sensitive to fairness in group situations. For example, it would have been evolutionarily very important to us to be sensitive to cheaters and free loaders, i.e., people who enjoy the benefits of others' labors with out doing any work themselves.

With this in mind, consider a third social contract variant of the selection task. In this one, the rule in question is: "If you have paid the cost, then you may enjoy the benefit." Each card has a statement about whether someone paid the cost on one side, and a statement about whether or not that same someone enjoyed the benefits on the other. The cards on the table look like this:

| This is some-one who has paid the cost. | This is some-one who has not paid the costs. | This is some-one who is enjoying the benefits. | This is some-one who is not enjoying the benefits. |
| --- | --- | --- | --- |

As with the original selection task, logic tells us that we should only pick the first and the last cards (the ones that represent p and not-q, respectively). The reasoning here is exactly as in the Introduction.

The second card (not-p) is not logically relevant, since even if the other side says that this person is enjoying the benefits, the rule in this case says nothing about people who don't pay the costs. It only says that if a person has paid the cost, then they should enjoy the benefits. Likewise for the third card (q). The rule only says what should be the case if someone has paid the costs, not if someone is enjoying the benefits. So no matter what the other side says, the third card is not logically relevant. Whether it says that this person has paid the cost or not, the rule in question will be neither confirmed nor disconfirmed.

In fact, in this version of the test, the second and third cards are the ones that subjects mostly pick. But according to the evolutionary psychologists who challenged the conclusions of the original Wason selection task, subjects are right to pick the second and the third cards, and would be wrong to follow logic and pick the first and the fourth cards, because people have evolved to detect cheaters. If what we are concerned to establish is that only those who pay costs get benefits, then the first and the last cards wouldn't be relevant to us at all. The person represented in the first card, after all, has paid, and so whether or not she gets benefits, the group would not be cheated either way. And the person represented in the last card is not enjoying benefits, so whether this person has paid a cost or not, there is no issue of the social unit being cheated by him either. But the people represented in the second and the third cards are potential cheaters. The second is a person that hasn't paid the cost, and so we want to make sure that she isn't enjoying benefits, and the third is a person who is enjoying benefits, and we want to make sure that he has paid the costs.

In response to the criticisms of the evolutionary psychologists, some have likened our propensity to give the wrong answers on tests like the Wason selection task to optical illusions. Consider this familiar optical illusion:

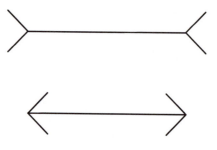

People see the bottom line as shorter than the top line, even after they have measured the lines and determined that the lines are the same length. Knowing that the lines are the same length doesn't stop us from seeing the bottom line as shorter.

According to this response to the evolutionary psychology critics, people are subject to "cognitive illusions" every bit as much as they are subject to optical illusions. The idea is that people tend to reason in certain illogical ways and even persist in that reasoning after they know the right answer. In both kinds of illusions, we are so gripped by the illusion that we still see it even when we know that it is not true. We can know that we shouldn't flip the card with the 4 on it, but it's hard not to want to do it, because it seems like the right thing to do. But just as no one would take our inability to see the above lines as equal in length as proof that they are equal in length, so too no one should take our propensity to want to flip that 4 card as evidence that we ought to flip the 4 card. In other words, just because people are prone to reason a particular way doesn't mean that that way of reasoning is correct.

The literature on what these tests show vis-a-vis our reasoning abilities is voluminous, and there is much more that could be said. While it is safe to conclude that people are giving logically incorrect answers (at least when the subject matter is more abstract), the real question is whether or not this means that people are not rational. Psychologists and philosophers disagree, and the tests themselves are inconclusive on that question. As interesting as these tests are, describing how people do reason leaves open how they should reason.

## II—THE IRRELEVANCE OF LOGIC

Let us, therefore, take a different approach to figuring out the relationship between logic and reasoning, and consider how central logic really is to our ability to reason. We'll start with a very radical claim concerning the relationship between logic and reasoning from the philosopher Gilbert Harman, namely that logic is not especially relevant to reasoning at all. According to Harman, we must distinguish between the mathematical logic that we have explored in this book and what he calls "reasoned change in view." The latter involves the acquiring of new beliefs and giving up of old beliefs which all of us engage in everyday. Harman argues that though certain logic-like principles may play a role in this change in view, the kind of logic that we have examined in this book really has nothing (or very little) to do with our everyday reasoning.

Harman begins with an ordinary story about someone named Mary and her search for breakfast. Mary wants to have Cheerios for breakfast, so she goes to the cupboard to get them. When she gets there, she doesn't find any Cheerios. So, she concludes that her roommate Elizabeth must have eaten them the day before, and settles for Rice Krispies instead.

As Harman points out, Mary goes to the cupboard with something like the following belief: If I look in the cupboard I will see a box of Cheerios. Upon looking in the cupboard, however, she doesn't see a box of Cheerios. So, Mary has a certain belief about the world that is frustrated (in the sense that the world is not as she expected it to be). How should she change her view?

Before she revises her belief set, Mary has the following beliefs:

1. If I look in the cupboard then I will see a box of Cheerios.

2. I am looking in the cupboard.

3. I don't see a box of Cheerios.

If her change in beliefs is determined purely by logic (and let us focus on classical logic for the purposes of this example), then by modus tollens and modus ponens she should also believe, respectively:

4. I am not looking in the cupboard.

5. I see a box of Cheerios.

Clearly, her three beliefs and those beliefs immediately entailed by her three beliefs are inconsistent. As we saw, in classical logic, anything follows from a contradiction. So classically, Mary should infer any belief whatsoever. Of course, even if she came to form either of the inconsistent beliefs (4) and (5) she would never think that she was entitled to believe anything whatsoever, and so classical logic seems to get it wrong.

In all fairness, no advocate of the role of classical logic in reasoning would claim that she should either form the contradictory beliefs or believe anything once she did so. People, Mary included, are not deductive machines. We use many different kinds of reasoning in contexts like this, and very few contexts are such that purely deductive reasoning is appropriate. According to a more realistic account of what's going on, Mary should evaluate her first three beliefs and consider which one is most likely to be false. In this case, beliefs (2) or (3) are, presumably, highly likely. Anyone who has taken an epistemology class will know that one can run skeptical arguments against them. Perhaps Mary is in a dream, or is a denizen of the Matrix, but none of these is really all that likely. The most likely belief to be false is belief (1), and since this belief is based on her assumption that there are still Cheerios left in the house, when she abandons (1), she also needs to abandon that assumption and have a plausible reason for doing so. It might be that aliens came down and ate all the Cheerios, or that the box spontaneously combusted, or that some kind of miracle of the Cheerios has occurred, but since the most likely explanation is that Elizabeth ate the rest of the Cheerios, Mary adds that to her other beliefs.

In Harman's story, of course, she just immediately drops her conditional belief that if she looks in the cupboard she will see a box of Cheerios, and she comes to acquire the new belief that she and Elizabeth are out of Cheerios. Because of this new belief, she simultaneously forms the entirely new practical intention to have Rice Krispies instead of Cheerios. But how does she go from her original intention and old beliefs to the new intention and accompanying new beliefs? The underlying assumption of this book has been that logic is normative, and that logical rules are supposed to help guide us in forming beliefs and intentions. Even if deductive logic can not be solely responsible for Mary's belief in this situation, it is supposed to add something. A defender of the role of logic in reasoning will say that deductive principles are playing some kind of implicit role in Mary's thinking. According to Harman, however, Mary's new beliefs and new intentions have very little to do with logic. In fact, put a little more strongly, Harman argues that what Mary does is influenced "in no significant way" by logic.

Why does Harman deny that logic has any significant role to play in reasoning? His argument has two essential parts. First, Harman argues that if logical principles were in any way to influence reasoned change in view like Mary's, it would presumably do so by something like the following principles:

"Logical Implication Principle: The fact that one's view logically implies P can be a reason to accept P."

"Logical Inconsistency Principle: Logical inconsistency is to be avoided."[2]

According to Harman, however, neither of these principles demonstrates that logic has a special role to play in reasoning. The essence of

---

[2] *Change in View*, Harman, Gilbert (1989) p. 11, Cambridge Mass., London: MIT Press

his criticism is that both are only default rules that hold other things being equal. For example, we have already seen that the Logical Implication Principle is faulty in Mary's case. The fact that Mary has beliefs (1) and (2) above don't really give her any reason at all to believe (5), nor do her beliefs (1) and (3) give her a reason to believe (4).

The Logical Inconsistency Principle fails by the same basic reasoning. It is, according to Harman, a default rule at best. Harman acknowledges that by and large we do try to avoid inconsistencies in our beliefs. However, he argues that sometimes we have neither the time nor the ability to really figure out the root of the inconsistencies that we believe. In these cases, Harman argues that the most rational thing for us to do is to acknowledge the inconsistency in our beliefs and try to avoid conclusions that exploit the inconsistency too much.

For example, we have already had several occasions in this book to consider the liar sentence, which indicates a clear inconsistency in our ordinary notion of truth. As I noted in Chapter 9, many of the proposed solutions to the liar paradox come with significant problems of their own. Given the usefulness of attributions of truth in ordinary language, and the difficulty of deciding what the best solution to the liar paradox is, it is neither unreasonable not irrational for a person to note the possibility of difficulties and just avoid predicating truth to itself. After all, should we really devote large portions of our lives to getting straight about truth before we feel comfortable using the term? Of course, some philosophers and logicians do just that, but should the rest of us wait until it has all been worked out before we use truth in ordinary contexts? That seems absolutely crazy. For most of us, our ordinary understanding of truth is good enough, and it's a good thing too, since truth, arguably, does important work for us in every day life. When my son comes home from school with some new, crazy bit of school-yard wisdom, it is very useful for me (aware as I am of the problems with the truth predicate) to be able to tell him that what he heard is emphatically not true.

The second part of Harman's argument is supposed to be the nail in the coffin for the role of logic in reasoning. According to Harman, ordinary people don't have any particular understanding of logical implication or logical inconsistency, and so these notions can't have any special role to play in reasoning. Though people certainly have some conception that certain beliefs follow from their other beliefs, Harman argues that this conception is not particularly logical. Certain kinds of immediate inferences may well be logical ones. For example, most people are immediately inclined to infer q from their beliefs p and if p then q. But many of the immediate inferences that people are inclined to make are not logical at all. Returning to the sweater argument again from Chapter 4, most people would be inclined to immediately accept that the belief "This sweater is not red" follows from the belief that "This sweater is green." Or, to use some of Harman's own examples, most people are inclined to think that "Today is Tuesday" implies that "Tomorrow is Wednesday", that "X is Y's brother" implies that "X is a male", and that "X plays defensive tackle for the Philadelphia Eagles" implies that "X weighs more than 150 pounds."[3] Harman argues that examples like these show that people have an inclination to immediately infer certain beliefs from other of their beliefs whether the inferences in question are logical or not. Furthermore, our inclination to make all of these kinds of immediate inferences is very important when it comes to reasoned change in view. For example, we are correct to infer that tomorrow is Wednesday from the fact that today is Tuesday. Thus, since there are many logical inferences that people are not immediately inclined to make (like *ex contradictione quod libetum*), and since people are immediately inclined to infer many good beliefs which are not simply logical consequences of the beliefs that they already accept (as in the examples we canvassed above), Harman doesn't think logic is playing any special role in reasoning.

Not surprisingly, Harman has his share of critics. With respect to the first part of his argument, that logical principles are default rules at best, some have tried to offer plausible rules that side-step Harman's criticism. But I think that there is a more general reason to be suspicious of his claim. Let me explain.

Default rules are rules that hold only other things being equal, and they are ubiquitous. For example, one default rule concerning the testimony of other people is that, in general, you should believe what others tell you. Many cynically balk at this claim, but if you think about it, you'll realize that the vast majority of the time, you are inclined to trust what people tell you. If you ask a stranger on the street what is the best way to get somewhere, in general you believe them. If someone tells you their name is Paul, you don't generally greet this pronouncement with a healthy dose of skepticism. These are banal examples, but that is precisely the point. In most of our ordinary interactions with others, we are inclined to believe what others tell us.

---

[3] *Change in View*, Harman, Gilbert (1989) p. 17, Cambridge Mass., London: MIT Press

Of course, there are contexts and situations where this default rule gets over-ridden. Politicians' promises should be taken with a grain of salt, used car salesmen are notoriously willing to stretch the truth, and if a cheating spouse has lied to you a lot in the past about her whereabouts when she is home late, that is a good reason to suspend trust the next time she doesn't show up for dinner. But that's just what makes it a default rule. It holds by and large, but under certain circumstances, it can and should be over-ridden.

Now, Harman's argument with respect to the Logical Closure Principle and the Logical Inconsistency Principle is, essentially, as follows: because the logical principles that he examines only hold other things being equal, these principles are not especially relevant to reasoning. The comparable argument in the case of testimony would be this: because the rule that you should believe others only holds other things being equal, testimony is not especially relevant to how we gain knowledge about the world.[4] Is the conclusion about testimony warranted?

It seems to me that it is not. Testimony is highly relevant to knowledge gathering, and a huge amount of things that we think we know about the world are things that we believe because someone else has told them to us. I know where my husband was born, that it rained yesterday in New York City, and that some friends of mine had a quiet New Year's Eve, all because someone (in each case a different person) told me so. By analogy, therefore, the fact that logical implication and inconsistency are only default guides to belief formation doesn't mean that they are not especially relevant to reasoning. Harman's conclusion just doesn't seem to follow.

Against the second part of Harman's argument, that people don't really distinguish logical from non-logical implications, a main complaint focuses on Harman's blurring of the descriptive and the normative. Harman focuses very much on what an individual person such as Mary takes herself to have reasons to believe. But commentators have argued that this focus has a cost. What about what she ought to believe, whether she thinks she should believe it or not? It is not clear that Harman has left room for this kind of perspective on Mary's beliefs. To be fair, part of the main overall point in Harman's book is that the distinction between the descriptive and the normative is not as easily drawn as many philosophers pretend it

---

[4] In epistemology, testimony generally comes up in discussions concerning our sources of knowledge, which is why I think that would be a comparable conclusion.

to be. Nevertheless, Harman does take himself to be engaged in a project that is both descriptive and normative. Even if he is right that the distinction between the two is often over simplified, many commentators feel he errs too much on the side of the descriptive.

Another important issue to raise is that Harman just assumes that classical logic is the correct account of logical consequence, and, as we have seen, this is something that is far from clear. Though no one would argue that Mary should infer "I am the Yeti" if she forms the inconsistent beliefs above, the question of whether she ought to is still an important one to answer. What's right about the classical account of logical consequence is that if someone believes a set of inconsistent sentences, that person has an extremely faulty set of beliefs. So faulty, in fact, that they might as well believe anything at all. As we have seen, many think this is a bit of an over reaction to the problem, but the question of what to do with inconsistent beliefs is far from obvious. In just assuming that classical logic is the correct account of reasoning if any logic is, Harman has assumed that at least some of the difficulties that he raises could not be addressed by giving a better account of logical consequence. Thus, advocates of non-classical logics might rightly charge Harman with throwing the baby out with the bathwater.

Indeed, if Harman is right that logic has little to do with reasoning, then it's hard to see how many of the arguments for non-classical logics that we've discussed could ever even get off the ground. For example, non-classical accounts of the conditional depend for their persuasiveness on the fact that classical logical consequence just seems to get things wrong in terms of ordinary reasoning. But if logic has nothing to do with reasoning, then ordinary reasoning should have nothing to do with which logic is correct, either.

One thing is certain. Harman raises extremely challenging and provocative questions that philosophers ought to deal with. To the extent that we are concerned with more than logical systems and their formal attributes, we need to be a lot clearer than we are about logic's role in actual reasoning.

## III—BEYOND LOGIC

Though I think that Harman's conclusions are a bit strong, this doesn't mean that I think that logic is all or even most of what takes place in good reasoning. After seeming to show that logic could be neither justified nor revised, I ended the last chapter on what I hoped was a more positive note by outlining two different approaches to the critical evaluation of logic. According to one of these, we just do seem to have the ability to assess logical principles by the light of reason. Even if we are sometimes prone to errors when being guided by this light of reason, it is still a reliable source for the justification of our beliefs, and it can still be used to correct errors when they happen. According to the reflective equilibrium approach, we consider how our logic fits in with our overall world views, and then we correct our logic and/or our world views in a process whose ultimate aim is to get the two in accord. Both of these approaches to the critical assessment of logic have their strengths and weaknesses, but each makes clear that we can and do assess our logical intuitions.

But recall that in both cases, to evaluate logic we must use something other than logic itself. In the first, we use some intuitive ability to "see" into the rational nature of things, and in the second, we go by some as yet loosely defined notion of overall fit and balance. When we critically assess logic, therefore, we are doing something that goes beyond logic. However this happens, one thing is clear. Being rational is not a matter of simply being logical, and so there is something to rationality over and above the rules of logic.

Really, this should come as no surprise. If the arguments of the last chapter were correct (and its hard to see why they aren't), then it is clear that logic itself can't do the job. Remember, though I argued that logic was justified a priori, the sense of justification there was practical, not logical, since a rule of logic cannot non-circularly justify itself. If we insisted that rationality consisted in thinking logically, we would have to say that logic itself was irrational (because it is not logically justifiable), and that is just too counter-intuitive.

It is important to note, by the way, that this conclusion holds for all the many formal and informal aspects of reasoning, not just for deductive logic. As I mentioned in the introduction, this book is focused on one aspect of logic, but there are others. There is inductive logic, which is the logic that takes us from premises to conclusions that are likely, but not certain, and there is decision theory, which is the formal study of how people should make their decisions given the information they have (decision theory is used in all kinds of practical contexts, like economics). Both of these branches of logic have achieved a level of sophistication and formalization very close to if not as good as that of deductive logics. But there is also a study of what is called *informal logic*. This is the study of reasoning fallacies that cannot be explored formally.[5] All of these different branches of the study of how people should think or act are subject to the arguments of the last chapter, because those arguments apply totally generally to any kind of evaluative tool. In assessing the goodness or badness of any rule of evaluation, be that rule formally or informally defined, a general strategy or something more concrete, we must appeal to some other tool of assessment. But since we can ask the same questions about the tool of assessment that we are asking about the rule of evaluation, justification will always prove elusive. And since reasoned revision, too, involves some kind of evaluative rules, the difficulties that we saw in the last chapter for the possibility of revising logic will also arise for these other branches of reasoning.

If this is right, then we face a dilemma. Either we can critically assess our reasoning methods, including the logical, but doing so requires us to appeal to cognitive abilities beyond the logical, or we can't critically assess our reasoning methods and so they cannot, themselves, be said to be logically justified. Whichever option is correct, however, we are left with the same conclusion vis-à-vis the relationship between logic and rationality. The logical may be a subset of the rational, but the two are not the same. On the first option this is so because our rational assessment of logic is not, itself, based on logic. On the second option this is so because it is rational for us to use logic, even if logic can't justify itself. Either way, therefore, logic is not all there is to rationality and reasoning.

## IV—WHY BOTHER?

So far in this chapter, I have presented various considerations to the effect that logic is not really the be all end all of reasoning. And though I have argued against Harman's very negative conclusions about logic's role in reasoning, my own thoughts on the matter are hardly a ringing endorsement of the primacy of logic. This raises a very important question. Why should we bother to study logic at all?

I can think of several good reasons.

---

[5] One example of an informal fallacy was given in Chapter 2, with the Johnson Daisy campaign commercial against Goldwater. Here the fallacy is to appeal to people's emotions (fear) rather than their reason in order to get them to make judgments.

Let's begin by returning to the history of logic. As I pointed out early on, the study of logic originated with a philosophical concern to distinguish good arguments from bad ones. This concern is still important, even if it turns out that the role of logic in our everyday reasoning is smaller than we might think. Perhaps Harman is correct that logical implication, for example, is only a default rule, but this does not mean that people don't make logical inferences. I began this book with an everyday ordinary example that involved a woman reasoning about her husband's whereabouts, and examples like these are pervasive in our daily lives. In addition, there certainly are contexts where we use logic more systematically (i.e., in puzzle solving, legal argument, or mystery solving, à la Sherlock Holmes), and even if these contexts tend to be more specialized, we *do* use logic in these contexts.

Furthermore, both in everyday use and in more specialized contexts, it makes a difference if we use logic well or poorly, and people show a sensitivity to this fact in many cases. Though some psychological tests seem to reveal a problem with our logical abilities, not all of them do. Decades of extensive testing of our logical abilities by psychologists has made clear that many good inferences come very easily to us, and we readily recognize some bad arguments, as well.[6] So even if we get our logic wrong some of the time, we don't all of the time. It seems unlikely that we would have whatever skills we do in recognizing good and bad arguments if logical rules and principles had absolutely no importance to us.

Moreover, it is not implausible to think that people can be taught to be more logical. For example, philosophy majors in college outperform their peers in the other humanities by significant margins on post-secondary education tests that require critical skills (like the LSAT's and the GRE's). This suggests that more careful attention to critical skills, either as a subject of study or through example, might actually improve our reasoning skills. Of course, it might just be that those already predisposed to like arguments and logic are drawn to doing philosophy, and to my knowledge no large scale controlled study has ever been done to show whether or not everyone could benefit from a rigorous education in good argument. But the optimist in me is hopeful. After all, everyone in college has had to make his or

---

[6] See Further Readings for Chapter 12 for references for just some of these psychological findings.

her way through high school geometry and algebra with at least passing grades, and we are certainly taught to do that. As we have seen, the skill sets involved in higher math and logic are not, in essence, all that different.

The logical systems that we've discussed in this book are highly abstract, formal systems. This has given us a remarkably clear and precise understanding of many logical concepts. But the downside of all this formalism is that it makes logic less clearly applicable to our everyday reasoning. It is formal logical systems in all their glory that are the foot in the door for criticisms of logic's role in reasoning, such as Harman's. In essence, formal logic is so grown up that it seems to have outgrown us as ordinary reasoners. And I don't mean this in a merely descriptive way, but normatively as well. I think Harman is quite correct to point out that there are classical logical consequences that we shouldn't pattern our own reasoning on, and, as we have seen, it is no easy task to get the normative for everyday reasoning in accord with any of the other logics that we have looked at either.

In spite of this, I don't think we should conclude that formal logic has no interest to those who want to study reasoning. An analogy may be helpful here. Physicists describe physical spaces in highly abstract and formal ways, and the laws of physics are written for extremely idealized circumstances. But in spite of all the idealization that goes on, we can use physics to make predictions about the behavior of ordinary objects, like billiard balls and apples. In the same way, I would suggest that we think of formal logic (both classical and non-classical) as abstract and formal idealizations of how deductive reasoning ought to proceed. In both cases, applying the abstract theory to the real world will be unproblematic in many, but not all cases.

This analogy is fruitful in yet another respect. Suppose that some physical law accounts for motion by considering two factors, X and Y, but that sometimes, some further unknown factor Z gets in the way, and so the calculations don't come out right. The hope would be that we might learn enough about Z to be able to include it in our calculations, and physicists would certainly work to discover what the correct formulation for Z was. And so too, with logic. If our reasoning seems as though it ought to diverge in some way from the recommendations of our favorite logic, the correct response is not to deny that logic is important to reasoning. Rather, it is to try to uncover what rules and principles would best account for that divergence, and then try to incorporate those in our theories. But such an endeavor requires our taking seriously the idea that logic has something to say about how we ought to reason.

To the extent that logic is at least a part of how we reason, formal logic has something to tell us about our reasoning. And to the extent that reasoning is a part of being rational, logic has something to tell us about our rationality as well. The philosopher Ludwig Wittgenstein once compared logic to scaffolding.[7] What I believe he meant by this was that logic is the basic structure that makes it possible for us to come to have a world view or know anything at all. What we have seen in this book is that there are questions about which scaffolding is really best to use, and we have explored the possibility that the scaffolding might itself require some further support. But Wittgenstein's analogy points to the fundamental reason why we should bother to study logic. Logic is an essential tool in the tricky business of organizing and understanding the world around us.

---

[7] *Tractatus Logico-Philosophicus*, Ludwig Wittgenstein, 6.124 , Translated by C. K. Ogden, first published 1922, London: Routledge and Kegan Paul.

# Further Readings

## LOGIC

### Chapter 1

A very nice, short introduction to the history of logic is in *Elementary Logic*, 2nd Edition, by Benson Mates (1972) (Oxford University Press). The canonical history of logic book is *The Development of Logic*, by William Kneale and Martha Kneale (1962) (Clarendon Press), though the reader should be warned that it is not written with the introductory student in mind. The first chapter of *The Game of the Name*, by Gregory McCulloch (1989) (Oxford University Press) is a readable and engaging introduction to Frege's insight into language as I discuss it above. Frege's views on the generality of logic, and against the theory that logic describes the laws of thought (psychologism), can be found in the Introduction to his *Foundations of Arithmetic*. *The Frege Reader*, ed. Michael Beaney (1997) (Blackwell Publishers) contains this reading, and the other Frege reading recommended in the further readings for Chapter 12.

### Chapter 2

There are a number of introductory textbooks in symbolic logic. I particularly recommend the following for their accessibility: *A Concise Introduction to Logic*, Patrick Hurley (Thomson Wadsworth); *Understanding Symbolic Logic*, Virginia Klenk, (Prentice Hall); *Introduction to Logic*, Irving Copi and Carl Cohen, (Prentice Hall).

## Chapter 3

For a nice introduction to the liar paradox, see *Paradoxes* 2$^{nd}$ Edition by Mark Sainsbury (1995) (Cambridge University Press). Tarski's solution to the liar paradox can be found in his seminal paper, "The Semantic Conception of Truth and the Foundations of Semantics," Alfred Tarski (1944) *Philosophy and Phenomenological Research*, Volume 4 (reprinted in many philosophy of language anthologies). *Truth, A Primer*, by Frederick Schmitt (1995) (Westview Press) is an introductory overview of the theories of truth canvassed in this chapter. For a slightly more advanced introduction to theories of truth, see *Theories of Truth: A Critical Introduction*, by Richard Kirkham (1992) (MIT Press). The anthology *Truth*, eds. Simon Blackburn and Keith Simmons (1999) (Oxford University Press) contains many of the seminal papers representing the views discussed here.

## PHILOSOPHY OF LOGIC

There are not many introductory readings for the chapters in this section of the book. That said, I very highly recommend *An Introduction to Non-Classical Logic*, Graham Priest (2001) (Cambridge University Press). It is a wonderfully clear technical introduction to modal logic and most of the non-classical logics that I discuss in this section. Beyond this, I supply references for each chapter to some of the more accessible and philosophical primary sources discussed in the text. Where I know of them, I also supply references for further readings that would be more engaging to the introductory student.

## Chapter 4

I have two recommendations for further readings on logical consequence. The first is Chapter 1 of *Thinking About Logic*, by Stephen Read (1995) (Oxford University Press). Read also discusses a number of the non-classical logics that I explore. Slightly more difficult than this book, Read's book would be an excellent next step for readers interested in pursuing more philosophy of logic. The other is the entry on logical consequence in the Stanford Encyclopedia of Philosophy (on-line) by J.C. Beall and Greg Restall, at *http://plato.stanford. edu/entries/logical-consequence/* The Stanford Encyclopedia has entries on a number of the logics that I discuss in this book, and it is an excellent source, but the reader should be warned that some of the entries will be harder for newcomers to follow.

## Chapter 5

The McCulloch book (recommended in further readings for Chapter 1) is an excellent introduction to the machinery of the quantifiers. The solution to the problem of non-being that I discuss can be found in "On What There is," W.V. Quine, first printed (1948) *Review of Metaphysics* (reprinted in *From a Logical Point of View*, 2nd Edition, by W. V. Quine (1980) (Harvard University Press)). Russell's parsing of definite descriptions can be found in *Introduction to Mathematical Logic*, Bertrand Russell (1919) (George Allen and Unwin Ltd.) (reprinted in (1993) (Dover Publications) and in many philosophy of language anthologies).

## Chapter 6

The Priest introduction to non-classical logic mentioned at the outset of the further readings for the Philosophy of Logic section is a good place to learn more about the technical aspects of modal logics, and will make clear why the various theorems discussed in section 2 of this chapter vary according to the accessibility relations on possible worlds. *On the Plurality of Worlds*, David Lewis (1987) (Oxford University Press) gives the most well known account of modal realism. *The Possible and the Actual*, ed. M. Loux (1979) (Cornell University Press) contains essays representing both sorts of actualism discussed in the text, plus another essay by Lewis on modal realism. One famous paper critical of modal logics is "Three Grades of Modal Involvement," by W. V. Quine, in *Ways of Paradox* (1976) (Harvard University Press). John MacFarlane has a very nice and fairly accessible discussion of the difficulty of distinguishing the logical from the non-logical in the Stanford Encyclopedia of Philosophy (on-line), at *http://plato.stanford.edu/entries/logical-constants/*

## Chapter 7

For a comprehensive discussion of many-valued logics and their motivations, see *Many – valued Logics,* by Nicholas Rescher (1969) (McGraw-Hill). *Deviant Logic, Fuzzy Logic*, Susan Haack (1996) (University of Chicago Press), has a good discussion of future contingents and Aristotle's argument in particular. Haack discusses many of the non-classical logics that I have explored in the text, and is another excellent introduction to the philosophy of logic at a more advanced level than this book. The Sainesbury book, *Paradoxes* (see further readings for Chapter 3) also has a chapter on the sorites paradox and its possible solutions. For a very thorough discussion of the problem of vagueness and proposed solutions, see *Vagueness*, by Timothy Williamson (1996) (Routledge).

## Chapter 8

The Gricean defense of the material conditional comes from "Logic and Conversation," in *Syntax and Semantics*, Vol. 3, eds. Peter Cole and Jerry Morgan (1975) (Academic Press) (reprinted in *Conditionals*, ed. Frank Jackson (1991) (Oxford University Press)). For a defense of classical logic along similar lines see *Conditionals*, Frank Jackson (1987) (Basil Blackwell). Essays on conditionals, generally, and the various versions of possible world conditional logics, in particular, can be found in the collection *If*, eds, W. Harper, R. Stalnaker, and G. Pearce (1981) (Reidel Publishers). Stephen Read's *Relevance Logic* (1988) (Blackwell Publishers) is an excellent introduction to relevance logics.

## Chapter 9

Early mathematical constructivist arguments for intuitionism most famously come from L.E.J. Brouwer and Arend Heyting. Important early papers of theirs can be found in the anthology *Philosophy of Mathematics, Selected Readings*, 2nd Edition, eds. Paul Benaceraff and Hilary Putnam (1983) (Cambridge University Press). That same volume also contains one of Dummett's most important papers on the topic, "The Philosophical Basis of Intuitionist Logic." The example about Jones and bravery came from Dummett's early paper "Truth," originally published in 1959, and reprinted in a collection of Dummett's work, *Truth and Other Enigmas* (1958) (Harvard University Press). (This collection also contains "The Philosophical Basis of Intuitionist Logic"). A very nice short introduction to dialetheism can be found in, "What's So Bad About Contradictions?" by Graham Priest, *Journal of Philosophy*, 95 (8) (1998). A fuller, more advanced study is *In Contradiction; A Study of the Transconsistent*, by Graham Priest (1987) (Martinus Nijhoff Publishers). The Lewis letter in the Chapter is taken from a recent anthology devoted to the principle of non-contradiction (reference in chapter).

## Chapter 10

In addition to the Putnam paper cited in the chapter, two other papers by Putnam on quantum mechanics and quantum logic are "A Philosopher Looks at Quantum Mechanics," (1965) in *Beyond the Edge of Certainty: Essays in Contemporary Science and Philosophy*, ed. Colodny, R.G, (reprinted in *Mathematics, Matter, and Method, Philosophical Papers, Vol. 1*, 2nd edition (1979) (Cambridge University Press)), and "How to Think Quantum Logically" (1974) *Synthese* 29. Discussions of quantum logic tend to be pretty technical (both on the logic and the science side). One exception is Arthur Fine's "Some Conceptual Problems with Quantum Mechanics" from *Paradigms and Paradoxes*, ed. Robert Colodny (1972) (University of Pittsburgh Press).

John Stachel's "Do Quanta Need a New Logic?" in *From Quarks to Quasars*, eds. R.G Colodny, and A. Coffa (1986) (University of Pittsburgh Press) is a paper that I found particularly informative and thought provoking, though the reader should be warned that it is long and very tough going in places.

## Chapter 11

The reference for Prior's paper on tonk is in the chapter. Haack has a very thorough discussion of the change of logic, change of subject argument (see further readings for Chapter 7). The original version of this argument comes from W. V. Quine. See his "Carnap and Logical Truth" reprinted in *Ways of Paradox* (see further readings for Chapter 6). Quine's fullest discussion of this argument is in Chapter 5 of his *Philosophy of Logic* (1970) (Prentice Hall).

# SOME TRADITIONAL PHILOSOPHICAL QUESTIONS RAISED BY LOGIC

## Chapter 12

For a nice survey of the many metaphysical views in logic, see "Ought There to be but One Logic?" Michael Resnik (1996) in *Logic and Reality: Essays on the Legacy of Arthur Prior*, ed. Copeland, B.J., (Clarendon Press). Frege's rationalist account of logic is hinted at in several places, most notably in the preface of his *Grundgesetze der Arithmetik, Volume 1*, in the Beaney reader (see further readings for Chapter 1—the reading recommended for Chapter 1 is also a source for Frege's rationalist views). Conventionalist views are generally associated with the logical positivist movement. *Language, Truth, and Logic*, A. J. Ayer, (1952) (Dover Publications Inc.) is an accessible introduction to logical positivism and conventionalism. The Carnapian idea that philosophers ought to "let a thousand flowers bloom" (as I put it), can be found in section 17 of Carnap's *The Logical Syntax of Language* (2002) (Open Court Press). This book also contains a full development of his conventionalist views. Two papers on logical non-cognitivism are "Against Logical Realism," Michael Resnik, (2000) in *History and Philosophy of Logic*, 20, and "Revising Logic" Michael Resnik (2004) in the Priest, Beall, and Armour-Garb anthology on non-contradiction (reference in Chapter 9). The two theories about the psychology of logic that I mention in the footnote are due primarily to Lance Rips and Phillip Johnson-Laird. Rips' theory is that people are born with innate deduction rules. Johnson-Laird argues that people construct logical rules based on what he calls mental models. Both psychologists have written extensively on their proposed views, but for an example of each and further references see *The Psychology of Proof,* Lance Rips (1993) (MIT Press:) and *Deduction* Phillip Johnson-Laird and Ruth Byrne (1991) (Lawrence Earlbaum Associates)

## Chapter 13

In addition to the Haack paper cited in the chapter, a very nice discussion of the problems with justifying logic can be found in "Knowledge of Logic," Paul Boghossian, (2000) in *New Essays on the A Priori* eds, P. Boghossian and Christopher Peacocke (Oxford University Press). The problem with revising logic for empirical reasons comes from a series of papers by Hartry Field: "The A Prioricity of Logic," (1996) *Proceedings of the Aristotelian Society* 96, "Epistemological Nonfactualism and the A Prioricity of Logic" (1998) *Philosophical Studies*, 92, and "A Priority as an Evaluative Notion," (2000) in the Boghossian and Peacocke book cited for Boghossian. (Both the Boghossian and the Field papers also contain nice discussions of some of the issues in the metaphysics of logic that I discuss in Chapter 12.) For a version of the conceptual problem with revising logic, see *Realistic Rationalism,* Jerrold J. Katz, (1998) (Cambridge, MA: MIT Press). Katz's argument is directed against a particular version of naturalism, but as I argue in the text, his arguments apply purely generally. The "light of reason" approach to revising logic has been developed by Katz, and can also be found in *In Defense of Pure Reason*, Lawrence Bonjour (1998) (Cambridge University Press). The reflective equilibrium approach was first developed by Nelson Goodman in *Fact, Fiction and Forecast* (1955) (Harvard University Press), and has been pursued by Michael Resnik in the papers recommended in further readings for Chapter 12.

## Chapter 14

*Inevitable Illusions, How Mistakes of Reason Rule Our Minds*, by Piatelli-Palmarini, Massimo, (1994) (John Wiley and Sons, Inc.) discusses the Wason selection task and its critics, as well as other psychological tests about reasoning and their implications. Piatelli-Palmarini is the advocate of the view, discussed in this chapter, that people are subject to cognitive illusions. Another good overview of the Wason selection task and its many iterations is in *Rationality and Reasoning* by J. T. Evans and D. E. Over, (1999) (Psychology Press, Publishers). An early paper representing the evolutionary psychologist reaction is by Leah Cosmides, "The Logic of Social Exchange: Has Natural Selection Shaped How Humans Reason? Studies with the Wason Selection Task", in *Cognition* (33) (1989). For a fuller presentation of the evolutionary psychologist perspective, and for one source for the figure cited in the Introduction concerning the 80–90% failure rate of subjects on the original version of the Wason selection task, see *Adaptive Thinking: Rationality in the Real World*, by Gerd Gigerenzer (2000) (Oxford University Press). In addition to *Change in View* (reference in chapter), Harman pursues similar conclusions in *Reasoning, Meaning and Mind*, Harman, Gilbert (1999) (Clarendon Press).

# Glossary

*abstract objects* objects of reason that exist independently of human thought though not in space and time.

*accessibility relation* the relation that defines accessibility between possible worlds in possible world semantics.

*Addition* (Add) a valid rule of inference with the following form:

p

So, p ∨ q (p or q)

*additive pattern* in the two hole experiment, the pattern that appears on the detector screen when the experiment is performed with one hole open at a time. Demonstrates the particle-like behavior of subatomic particles.

*Affirming the Consequent* an invalid rule of inference with the following form:

p ⊃ q    (if p then q)

q

So, p

*antecedent* the complete declarative sentence that is the 'if' part of a conditional.

*a priori knowledge* (from the Latin, meaning from what comes before) A priori knowledge is supposed to be knowledge that is justifiable independently of any experiences we might have.

*a posteriori knowledge* (from the Latin meaning from what comes after). A posteriori knowledge is knowledge that requires experience for its justification.

*argument* a set of sentences in which some sentence (sentences) is (are) supposed to give some kind of support to another sentence.

*biconditional* a logical function that expresses an 'if and only if' relation between two complete declarative sentences.

*bivalence* (literally, two valued) the claim that sentences must be either true or false.

*box* (symbolized □) the symbol used to represent 'it is necessary that' in modal logics.

*categorical syllogisms* an argument with three terms whose premises and conclusion are all categorical sentences.

*categorical sentences* a sentence relating things belonging to one group to things belonging to a different group.

*circular reasoning* a poor form of reasoning that goes in a circle, either by assuming the truth of the conclusion in one or more of the premises or by assuming the legitimacy of some rule in a derivation meant to establish the justification for that same rule.

*class* a set of things all of which share some particular quality.

*classical logic* the logic that Frege helped develop, classical logic has dominated philosophical thinking for much of the 20th Century, and it is the theory most commonly taught in standard symbolic logic textbooks (at least in English speaking countries).

*coherence theories of truth* theories of truth whereby the unit to be evaluated for truth is not single sentences, but rather, sets of sentences and entire theories. What makes a theory true is overall internal coherence, i.e, that it is consistent, that it draws conclusions according to accepted logical rules, and so on.

*complete* a logical system in which everything that is true can also be proven.

*conclusion* the sentence that is being supported by reasons in an argument.

*conditional* a logical function that expresses a conditional relation between two complete declarative sentences. In English, conditionals are 'if . . . then' sentences.

*concrete objects* material objects that exist independently of human thought in space and time.

*conditional logics* logics that attempt to improve on the material conditional by formally clarifying the intuitive idea that there is supposed to be connection between antecedent and consequent. One class of conditional logics give the truth conditions for conditionals in terms of possible worlds and a notion of similarity between worlds. Another tries to define conditionals by a relation of relevance between antecedent and consequent.

*conjunct* a complete declarative sentence which is a component of a conjunction.

*conjunction* a logical function that conjoins two complete declarative sentences. In English, conjunctions are 'and' sentences.

*Conjunction* (Con) a valid rule of inference with the following form:

p

q

So, p • q (p and q)

*consequent* the complete declarative sentence that is the 'then' part of a conditional.

*constructivism* a view in the philosophy of mathematics according to which mathematical objects, and hence the truths about them, are constructed by the operations of human thought.

*content* what the sentences of an argument are about.

*contingent* a sentence that is sometimes true and sometimes false. On a truth table a contingent sentence is one that is true for some possible truth value of its constituent parts and false for others.

*contonktion* a sentence that contains tonk.

*contradiction* a sentence that is always false. On a truth table a contradiction is a sentence that is false for every possible truth value of its constituent parts.

*conventionalism* the view that truths of logic are given by the conventions that govern language.

*correspondence theories of truth* theories of truth whereby a sentence is true in virtue of its ability to accurately represent or picture the world the way it is. These theories make truth a matter of whether or not words in a sentence correspond to the world.

*counter-example* providing counter-examples is one way of showing that an argument form is not a valid one. To show that some argument form is invalid by providing a counter-example to it, one simply replaces each variable in the argument with sentences that clearly make the premise(s) true, but the conclusion false.

*counterfactuals* conditional sentences that say what follows if we assume something contrary to the facts in the antecedent.

*deductive arguments* an argument whose premise or premises are supposed to necessitate or guarantee the truth of the conclusion.

*deflationary theories of truth* theories of truth whereby truth is not a property at all. Rather, truth is nothing but a meta-linguistic device for talking about language.

*definite descriptions* predicates that behave logically like names, in the sense that they are meant to designate one particular thing.

*decision theory* a formalization of the rules and principles for correct decision making.

*DeMorgan's Rules* the rules that state the logical equivalence of the following:

$\sim (p \lor q) :: (\sim p \cdot \sim q)$      (not either p and q)::(not p and not q)

$\sim (p \cdot q) :: (\sim p \lor \sim q)$      (not both p and q)::(not p or not q)

*Denying the Antecedent* an invalid rule of inference with the following form:

$p \supset q$     (if p then q)

$\sim p$        (not p)

So, $\sim q$    (not q)

*deontic logics* modal logics that express the logic of moral and other obligations.

*descriptive* that part of theory that describes what is the case.

*designated values* the values that get preserved in valid inference.

*dialetheism* a theory that endorses the idea that there are true contradictions.

*diamond* (symbolized $\lozenge$) the symbol used to represent 'it is possible that' in modal logics.

*disjunct* a complete declarative sentence which is a component of a disjunction.

*disjunction* a logical function that disjoins two complete declarative sentences. In English, disjunctions are 'or' sentences.

*Disjunctive Syllogism* (DS) a valid rule of inference with the following form:

$p \lor q$     (p or q)

$\sim p$       (not p)

So, q

*Distributive Rules* the rules that state the logical equivalence of the following:

$(p \cdot (q \lor r)) :: ((p \cdot q) \lor (p \cdot r))$ (p and either q or r)::(either p and q or p and r)

$(p \lor (q \cdot r)) :: ((p \lor q) \cdot (p \lor r))$ (either p or both q and r)::(both p or q and p or r)

*domain of discourse* the things that are quantified over in relational predicate logic. Unless otherwise specified, the domain of discourse is generally supposed to include everything that there is.

*dot* (symbolized $\cdot$) one of several symbols commonly used to represent 'and' in symbolic logic.

*Double Negation* a rule that states the logical equivalence of the following:

$p :: \sim \sim p$ (not not p)

*Dysfunctional Syllogism* an invalid rule of inference with the following form:

p ∨ q     (p or q)
~ p       (not p)
So, ~ q   (not q)

*epistemic logics* modal logics that express the logic of knowledge claims.

*epistemology* (deriving from the ancient Greek 'episteme,' which means to know) the theory of knowledge.

*essentialism* the idea that everything has an essence, or something that makes it what it is.

*ex contradictione quod libetum* (literally, from contradictions comes anything you like, or more colloquially, anything follows from a contradiction) the consequence in many logics that allows one to infer any q whatsoever from a contradiction.

*exclusive 'or'* one of two senses of 'or' in English. Sentences with exclusive 'or' are false when both disjuncts are true.

*Existential Generalization* a valid rule of inference with the following form:

Φa         (a is Φ)
So, (∃x) Φx   (Something is Φ)

*existential quantifier* (symbolized ∃) the symbol used to represent 'There is some thing such that ...' in symbolic logic.

*explosion* a more colorful way to indicate that *ex contradictione quod libetum* is a consequence in some logic. A set of sentences that contain a contradiction explodes in the sense that any and every sentence will then be a consequence of that set.

*equivalence rules* logical rules that make clear how to rephrase sentences in a way that preserves their logical import.

*fallacy* a mistake in reasoning.

*fatalism* the idea that there is no way for us to change the future.

*function* an operation that takes inputs and yields outputs according to certain specified rules.

*future contingent* a sentence whose truth value can only be determined in the future.

*fuzzy logic* many valued logics that allow objects to have properties in greater and lesser degrees.

*global revision* when a revision of logic is recommended for all domains.

*horseshoe* (symbolized ⊃) one of several symbols commonly used to represent 'if ... then' in symbolic logic.

*identity* (symbolized =) the symbol used to represent 'is identical with' in symbolic logic.

*identity of indiscernibles* a law of identity due to W. G. Leibniz which posits that if thing a has every property that thing b has, then a is identical to b.

*inclusive 'or'* one of two senses of 'or' in English. Inclusive 'or' is like and/or. Sentences with inclusive 'or' are true when both disjuncts are true.

*indirect proof* A rule of inference that says that if one can derive a contradiction from an assumption, then the negation of that assumption must be true.

*inductive argument* an argument whose premise or premises is/are supposed to make the conclusion more likely.

*inductive generalization* an argument form in which particular observations of some things in a domain are used to make generalizations about all things in that domain. The form of inductive Generalizations is:

n% of observed A's are B's.

So, it is likely that n% of all A's are B's.

*inference,* in reasoning, when one belief is thought to follow in some way from some other belief or set of beliefs.

*informal logic* the study of reasoning and fallacies that can not be formally evaluated.

*interference pattern* in the two hole experiment, the pattern that appears on the detector screen when the experiment is performed with both holes simultaneously open. Demonstrates the wave-like behavior of sub-atomic particles.

*intuitionist logic* a non-classical logic in which LEM (among other things) is not a logical truth. Intuitionist logic arose as a challenge to classical logic in the world of mathematics. Later arguments for it came from considerations about meaning.

*invalid argument* a deductive argument in which the truth of the conclusion is not guaranteed by the truth of the premises.

*law of excluded middle* (or the *law of the excluded third*) $p \lor \sim p$ (either p or not p). A logical truth in many logics.

*law of non-contradiction* $\sim (p \bullet \sim p)$ (not both p and not p, or colloquially, it can't be the case that a sentence and its negation are both true). A logical truth in many logics.

*liar sentence* a paradoxical sentence that attributes falsity to itself. For example:

(L) This sentence is false.

*Leibniz's Law,* the law of logic attributed to the philosopher W. G. Leibniz, which posits that identical objects have identical properties. Can be expressed as a valid rule of inference as follows:

a = b (a is identical with b)
Φa (a is Φ)
So, Φb (b is Φ)

*local revision* when a revision of logic is recommended for only one particular domain.

*logical consequence* what follows logically from what and why. A proper analysis of the concept of logical consequence will be one that clarifies the relation 'logically follows from.'

*logical necessity* a very strong sort of necessity. In modal logics that represent logical necessity, the accessibility relation is reflexive, symmetric, and transitive (among other things).

*logical truth* a sentence that is true in virtue of its logical form.

*logically equivalent* two sentences are logically equivalent if they have the same logical content.

*logical form* an argument's basic logical structure, what remains when all non-logical terms are removed, leaving the logical terms in their place.

*material conditional* the definition of the conditional in classical logic, according to which a conditional is false when its antecedent is true and its consequent is false, and true otherwise. The material conditional gives rise to number of counter-intuitive consequences.

*mathematical realism* (also known as *Platonism*) the idea that there is a world of mathematical objects which is independent of humans and their ways of thinking, but which is accessible to humans through the exercise of reason.

*meta-language* the language used to talk about the object-language.

*metaphysics* the study of the fundamental nature of reality.

*modal actualism* a philosophical interpretation of possible worlds semantics according to which possible worlds exist as abstract objects.

*modal realism* a philosophical interpretation of possible worlds semantics according to which possible worlds really exist, just as surely as the actual world does.

*modality* a way of qualifying the truth of a sentence.

*modal logics* the logics that attempt to capture, in formal symbolic form, the inferential connections in arguments containing modal terms.

*Modus Ponens* (MP) a valid rule of inference with the following form:

p ⊃ q    (If p then q)

p

So, q

*Modus Tollens* (MT) a valid rule of inference with the following form:

p ⊃ q    (If p then q)

~q       (not q)

So, ~p    (not p)

*names* in modern logic, lower case letters that stand for particular individuals or things in the world.

*natural deduction* a method for characterizing good arguments in a way which is supposed to closely mimic how we actually reason.

*negation* a logical function used to deny a complete declarative sentence. In English, negation are sentences containing 'not'.

*non-cognitivism* the view that there are no facts that determine the truths of logic. In addition, non-cognitivists believe that sentences of logic are neither true nor false.

*normative* that part of theory that prescribes what ought to be the case.

*object language* the language being talked about.

*ontology* the study of what exists.

*paraconsistent logic* non-classical logics in which explosion or *ex falso quod libetum* fails.

*paradox of the heap* an ancient argument that goes from obviously true premises (that one grain of sand is not a heap of sand and that if one grain of sand is not a heap of sand, then adding another won't make it so) to an obviously false conclusion (that 1,000,000 grains of sand is not a heap of sand) using only valid rules of inference. The paradox is used to exemplify the problem properly accounting for vague language.

*particle-wave duality* the idea that sub-atomic particles behave in both a wave-like and a particle-like fashion.

*Platonism* (also known as *mathematical realism*) the idea that there is a world of mathematical objects which is independent of humans and their ways of thinking, but which is accessible to humans through the exercise of reason. The name comes from Plato, who thought that the world of concrete objects could never be the source of knowledge and that real knowledge could only be attained by considering abstract objects.

*pluralism* the view that many different logics might be true.

*possible worlds* worlds that might have been.

*possible world semantics* the interepretation of modal and other logics that appeals to truth conditions in possible worlds.

*pragmatic theory of truth,* a coherence theory of truth associated with the philosophers William James and John Dewey according to which true theories are simply those that are instrumentally useful to us.

*precisification* in a supervaluational logic, a way of making the applications for a vague term more precise without actually specifying strict criteria.

*predicate* a word or phrase that stands for a class or set. In modern logic, predicates are incomplete and get completed by names to form sentences, and they are symbolized by upper case letters.

*premises* in an argument, the sentence or sentences that is/are supposed to provide the support for the conclusion.

*problem of non-being* a very famous philosophical problem dating back to the time of Plato and Socrates, according to which we can not deny the existence of something without presupposing that thing's existence.

*proof* makes each step of an argument from the premises to the conclusion explicit. In a proof, one numbers the lines and puts the justification for each line next to it. The only justifications allowed are that a line is a premise, or that it is derived from a previous line in the proof using one of the rules of the system, which is indicated by citing the line (or lines) and the rule used.

*psychologism* the view that truths of logic are determined by the logic we use.

*quantifiers* the logical functions used to indicate the quantity of the subject in sentences of predicate logic. In English, quantified sentences are those containing 'some' and 'all'.

*quantum logic* a non-classical logic proposed as a solution to certain long-standing interpretive difficulties in quantum mechanics. In quantum logics, the validity of some of the distributive rules is restricted.

*rationalism* the view that truths of logic are determined by abstract facts accessible to reason.

*reasoning* what people do when they go from one set of beliefs to another belief or set of beliefs.

*reductio ad absurdum* an argument form whereby a sentence, p, is said to be true if a contradiction follows from the negation of that sentence, ~p. This form is valid in classical logic, but not in intuitionist logic.

*reflective equilibrium* from the political philosopher John Rawls, describes the process necessary for determining which principles of justice are best. Applied to logic, it describes a logical theory in which intuitions about good inference are fully captured by a logical theory and the theory no longer has any counter-intuitive consequences.

*reflexivity* if a relation R is reflexive, then it relates things to themselves. An example of a reflexive relation is 'is identical with', since everything is identical with itself. Reflexivity is one of several relations that define the accessibility relation in modal logics.

*relational phrases* a word or phrase that stands for the relations between objects. Like predicates in modern logic, these are symbolized by upper case letters and completed by names to make sentences.

*relational predicate logic* the logical functions that operate on sentences in which subject and predicate/relational structures are fully expressed. The symbols of relational predicate logic with identity are •, ∨, ⊃, ≡, ~, ∃, and ∀.

*relational predicate logic with identity* the logical functions that operate on sentences in which subject, predicate/relational, and identity structures are fully expressed. The symbols of relational predicate logic are •, ∨, ⊃, ≡, ~, ∃, ∀, and =.

*relevance logics* (in some parts of the world, called *relevant logics*) non-classical logics that attempt to improve on the material conditional by requiring that the antecedent of a conditional be somehow relevant to its consequent.

*revision* what happens when we change our beliefs by adding new ones and/or deleting old ones.

*rule of inference* an idealization of our ordinary inferential practices, says how to go from one set of sentences to another.

*schema* a pattern or template that can be used in many different instances or situations.

*semantics* the study of meaning, truth and reference.

*sentential or propositional connectives* the symbols •, ∨, ⊃, ≡, and ~, so named because they connect whole complete declarative sentences.

*sentential or propositional logic* the fragment of logical functions that operate on whole sentences or propositions. The symbols of sentential logic are •, ∨, ⊃, ≡, and ~.

*Simplification* (Simp.) a valid rule of inference with the following form:

p • q     (p and q)
So, p

*sophists* from the Greek 'sophistes', meaning expert. A group in ancient Greece who were known for using any argument (good or bad) to persuade others of a claim, and who would defend any claim that they were paid to defend, whether or not the claim had any real worth. The word *sophistry* is still used to refer to the practice of making bad arguments sound like good ones.

*sorites* a series of arguments strung together.

*sound* a valid argument with true premises.
a logical system in which everything that is provable is true.

*strength* a measure of the number of sentences that can be proven in a logical system.

*syllogism* an argument with two premises and one conclusion.

*symmetry* if a relation R is symmetrical, then if a thing a is related to a thing b, b is also related to a. An example of a symmetrical relation is 'is a sibling of', since if one person is a sibling of another person, that second person must also be a sibling of that first person. Symmetry is one of several relations that define the accessibility relation in modal logics.

*syntax* the study of the structure or form of languages.

*supervaluational logic* a logic with a specified supervalution function. A supervaluation function assigns to compound sentences with indeterminate truth values whatever classical logic would assign to the compound, if there is a unique such value, and otherwise it assigns it no value.

*tautology* a sentence that is always true. On a truth table a tautology is a sentence that is true for every possible truth value of its constituent parts.

*temporal logics* modal logics that express the logic of time relations.

*terms* the predicates and noun phrases that denote classes in a categorical sentence.

*theorem* a sentence that is provable using no assumptions or premises whatsoever.

*tilde* (symbolized ~ ) one of several symbols commonly used to represent 'not' in symbolic logic.

*tonk,* a very poor logical function defined by the following two rules of inference:

p
So, p tonk q

p tonk q
So, q

A language with tonk would license belief in anything and everything.

*topic neutral* a phrase commonly used to express the fact that logical functions and rules of inference place no restrictions on the subject matter of the sentences that the functions/rules operate with.

*transitivity* if a relation R is transitive, then if a thing a is related to a thing b, and b is related to c, a is related to c. An example of a transitive relation is 'is to the right of', since if one thing is to the right of a second thing and that second thing is to the right of a third thing, the third thing must be to the right of the first thing. Transitivity is one of several relations that define the accessibility relation in modal logics.

*triple bar* (symbolized ≡) one of several symbols commonly used to represent 'if and only if' in symbolic logic.

*truth-function* a logical function that takes truth values as input and yields truth values as output.

*truth table* a way of laying out all the possible semantic values of complex sentences, useful for demonstrating important logical properties such as validity and logical truth.

*truth-value gap* in a 3 or more valued logic, a sentence that is neither true not false.

*truth-value glut* in a 3 or more valued logic, a sentence that is both true and false.

*two hole experiment* (also known as the *two slit experiment*) the famous experiment in quantum mechanics that best illustrates particle wave duality.

*Universal Instantiation* a valid rule of inference with the following form:

(∀x) Φx   (All x are Φ)

So, Φa      (a is Φ)

*universal quantifier* (symbolized ∀) One of the symbols commonly used to represent 'All things are such that . . . ' in symbolic logic.

*vague* a term that doesn't have clear truth conditions in every case.

*valid argument* a deductive argument in which the truth of the premises guarantees the truth of the conclusion.

*variables* letters in symbolic logic (usually p and q) for which any complete declarative sentence could be substituted.

*Wason selection task* a psychology test first performed it in 1966, designed to assess ordinary people's logical abilities by measuring their understanding of conditionals.

*wedge* (symbolized ∨) one of several symbols commonly used to represent 'or' in symbolic logic.